THE MAKING OF THE MODERN WEST:
Western Canada Since 1945

Edited by A.W. RASPORICH

THE UNIVERSITY OF CALGARY PRESS

Published by The University of Calgary Press
        2500 University Drive N.W.
        Calgary, Alberta, Canada T2N 1N4

Order from The University of Calgary Press

Price: $10.95

Cover Photo: ''Oil Tanker Train - NISKU, 1947''
        By H. Pollard, #P 1444
        Courtesy of the Provincial Archives of Alberta

TABLE OF CONTENTS

LIST OF CONTRIBUTORS

(1) Gerald Friesen
     Department of History, University of Manitoba

(2) Roger Gibbins
     Department of Political Science, The University of Calgary

(3) David K. Elton
     Department of Political Science, The University of Lethbridge
     Director, Canada West Foundation, Calgary

(4) Donald E. Blake
     Department of Political Science, The University of British Columbia

(5) Kenneth H. Norrie
     Department of Economics, University of Alberta

(6) Brenton M. Barr
     Department of Geography, The University of Calgary

(7) Walter G. Hardwick
     Department of Geography, The University of British Columbia
     President, Knowledge Network of the West

(8) John J. Barr
     Director, Public Affairs, Syncrude Canada Ltd., Edmonton

(9) R.W. Wright
     Department of Economics, The University of Calgary

(10) Max Foran
     Historian, Calgary

(11) Peter J. Smith
     Department of Geography, University of Alberta

(12) Brigham Y. Card
     Red Deer College; Emeritus, University of Alberta

(13) Leo Driedger
     Department of Sociology, University of Manitoba

(14) Murray J. Dobbin
     Gabriel Dumont Institute of Native Studies and Applied Research, Regina

(15) J.A. Boan
     Department of Economics, University of Regina

(16) Diane Bessai
     Department of English, University of Alberta

(17) Christopher Varley
     Curator, Edmonton Art Gallery

PREFACE

Such efforts as this collection of papers are collaborative ventures, and rest on a tradition of contributions to scholarship on western Canada. From their very inception a decade and a half ago, the Western Canadian Studies Conferences have made considerable contributions to mapping the historical landscape of the *terra incognita* of the western interior of Canada. We now know considerably more about the western plains in Canada as a result not only of this conference, but also of the collective efforts of western Canadianists largely centered at western universities. They have faithfully contributed to the longstanding success of this enterprise both as contributors of papers, and as conference participants. Without them (and I note sadly that some have passed on, such as W.L. Morton, Lewis H. Thomas and Robert Painchaud), western Canada would scarcely be understood as well as it is today. When one thinks of the mindscape of the West before this enterprise began in 1968 and its strong self-consciousness today, it is to some degree a reflection on the willing efforts of western academics, writers and thinkers who have sown and reaped a bountiful crop.

This particular chapter of western development, that is, the modern West or New West, began largely as a result of a chance meeting between myself and the keynote speaker, Gerald Friesen, at the Public Archives of Canada in Ottawa where, contrary to the regulations for total silence in the reading room, the subject of this conference was broached in a whisper. Upon retreat to a more convivial ground, he repeated what began *sotto voce*, that perhaps a conference on the postwar West was indeed appropriate since we had left off with recent conferences on the Depression and the wartime West. Not only was it timely but necessary in his view, since he had found in writing his survey of the history of western Canada, that the recent past was all but neglected by historians. It was also only partially understood by the several disciplines in the humanities and social sciences which had recently reflected upon the very dramatic changes in western society and culture. I must say that the process of convincing my colleagues upon return to Calgary proved easy—all agreed and the task was joined. I must also say that it was utterly without malice and with considerable conviction that I first asked Dr. Friesen to be our keynote speaker, and the 1983 conference was off to a good beginning. A whisper had, so to speak, become a roar.

The conference itself was a rather more substantial discourse than these selected papers and not all of the special events, panels and commentaries could be reproduced here. Indeed, we attempted in the public forum to present some of the practitioners and key participants in those events, such as the Hon. Justice Emmett Hall who forged the modern medicare system in western Canada; John Tootoosis, an Indian activist in Saskatchewan, and who was and is a passionate advocate for his people; the film-maker Fil Fraser who commented upon and presented extracts from his and other wonderful cinematic contributions on the historic West such as *Why Shoot the Teacher?*, *The Hounds of Notre Dame* and *Latitude 55;* and the Hon. Roy Romanow who concluded the conference with a vivid recollection of the political forces which were at play in the forging of the constitutional accord of 1981. Yet, the scholarly substance of what is presented here does capture that substantial attempt at understanding a complex series of changes in western Canada after the war. The Leduc era has come and gone, the urban cores of western cities are now scarcely recognizable in their prior incarnation, the scared cow of the Crow Rate has been dispatched, and a postwar baby boom has passed into middle age. Since more than a generation has passed by historical reckoning, this conference attempted a stock-taking, admittedly a very partial one, of some major events and policy changes which have marked these dynamic decades.

These collected papers on western development are clearly only a part of the kaleidoscopic changes which have occurred, but to have included all of them would have resulted in a much longer and more diffuse study. But we have addressed some of the major issues which have been at the center of change such as: political alienation versus integration of the New West; energy developments and economic modernization; the recent debate on economic growth and stagnation; the development of the rural and urban West; the social and ethnic character of the emergent West; and cultural development of the West in a national and international context. Its juxtapositions of viewpoint were also meant to stimulate an interdisciplinary or cross-disciplinary dialogue, and it is clear that some markedly differing points of view emerge here—on the "good" of modernization and rapid developments, the "necessity" of economic stagnation in the 1980s in a dependent hinterland, and the value of regional expression in the arts and culture. It is hoped that what has resulted is as much a dialogue about the postwar period in the West, as it is useful information to scholars and students of the modern West.

Some acknowledgments are also in order to various bodies and granting agencies which have made possible both the scholarly conference and these proceedings. First, to the University of Calgary, to the Head of the Department of History, T.H.E. Travers and to the Dean of the Faculty of Social Sciences, D.A. Seastone, must go our thanks for their continued support of the conference. For their financial assistance toward the hosting of the conference and special events, we owe a continuing debt of gratitude to the University Research Grants Committee and the Special Projects Fund of the University of Calgary Endowment Fund. Without these internal supports this conference and these proceedings would not exist. Finally, to the Social Sciences and Humanities Research Council must go an equal share of the credit for their very generous support of conference travel expenses and the partial costs of this volume. Individuals who have been particularly helpful to me as organizer of this conference were Madeleine Aldridge of the Conference Office, Cliff Kadatz of Com-Media Graphics, Pat Evans of the Research Grants Office, and Liesbeth von Wolzogen, Marjory McLean and David Finch of the Department of History, and Douglas Cass of the Glenbow-Alberta Institute. For the production of this book I owe special thanks to Marcy Laufer of the University of Calgary Press for her capable guiding of this manuscript through the various stages of publication. And finally to my colleagues in the Department of History who have unfailingly given of their time to this event and these proceedings over the years, I owe a special debt of gratitude.

Anthony W. Rasporich
April, 1984

THE PRAIRIE WEST SINCE 1945: AN HISTORICAL SURVEY

Gerald Friesen

It is a truism that prairie society changed rapidly in the four decades after 1940. Observers of the region might single out such local trends as the migration of farm residents to the cities, the entry of women into the workforce, and the participation of Indians in political debates as indicators of a social upheaval. But these particular changes also affected Argentina and Australia and midwestern America. Like the spread of transnational corporations and made-in-Hollywood "entertainment"—two other noteworthy developments of the era—these trends were not unique to the prairie West but, rather, affected many parts of the developed world. And yet, despite the apparent homogeneity of modern social history, the prairie community also witnessed a flowering of distinctive local cultural expressions and seemed to be the home of distinctive political and ethnic loyalties in these decades. What was the "state of the region"? Was it indeed just a neighborhood of a global metropolis? Or did elements of a distinctive society and culture continue to exist? This paper will sketch some of the political, economic, and social trends of the era in order to suggest the nature of the "delicate balance" which must be struck in the study of small communities in the modern world.

Prairie demographic trends demonstrate that significant social changes carried the region closer to international norms in the decades after 1945.[1] Of these trends, the most striking was the decline in rural population and the growth of cities. Though half of prairie residents lived on farms in 1941, only 10 percent did so in 1981. Because the village proportion of the total remained nearly constant, the proportion of prairie residents living in towns and cities over 1,000 population rose from 38 percent to 71 percent. By 1981, a demographic milestone had been passed: for the first time, over 50 percent of the prairie population lived in its five metropolitan centers. Within these generalizations is hidden an important change in the balance of urban power. Winnipeg, which was as large as the combined population of the other four prairie metropolises at the start of this period, was slightly smaller than Calgary and Edmonton by 1981. And the prairie population declined in relation to the national population because, despite a sharp rise in Alberta, neither Manitoba nor Saskatchewan kept pace with Canada's steady growth.

The nature of the prairie economy changed considerably in these four decades, as the urban-rural balance suggests. Agriculture's share of the wealth produced in the provinces (census value added) in 1941 was 50 percent of the regional total; in 1978 it was under 15 percent. In Alberta, indeed, agriculture contributed just 8 percent of census value added by 1978. The economic boom was based upon the mining sector, whose proportion of regional wealth (cva) grew from 8 percent in 1941 to 41 percent in 1978. With such changes in population concentration, in place of residence and in the nature of economic activity, the prairie provinces also experienced a significant redistribution of the labor force. The proportion engaged in agriculture declined from 48 percent in 1941 to 10 percent in 1981. The most important increase occurred in the tertiary sector, where the proportion of managerial, professional, clerical, sales, and service workers grew from 30 percent of the paid labor force in 1941 to 59 percent in 1981.

There were dramatic changes in the household, too, after World War II. Life expectancy rose sharply, from the low sixties to the low seventies for men, and from the mid-sixties to the high seventies for women. The number of divorces increased rapidly, from about 230 in each prairie province in 1941 to an average of over 4,000 per province per year in the early 1980s. Family size decreased. The proportion of women over fifteen years, including married women, in the paid labor force increased from 20 percent to 52 percent in these four decades. The level of education rose and, both in rural and in urban communities, the attainments of prairie children became comparable to those in the rest of Canada and North America.

To these numerical measures of change must be added the qualitative evidence which suggested the transcendence of urban and rural differences. Farm people moved to the cities by the tens of thousands in these decades, it is true, but the life of the city also invaded the countryside. The rapid adoption of the car, truck, combine and tractor, the spread of rural electrification and the consequent changes in the farm household, the complex demands of crop selection and cultivation, the growing importance of farm finance, as well as school consolidation and centralization of economic and social services brought rural work processes and material culture closer to their urban counterparts than at any time in the preceding century. The prairie provinces also led the continent into another international trend of the era, the welfare state. It was quite possible in the 1930s to live in fear of illness, to suffer serious food shortages, and to be clothed and housed at the barest minimum standard. These problems were mitigated in the postwar decades as the prairie West joined western Europe in attempting to guarantee that the state would intervene to provide health and income assistance.

The Canadian West became increasingly homogeneous and increasingly like the rest of the developed world between 1945 and the early 1980s. It was much more urban than rural; it was less dependent on agricultural income; the largest proportion of its labor force was in the so-called tertiary-sector occupations including the liberal professions and managerial and clerical jobs; it was still heavily engaged in natural resource production and tied to world markets, true, but it had a reasonably diversified base of resources and its per capita personal income hovered around the national average; it had been swept by new trends in family formation, as had the rest of the developed world, and it had succumbed to the trappings of material culture that guided, amused, adorned or eased daily living in Lyons and Belgrade and Wichita and Leeds. Finally, it was part of the North Atlantic welfare state and, depending upon the perspective of the observer, might have seemed just another neighborhood within a single homogenized global metropolis.

This assumption of growing global uniformity which would swallow up a distinctive prairie society was prominent in Canadian scholarship. One influential work of this type was George Grant's *Lament for a Nation*. Grant argued that, in the years after 1945, Canada's ruling class, the people who controlled its great corporations, became a northern extension of the continental ruling class, just as the nation's economy became a branch plant and the nation's military became an errand boy. In the modern age, he wrote, it was impossible for many citizens to live outside the dominant assumptions of their world: democracy could not save Canadians from absorption into a ''homogenized continental culture.'' His argument was based upon the assumption that Canada was ''a local culture'' and upon the assertion that ''modern civilization,'' especially ''modern science,'' made all local cultures obsolete. His essay reached a stinging conclusion: because conservatism was impossible, and because Canadian existence had hitherto been predicated upon the conservatism of Canadian society and its leaders, then the existence of Canada—a local conservative culture—was impossible.[2]

Grant had considerable support for his generalizations in the 1960s. A distinguished Canadian economist, Harry Johnson, argued that Canada was increasingly a part of the larger North American economy: ''Both politically and economically, the general trend of world evolution is toward...political and economic organization on a continental... rather than national scale.''[3] The best known Canadian student of communications in the 1960s, Marshall McLuhan, was making comparable statements about the effects of the electronic media, though one was never certain whether he saw the global village as a harmonious utopia or a centralized tyranny.[4] A paper presented by E.K. Brown upon the proper audience and context of Canadian imaginative writing, though published in 1943, remained an important force in literary criticism. Brown deplored the possibility of a descent into ''regionalist art'' in Canada, arguing that such art would ''fail because it stresses the superficial and the peculiar at the expense, at least, if not the exclusion, of the fundamental and universal. The advent of regionalism may be welcomed with reservations as a stage through which it may be well to pass, as a discipline and a purgation. But if we are to pass through it, the coming of great books will be delayed beyond the lifetime of anyone now living.''[5] Finally, John Porter's studies of Canadian society denied the existence of coherent class cleavages and suggested that Canadians were becoming more like each other: ''the maintenance of national unity has over-ridden any other goals there might have been, and has prevented a polarizing, within the political system, of conservative and progressive forces.'' He also argued that ''There is...little conflict between those who have power and those who do not. It is not a question of conflicts between the 'ins' and the 'outs', but rather of conflicts between those who are 'in'.''[6] Prairie Canadians, in this perspective, were entering a new phase in national existence. They were moving beyond regionalist art and regional or even national economic policy; they were accepting greater homogeneity in culture and, apparently, were less distinguishable from other communities in the developed world.

The perspective which emphasized homogeneity and internationalism has shaped aspects of prairie scholarship. The economist, Paul Phillips, based a recent essay upon the assumption that regionalism had always been a central characteristic of the Canadian economy but that, in recent decades, the multinational corporation and continental capital integration, not the Canadian government, were the crucial forces in decision making.[7] The historian, J.E. Rea, in his discussion of ''the most persistent social theme'' in prairie history, ''the struggle for cultural dominance,'' suggested that ethnic minorities were assimilated in the post-1945 decades: ''What has evolved is a Prairie culture which is more diverse, but not essentially different from that established at the end of the nineteenth century. The premises of the Ontario migrants, and the social institutions which they planted, have generally remained intact.''[8] The political scientist, Roger Gibbins, perceived a ''decline of political regionalism'' in the prairie West and made it the central theme of his *Prairie Politics and Society*. Among the reasons for the decline, he argued, were the urbanization of the population, the erosion of ethnicity, the transformation of agriculture and, finally, ''the loss of a distinctive prairie culture, or the lost opportunity to create a distinctive prairie culture'' which he associated with pressures from urban multinational mass media.[9] What these prairie scholars had in common was the assumption that the forces of modern economic organization, modern transportation and communications technology, and even of modern politics were eliminating the possibility of local autonomy, region-wide political identity, and a distinctive local culture.

There is merit in this view. No one would wish to deny it. But it is only half a story for a student of regional society. We must also look at the other side under these same headings of economic structure, social organization and regional perspective. The argument for a decline of local control over the economy, for example, should be tempered by recognition of areas of considerable regional power. As long as prairie-based cooperatives owned three-quarters of the country elevators and were relatively responsive to their membership, there was a measure of local control in the wheat economy. As long as the Wheat Board acted as the central agency for the sale of Canadian grain, and was reasonably responsive to the needs and desires of its constituents, its important functions were subject to a measure of local control. And as long as decisions on freight rates remained within the political system, even there a measure of local control was possible. It is true that determinants of prices and yields were still beyond the farmers' grasp but security of return had become greater than ever before, due in good measure to the efforts of the local Pools and the local agricultural scientists and extension educators. These trends did not suggest homogenization or loss of local autonomy.

Within the rest of the prairie economy, the strength of the thesis regarding international capital flows and transnational enterprises must be acknowledged. But, at the same time, given the inevitable context of an increasingly integrated global economy, the degree of local control over the nonagricultural portions of the prairie economy merits a closer look. Three developments contradict the conventional wisdom. First, cooperative enterprises and credit unions were extremely important in the prairie economy. In the early 1980s, five of Canada's ten largest cooperatives were based in the prairie West and the prairie credit unions possessed assets of nearly $7 billion.[10] Second, the number and importance of prairie-based industrial enterprises grew substantially in the four decades. Though in several cases these corporations were themselves transnational enterprises, their owners, the prairie super-rich, demanded recognition as local entrepreneurs who reflected a regional bias in their approach to the economy. The power associated with such families as Richardson, Poole, Mannix, Southern, Webster, Child, Seaman, Scurfield, Simpson, Banister, Cohen, Searle, McKinnon, Asper, Simkin, Torchinski, Friesen, Lyons and Ward could not be discounted. And, to the degree that this power was exercised with the future of the community or the region in mind, must be recognized as another kind of local control.[11] The third theme in prairie economic self-determination concerned the role of the state. Prairie governments had always been prepared to intervene in the economy on behalf of local citizens. By the early 1980s, it was a rule of thumb that Canadian governments—that is, all levels of government—spent, on direct purchases and transfers of income, roughly 40 percent of the total value of goods and services produced in Canada.[12] Large state-owned institutions such as the three prairie telephone corporations, the two power corporations, the Alberta airline (Pacific Western), the Alberta Energy Company and Treasury Branches, the Saskatchewan Crown Investments Corporation and the Alberta Heritage Fund and even that unusual hybrid, "NOVA-An Alberta Corporation," were subject to direction from the people's representatives. Though one might debate the true nature of state capitalism and corporate socialism, one must still acknowledge that the degree of local control over the local economy was much greater in 1980 than in 1940.

If the argument for increasing international homogeneity and multinational power could be contrasted with a trend to local control in the case of the prairie economy, a similar duality could be posited in the case of social organization and social structure. Ethnicity, native-white relations and social class were the chief subjects at issue. The conventional wisdom in North American sociology, a product of Robert Park's work many years ago, was that ethnic minorities inevitably were assimilated during the passage of several generations. This perspective seemed reasonable because it corresponded to daily observations on the replacement of folk architecture by suburban tract home, the decline of traditional language use, the exogamy of young people and the uniform secularism of daily life, to cite but a few obvious illustrations. But the field work of prairie sociologists such as Alan Anderson and Leo Driedger in the early 1970s found evidence which did not entirely confirm the Park thesis. Despite a significant provincewide decline in the use of traditional languages, Anderson discovered widespread use of ethnic languages and other important characteristics of group identity in the rural bloc settlements of north-central Saskatchewan.[13] Driedger catalogued continuing minority group loyalties and institutional completeness within Winnipeg's ethnic communities and then adopted the concept of "cultural pluralism" to depict the social organization of the prairie West. He had found relatively meltable and unmeltable individuals and groups, in other words, and the latter—the "unmeltables"—created institutions parallel to those of the mainstream and climbed parallel ladders to success.[14]

This distinction between cultural assimilation, defined as adaptation to mainstream values and material culture, and structural assimilation, defined as entry into the important institutions of mainstream society, itself raised problems but it did emphasize the continuing importance of ethnic identity in the prairie West. Similarly John Porter, Wallace Clement and Raymond Breton noted the "gatekeeping" activities and the overrepresentation in the national elite of Canada's "charter" ethnic groups.[15] If some groups were rewarded, others were denied. Surely ethnic consciousness was the product of such experiences. Howard Palmer recently associated the tides of nativism in twentieth-century Alberta with the rise and fall of prejudice throughout the English-speaking world, but he did not argue that nativism had disappeared. Indeed, the hostility expressed toward the so-called "visible minorities" from South and East Asia, the "indigenous minorities" —Canada's native peoples—and the "unassimilable minorities," such as the Hutterites, ensured that ethnic identity and conflict remained a part of prairie society.[16]

Native identity, like ethnic identity, did not disappear during these forty years. There were 68,000 native people in the prairie West in 1941, most of whom lived in rural surroundings, and about 200,000 in 1981. By the latter date, natives constituted about 7 percent of the Manitoba and Saskatchewan populations and about 4 percent of the Alberta population. About one-quarter of the registered Indians lived off their reserves by 1976 and it was estimated that this proportion would reach one-third by the mid-1980s. In the five prairie cities in 1981 estimates of the native proportion of the population varied from about 2 percent in Calgary (about 7,000), to 4 percent in Edmonton (about 15,000), 15 percent in Regina (about 20,000), 6 percent in Saskatoon (about 7,000), and about 5 percent in Winnipeg (about 22,000).[17] Generalizations concerning the economic and social status of the urban and rural native population appeared frequently in the press and, almost without exception, emphasized that native birth rates were higher than white, that native unemployment rates were higher and native household incomes lower than whites, that transfer payments were a primary source of native income, and that violence was endemic in native communities. The catalogue of negatives was so well-known that it must have had some accuracy but it also rang chords which were familiar to students of prairie immigration history. The questions asked and the values implicit in the analysis sounded very much like the social surveys of central European immigrant communities in the prairie West before 1930. Like those surveys, contemporary reports reflected a concern for the members of the native community but they also imposed goals that were not necessarily those of the natives.

A different perspective upon the prairie native community was presented by the sociologist, Linda Gerber, whose research into reserve communities was based upon the concepts of institutional completeness and personal resource development. Her survey of over 500 reserve bands in Canada demonstrated that adaptive strategies which concentrated upon either the development of individual skills or upon community development policies had become a focus of local native politics. In the late 1960s and early 1970s, she wrote, the bands in the southern two-thirds of each prairie province differed from their counterparts in the rest of Canada: "The typical prairie band is larger and grows rapidly due to the unusually high fertility rates. It is remarkably cohesive, well-developed at the community level, and relatively likely to retain the use of native languages. The typical nonprairie band is the obverse in many respects, being more fully integrated into the mainstream through education, employment, and off-reserve residence." Her conclusion was that "the communal prairie bands and the individualistic bands of the other provinces employed different strategies of adaptation to modern conditions," and that "ethnic differentiation" and the development of an Indian "institutional framework" were becoming more evident in the prairie West.[18]

Native identity in the region was consolidated in the decades after 1945. Campaigns for native rights and celebrations of native culture produced a clearer and more insistent articulation of native perspectives than had occurred in the preceding half century. Despite the assimilationist drive of the federal government, indeed, the natives forced the larger society to acknowledge a new political status —or statuses—for them. And within the larger Canadian native community, the distinctive characteristics of the three prairie provincial associations and of the Métis and nonstatus Indian communities were evident.

Ethnic and native studies are familiar aspects of social history. Class analysis is not. It has not always enjoyed favor in national historical scholarship and it continues to pose serious problems even for its most committed practitioners. And yet a tentative version of class appeared in discussions of the prairie experience between 1880 and 1940 and, as a clear trend in modern political studies literature suggests, class-based analysis of the post-1945 era preoccupied a number of Canadian scholars. Tom Peterson's interpretation of Manitoba politics, for example, argued that the fundamental cleavage in the province between the early 20th century and the 1960s had been ethnicity, but that class loyalties transcended ethnic divisions in the late 1960s and 1970s. Nelson Wiseman and Wayne Taylor measured class and ethnic loyalties in Winnipeg elections in the 1940s and 1950s and found them to be significant. Other recent studies, such as Richards and Pratt's *Prairie Capitalism*, suggested similar conclusions for rural society. The crude categories of the Marxian dialectic might not have been the proper abstract formulation of social divisions in the postwar prairie West but some type of categorization still seemed necessary. Prairie people were not, as the pioneer cliché had it, "all just folks together," nor did they lose their class identity in a modern homogeneous society.[19]

Studies of prairie literature took a different course. Dick Harrison, the literary critic, recently suggested that the history of prairie literature must first treat the "struggle for an indigenous prairie fiction;" its task was to reconcile "the incongruities between the culture and the land." W.L. Morton's literary confession emphasized similar themes.[20] Even Wallace Stegner contended with this kind of problem:

> Contradictory voices tell you who you are. You grow up speaking one dialect and reading and writing another…all the forces of culture and snobbery are against your *writing* by ear and making contact with your natural audience. Your natural audience, for one thing, doesn't read—it *isn't* an audience. You grow out of touch with your dialect because learning and literature lead you another way unless you consciously resist.[21]

This is the gap between nature and culture, America and Europe, West and East, country and city, body and mind which has been expressed many times from many perspectives. But in the decades after 1945 in the prairie West, one was struck not by an exceptionally-wide gap between literature and life, nor indeed by the absence of an audience, but by the very eagerness for locally-created, locally-inspired art, and by a distinctive but not exceptional quest to bridge the gap between "memory" and "history." Was this not the inspiration for the Golden and seventy-fifth provincial birthdays in Alberta and Saskatchewan, the centennials of Manitoba, Winnipeg, Saskatoon, Regina and Canada and the boom in local history publications, heritage movements and family reunions?[22] A regional voice and a regional audience—two very different things—had developed in the prairie West after World War II. As John Hirsch said of the Manitoba Theatre Centre, which was founded in 1957-58 but whose formative years were in the preceding decade, there came together in Winnipeg the physical and financial support, the artistic talent, and best of all, the audiences to support an institution devoted to drama. In the postwar decades, the prairie West was prepared to see its life translated into and its perceptions shaped by literature.

The expression of this interest in one's past and one's environment often began at an artistic level inferior to that of the metropolises of the English-speaking world. Despite a continuing self-consciousness, however, there was, especially in literature, and here the growing influence of the university was evident, a growing maturity. The finest prairie writers had learned to speak of local concerns in an international idiom. And, for that reason, the language of their imagination created a vision that became a focus for the community. It also attracted international attention. Northrop Frye has suggested that the best literature seems to depend upon local identification. And he went on to defend its quality in Canada, to argue that the gap between colonialism and maturity had narrowed:

> ...there is no reason for cultural lag or for a difference between sophisticated writers in large centres and naive writers in smaller ones. A world like ours produces a single international style of which all existing literatures are regional developments. This international style is not a bag of rhetorical tricks but a way of seeing and thinking in a world controlled by uniform patterns of technology, and the regional development is a way of escaping from that uniformity.[23]

Every type of cultural expression has its own technology and its own historical rhythms of patronage, circulation, production, content or language and form. Thus, what may have been true for prairie literature had no necessary relationship to developments in architecture, film, television, newspapers, painting or other kinds of cultural production. Two brief observations upon their development might be hazarded. First, one saw in each of these areas the contradictory pressures toward a distinctive indigenous expression, on the hand, and toward international uniformity, on the other. Second, communications technology was changing so rapidly in these decades that generalizations about international cultural homogeneity—as in the common fear of Hollywood and American network television—like generalizations about the disappearance of ''genuine culture'' entirely, were premature.

This discussion of economic decision making, social composition, cultural expression and literary achievement in the prairie West omits one theme that is central to society and to historians' analysis of its evolution. That is politics. As the decades of the twentieth century passed provinces became increasingly important units in Confederation. With the growth of provincial responsibilities, provincial wealth, and local bureaucracies, as Alan Cairns has suggested, provincial identities began to take shape.[24] One aspect—even creator of—these identities was the provincial party system. A distinctive local blend of personalities and popular preferences molded distinctive provincial governments and political institutions. In the years after 1945, the various communities in each province— native, ethnic, class, occupational, rural and urban—became more closely integrated into a single community. The political parties reinforced provincial distinctiveness by pursuing significantly different brands of political education. The result was the development of ideological divisions within each prairie province and, thus, an indigenous two-party system. These were not simply brokerage parties, in other words, but rather were parties based upon ideological differences. The disappearance of the national governing party, the Liberals, from the prairie scene ensured that federal-provincial conflict would be bitter; disagreement between the two levels of government was probably inevitable but the Liberal failure made such disagreement a more serious event. Finally, despite the separatist backlash, which was the right-wing ideological expression in Alberta, the prairie West continued to be Canadian.[25] Its local politics possessed distinctive elements, but its distinctiveness did not imply disloyalty.

In these forty years, the prairie West was affected profoundly by international forces but it also retained elements of individuality. The sweeping generalizations concerning cultural homogeneity and the concentration of global decision making presented only one perspective on a complex story. As W.L. Morton commented, "there are sections as well as nations, nations as well as civilizations. The sub-society which is a section,...possesses some degree of integrity and character. That character...may be defined, and the relations of the sub-society with other societies explored." In a later essay, he added: "Federally created, the West was self-defined...(It) knew in its bones that it was an independent creature which had determined its own life within known and accepted limits."[26] The West was a distinctive community from the mid-seventeenth to the mid-nineteenth century; the diplomatic and economic rhythms of native-European relations ensured that the dramatic changes of these two centuries would occur in relative peace and according to the dictates of local forces. The prairie West adapted to the industrial capitalism of the North Atlantic world in the last half of the nineteenth century, as did much of the globe, and became a separate Canadian region with interests, issues, and an outlook of its own despite vast areas of experience in common with Canadians from other parts of the country. In the first four decades of the twentieth century, it adjusted to the strains of rapid population change, the challenges of ethnic and political disagreements and the crises of the Great Depression and two World Wars while remaining within the Canadian economic structure and the parliamentary system. Its experience was no less distinctive in the four decades after 1945. As in the past, so in recent years, world issues were also prairie issues. But it would be one-sided to talk about international homogeneity and transnational decision making as if they were the only aspects of prairie experience that mattered. As ever, local will, local interest and local memory constituted the other side of the "delicate balance" that was prairie experience.[27]

Footnotes

1. The following paragraphs are based upon the appended tables.

2. George Grant, *Lament for a Nation: The Defeat of Canadian Nationalism* (Toronto: 1965).

3. Harry G. Johnson, *The Canadian Quandary: Economic Problems and The Policies* (Toronto: 1963, 1977), p. 103.

4. Marshall McLuhan, *Understanding Media: The Extensions of Man* (Toronto: 1964, 1966).

5. E.K. Brown, "Canadian Poetry," in *Contexts of Canadian Criticism*, edited by Eli Mandel (Chicago: 1971), pp.29-47.

6. John Porter, *The Vertical Mosaic: An Analysis of Social Class and Power in Canada* (Toronto: 1965), pp. 27, 369.

7. Paul Phillips, "National Policy, Continental Economics, and National Disintegration," in *Canada and the Burden of Unity*, edited by David Jay Bercuson (Toronto: 1977), pp. 19-43. I would like to thank Doug Owram for an advance copy of his "The Economic Development of Western Canada: An Historical Overview," Discussion Paper 219, *Economic Council of Canada* (November 1982).

8. J.E. Rea, "The Roots of Prairie Society," in *Prairie Perspectives I*, edited by David Gagan (Toronto: 1970), p. 54.

9. Roger Gibbins, *Prairie Politics and Society: Regionalism in Decline* (Toronto: 1980), p. 93.

10. Canadian Co-operative Credit Society Limited, *Annual Report* (1982), p. 20; *The Financial Post 500* (June 1982), p. 100.

11. Based upon *The Financial Post 500* (June 1982).

12. Marsha Gordon, *Government in Business* (Montreal: 1981), p. 1.

13. Alan Anderson, "Linguistic Trends among Saskatchewan Ethnic Groups," in *Ethnic Canadians: Culture and Education*, edited by Martin L. Kovacs (Regina: 1978), pp. 63-86 and "Ethnic Identity in Saskatchewan Bloc Settlements: A Sociological Appraisal," in *The Settlement of the West*, edited by Howard Palmer (Calgary: 1977).

14. Leo Driedger, "In search of cultural identity factors: a comparison of ethnic students," *Canadian Review of Sociology and Anthropology* 12 (1975), pp. 150-62.

15. Leo Driedger, "Multicultural Regionalism: Toward Understanding the Canadian West," in this volume. I would like to thank Professor Driedger for permitting me to see an early draft of this paper.

16. Howard Palmer, *Patterns of Prejudice: A History of Nativism in Alberta* (Toronto: 1982).

17. Stewart J. Clatworthy and Jonathan P. Gunn, "Economic Circumstances of Native People in Selected Metropolitan Centres in Western Canada" (Institute of Urban Studies, University of Winnipeg, December 1981).

18. Linda Gerber, "The development of Canadian Indian communities: a two-dimensional typology reflecting strategies of adaptation to the modern world," *Canadian Review of Sociology and Anthropology* 16 (1979), pp. 404-24.

19. Nelson Wiseman and Wayne Taylor, "Class and Ethnic Voting in Winnipeg during the Cold War," *Canadian Review of Sociology and Anthropology* 16:1 (1979), pp. 60-76; Wiseman and Taylor, "Ethnic vs Class Voting: The Case of Winnipeg, 1945," *Canadian Journal of Political Science* 7 (1974), pp. 314-28; John Richards and Larry Pratt, *Prairie Capitalism: Power and Influence in the New West* (Toronto: 1979).

20. Dick Harrison, *Unnamed Country: The Struggle for a Canadian Prairie Fiction* (Edmonton: 1977), p. xii and W.L. Morton, "Seeing an Unliterary Landscape," *Mosaic* 3:3 (Spring 1970), pp. 1-10; also Eli Mandel, "Writing West: On the Road to Wood Mountain," in *Another Time*, edited by Mandel (Erin: 1977), pp. 68-78.

21. Wallace Stegner, *Wolf Willow: A History, A Story and a Memory of the Last Plains Frontier* (New York: 1955, 1966), pp. 25-6.

22. David E. Smith, "Celebrations and History on the Prairies," *Journal of Canadian Studies* 17:3 (Fall 1982), pp. 45-57.

23. Northrop Frye, "Across the River and Out of the Trees," in *Northrop Frye: Divisions on a Ground: Essays on Canadian Culture*, edited by James Polk (Toronto: 1982), p. 31.

24. Alan C. Cairns, "The Governments and Societies of Canadian Federalism," *Canadian Journal of Political Science* 10:4 (December 1977), pp. 695-725.

25. Larry Pratt and Garth Stevenson, eds., *Western Separatism: The Myths, Realities and Dangers* (Edmonton: 1981); David E. Smith, *The Regional Decline of a National Party: Liberals on the Prairies* (Toronto: 1981).

26. W.L. Morton, "The Bias of Prairie Politics," in *Contexts of Canada's Past: Selected Essays of W.L. Morton*, edited by A.B. McKillop (Toronto: 1980), p. 159 and Morton, "A Century of Plain and Parkland," in *A Region of the Mind*, edited by Richard Allen (Regina: 1973), p. 179.

27. Carl Berger, *The Writing of Canadian History: Aspects of English-Canadian Historical Writing: 1900-1970* (Toronto: 1976) contains a chapter on "William Morton: The Delicate Balance of Region and Nation," pp. 238-58.

Appendix

TABLES

1. Prairie Population and Canadian Population: 1941-81.

2. Prairie Population: Rural, Rural Non-Farm and Urban: 1941-81.

3. Population of Five Prairie Cities: 1941-81.

4. Prairie Census Value Added by Province and Sector: 1941-78.

5. Prairie Labor Force by Occupational Division and Province: 1941-71.

6. Tertiary and Agricultural Workers as Proportion of Prairie Workforce by Province: 1941-81.

7. Prairie Native Population: 1941-81.

8. Women in Prairie Workforce by Province: 1941-81.

9. Some "Prairie" Corporations on the *Financial Post 500: Industrials, 1981.*

10. Some "Prairie" Firms among the 50 Big Subsidiaries: 1981 (FP 500).

11. Canada's 10 Largest Crown Corporations: 1981 (FP 500).

12. Some "Prairie" Firms among the 75 Banks/Financial Institutions: 1981 (FP 500).

13. Canada's 10 Largest Cooperatives: 1981 (FP 500).

14. Credit Unions and Caisses Populaires, Western Provinces and Canada: 1982.

15. Divorces in Prairie West by Province: 1921-81.

16. Life Expectancy at Birth, By Sex, Alberta and Saskatchewan: 1931-71.

17. Personal Income per person and as % of National Average, Prairie Provinces: 1954-1981.

I would like to thank Richard Enns, who prepared these valuable tables, for his assistance.

TABLE 1:
Number and % of Total Prairie Pop'n in Each Province: 1941-81

	1941		1951		1961		1971		1981	
	#	%	#	%	#	%	#	%	#	%
Manitoba	729,744	30.1	776,541	30.5	921,686	29.0	988,250	27.9	1,026,240	24.2
Saskatchewan	895,992	37.0	831,728	32.6	925,181	29.1	926,240	26.1	968,315	22.9
Alberta	796,169	32.9	939,501	36.9	1,331,944	41.9	1,267,875	46.0	2,237,725	52.9
Prairie Total	2,421,905	(100)	2,547,770	(100)	3,178,811	(100)	3,542,365	(100)	4,232,280	(100)

Prairie Pop'n and BC Pop'n As % of Cdn Pop'n 1941-1981

	Canada	Prairie Pop'n	Prairie pop as % of Cdn. pop.	B.C. pop	B.C. pop as % of Cdn. pop.
1941	11,506,655	2,421,905	21.0%	817,861	7.1%
1951	14,009,429	2,547,770	18.2%	1,165,210	8.3%
1961	18,238,247	3,178,811	17.4%	1,629,082	8.9%
1971	21,568,315	3,542,365	16.4%	2,184,621	10.1%
1981	24,343,180	4,232,280	17.4%	2,744,467	11.3%

TABLE 2:
Prairie Population: urban and rural (farm and non-farm): 1941-1981

	1941[1]		1941[2]		1951[2]	
	#		#		#	
Manitoba						
Rural Farm					214,435	27.6
Non-Farm					122,526	15.8
Total	407,871	55.9	370,066	50.7	336,961	43.4
Urban	321,873	44.1	359,678	49.3	439,580	56.6
Total	729,744		729,744		766,541	
Sask.						
Rural Farm					398,279	47.9
Non-Farm					180,979	21.8
Total	600,846	67.1	703,710	78.5	579,258	69.7
Urban	295,146	32.9	192,282	21.5	252,470	30.3
Total	895,992		895,992		831,728	
Alberta						
Rural Farm					339,955	36.2
Non-Farm					149,871	16.0
Total	489,583	61.5	530,640	66.6	489,826	52.2
Urban	306,586	38.5	265,529	33.4	449,675	47.8
Total	796,169		796,169		939,501	
Prairie Region						
Rural Farm					952,669	37.4
Non-Farm					453,376	17.8
Total	1,498,300	61.9	1,604,416	66.2	1,406,045	55.2
Urban	923,605	38.1	817,489	33.8	1,141,725	44.8
Total	2,421,905		2,421,905		2,547,770	
Canada						
Rural Farm					2,827,732	20.2
Non-Farm					2,553,444	18.2
Total	5,254,239	45.7	5,003,876	43.5	5,381,176	38.4
Urban	6,252,416	54.3	6,502,779	56.5	8,628,253	61.6
Total	11,506,655		11,506,655		14,009,429	

[1]Rural and urban as defined by 1941 Census. Rural population includes persons living outside of the boundaries of incorporated cities, towns or villages. Urban population includes those resident within the boundaries of incorporated cities, towns or villages regardless of the size.

[2]Rural and urban as defined by 1951 Census. Urban population includes all persons residing in cities, towns, or villages of 1,000 people and over, whether or not they are incorporated, as well as the population of all census metropolitan areas.

[3]Rural and Urban as defined by 1961 Census. The urban population includes all those resident within cities, towns and villages of 1,000 people and over, whether incorporated or not, as well as the urbanized fringes of (a) cities classified as metropolitan areas (b) those classed as other major urban areas (c) certain smaller cities if the city together with urbanized fringes is 10,000 or over.

TABLE 2: CONTINUED
Prairie Population: urban and rural (farm and non-farm): 1941-1981

1961[3]		1971[4]		1981[5]	
#		#		#	
171,472	18,6	130,410	13,2	96,390	9.4
161,407	17.5	171,390	17.3	199,190	19.4
332,879	36.1	301,800	30.5	295,585	28.8
588,807	63.9	686,445	69.5	730,660	71.2
921,686		988,250		1,026,240	
304,672	32.9	233,335	35.2	180,255	18.6
222,418	24.0	202,275	21.8	224,890	23.2
527,090	56.9	435,610	47.0	405,150	41.8
398,091	43.1	490,630	53.0	563,165	58.2
925,181		926,240		968,315	
285,823	21.5	236,000	14.5	190,755	8.5
202,910	15.2	195,595	12.0	319,425	14.3
488,733	26.7	431,620	26.5	510,180	22.8
843,211	63.3	1,196,255	73.5	1,727,545	77.2
1,331,944		1,627,875		2,237,725	
761,967	24.0	599,770	16.9	467,400	11.1
586,735	18.5	569,260	16.1	743,505	17.5
1,348,702	42.5	1,169,030	33.0	1,210,915	28.6
1,830,109	57.5	2,373,325	67.0	3,021,370	71.4
3,178,811		3,542,365		4,232,280	
2,072,785	11.4	1,419,795	6.6	1,039,850	4.3
3,465,072	19.0	3,737,730	17.3	4,867,405	20.0
5,537,857	30.4	5,157,525	23.9	5,907,255	24.3
12,700,390	69.6	16,410,785	76.1	18,435,925	75.7
18,238,247		21,568,315		24,343,180	

[4]Rural and Urban as defined by 1971 Census. The urban population
includes (1) those resident within incorporated cities, towns or
villages with 1,000 people or more (2) those residing within the limits
of any unincorporated city, town or village with 1,000 people or more a
density of at least 1,000 people per sq. mi. (3) those resident within
the built fringes of either the above where the population exceeds 1,000
people or a density of at least 1,000 people per sq. mi.

[5]Rural and Urban as defined by 1981 Census. The urban population refers
to persons living in an area having a concentration of 1,000 people or
more and a density of 400 or more per square kilometer.

Sources:

- 1951 Census; CS98-1951f, 1951 Fol. 1 "Pop: Gen'l Characteristics",
  Tables 14 & 15.
- 1961 Census; CS92-536, 1961 Vol. 1. Pt. 1., Table 13
- 1971 Census; CS92-709, 1971 Vol. 1, Pt. 1, Table
- 1981 Census; CS92-901, 1971 "Pop: Age, Sex and Marital Status", Table 7.

TABLE 3:
Population of 5 Prairie Cities: 1941-81[1]

	1941	1951	1961	1971	1981
Total Pr. Pop.	2,421,905	2,547,770	3,178,811	3,542,365	4,232,280
Number resident in:	% of Total Prairie Population in:				
Wpg.	285,957 11.8%	356,813 14.0%	475,989 15.0%	540,262 15.3%	584,842 13.8%
Saskatoon	43,027 1.7%	53,268 2.1%	95,526 3.0%	126,449 3.6%	154,210 3.6%
Regina	58,245 2.4%	71,319 2.8%	112,141 3.5%	140,734 4.0%	164,313 3.9%
Edmonton	93,817 3.9%	176,782 6.9%	337,568 10.6%	495,702 14.0%	657,057 15.5%
Calgary	88,904 3.7%	142,315 5.6%	279,062 8.8%	403,319 11.4%	592,743 14.0%
Total	569,950 23.5%	800,497 31.4%	1,300,286 40.9%	1,706,466 48.3%	2,153,165 50.8%

[1] Population for all cities, 1951-1981, includes, where applicable, both urbanized core and fringe areas

Source: Canada Census

TABLE 4:
Census Value Added in goods producing industries by province sector & % of total by sector:
1941-1978 (Canada & Pr. totals included) ($000)

	1941		1951	
	#		#	
Manitoba				
Agriculture	77,776	38,36	230,371	40.63
Forestry	2,290	1.14	10,536	1.86
Fishing	2,448	1.22	4,263	.74
Trapping	2,002	1.00	3,394	.60
Mining	9,861	4.93	20,804	3,67
Electric Power	9,326	4.66	18,443	3.25
Manufacturing	74,451	37.20	192,849	34.01
Construction	22,000	10.99	86,400	15.24
Total	200,154		567,060	
Saskatchewan				
Agriculture	123,416	64.16	664,931	77.67
Forestry	2,518	1.31	4,532	.53
Fishing	262	.14	910	.11
Trapping	1,948	1.01	1,985	.23
Mining	6,142	3.19	38,723	4.52
Electric Power	4,889	2.54	11,059	1.29
Manufacturing	28,172	14.65	61,089	7.14
Construction	25,000	13.00	72,900	8.50
Total	192,347		856,129	
Alberta				
Agriculture	116,349	46.80	502,440	49.61
Forestry	3,714	1.49	10,151	1.00
Fishing	197	.08	544	.05
Trapping	1,952	.79	2,531	.25
Mining	34,129	13.72	151,554	14.96
Electric Power	6,323	2.54	16,591	1.64
Manufacturing	45,958	18.49	141,649	13.99
Construction	40,000	16.09	187,400	18.50
Total	248,622		1,012,860	
Prairie Rgn.				
Agriculture	317,541	49.53	1,397,742	57.38
Forestry	8,522	1.33	25,219	1.04
Fishing	2,907	.45	5,717	.24
Trapping	5.902	.92	7,910	.32
Mining	50,132	7.82	211,081	8.66
Electric Power	20,538	3.20	46,093	1.89
Manufacturing	148,581	23.18	395,587	16.24
Construction	87,000	13.57	346,700	14.23
Total	641,123		2,436,049	
Canada				
Agriculture	730,280	15.99	2,448,085	18.64
Forestry	163,734	3.59	660,420	5.03
Fishing	34,378	.75	102,027	.78
Trapping	15,138	.33	19,792	.15
Mining	356,244	7.80	770,143	5.86
Electric Power	183,146	4.01	363,643	2.77
Manufacturing	2,605,120	57.04	6,940,947	52.83
Construction	479,000	10.49	1,831,900	13.94
Total	4,567,050		13,136,957	

Source: Stats Canada 61-202 "Survey of Production" Tables 5-13 for
          1941-61; Table 3 for 1971 and 1978.
Note: Any discrepancies in total cited appear in Stats Canada material

TABLE 4: CONTINUED

Census Value Added in goods producing industries by province sector & % of total by sector:
1941-1978 (Canada & Pr. totals included) ($000)

	1961		1971		1978	
	#		#		#	
Manitoba						
Agriculture	111,949	15.98	242,504	18.34	646,131	19.80
Forestry	4,261	.61	4,692	.36	15,619	.49
Fishing	3,174	.45	2,403	.18	10,469	.32
Trapping	1,601	.23	2,189	.17	6.499	.20
Mining	34,060	4.86	148,195	11.20	222,993	6.83
Electric Power	37,864	5.40	81,005	6.12	326,303	10.00
Manufacturing	315,235	44.99	558,920	42.26	1,338,676	41.03
Construction	192,577	27.48	282,674	21.37	695,897	21.33
Total	700,722		1,322,582		3,262,587	
Saskatchewan						
Agriculture	215,054	28.43	737,270	45.70	1,734,887	38.24
Forestry	3,556	.47	6,626	.41	21,237	.47
Fishing	1,385	.18	1,802	.11	3,199	.07
Trapping	1,591	.21	1,710	.10	7.767	.17
Mining	170,208	22.50	349,009	21.64	1,215,717	26.79
Electric Power	36,192	4.78	67,952	4.21	142,614	3.14
Manufacturing	120,972	16.00	217,941	13.51	567,984	12.52
Construction	207,487	27.43	231,115	14.32	843,920	18.60
Total	756,444		1,613,425		4,537,325	
Alberta						
Agriculture	357,151	20.68	441,300	11.82	1,359,370	7.69
Forestry	17,330	1.00	10,024	.27	31,733	.18
Fishing	883	.05	729	.02	1,262	.01
Trapping	1,715	.10	2,566	.07	10,406	.06
Mining	460,199	26.64	1,486,366	39.83	9,109,848	51.45
Electric Power	52,608	3.05	110,262	2.95	369,037	2.08
Manufacturing	346,732	20.07	785,347	21.04	2,544,160	14.37
Construction	490,651	28.41	895,412	24.00	4,279,369	24.17
Total	1,727,269		2,732,007		17,705,185	
Prairie Rgn.						
Agriculture	684,154	21.48	1,421,074	21.31	3,740,388	14.67
Forestry	25,147	.79	21,343	.32	68,589	.27
Fishing	5,442	.17	4,934	.07	14,930	.06
Trapping	4,907	.15	6,465	.10	24,672	.10
Mining	664,467	20.87	1,983,570	29.75	10,548,558	41.35
Electric Power	126,664	3.98	259,219	3.89	837,954	3.29
Manufacturing	782,929	24.59	1,562,208	23.43	4,450,820	17.45
Construction	890,715	27.97	1,409,201	21.13	5,819,186	22.81
Total	3,184,435		6.668,014		25,505,097	
Canada						
Agriculture	1,613,020	8.40	2,610,349	6.55	6,739,034	6.51
Forestry	666,414	3.47	697,634	1.75	1,647,303	1.59
Fishing	111,188	.58	205,568	.52	703,992	.68
Trapping	11,704	.06	13,770	.03	60,829	.06
Mining	1,561,989	8.14	3,826,265	9.60	14,912,401	14.39
Electric Power	840,397	4.38	1,736,678	4.36	5,278,520	5.09
Manufacturing	10,682,138	55.67	23,187,880	58,17	54,634,610	52.72
Construction	3,700,866	19.29	7.580,945	19.02	19,647,660	18.96
Total	19,187,716		39,859,089		103,624,349	

TABLE 5:
Prairie Labor Force 15 Years and Over By Occupational Division: 1941-1971

	1941		1951	
	#		#	
Manitoba				
Managerial	14,959	5.6	22,738	7.6
Technical and Professional	16,589	6.3	19,034	6.4
Clerical	21,343	8.1	35,250	11.8
Sales	12,462	4.7	16,022	5.4
Service & Recreation	29,496	11.1	30,220	10.1
Transportation and Communication	12,902	4.9	17,807	6.0
Farmers and Farm Workers	91,784	34.6	73,576	24.7
Loggers and Related Workers	1,493	.56	1,288	.43
Fishermen, Trappers and Hunters	5,130	1.9	1,546	.52
Miners, Quarrymen and Related Workers	2,119	.80	2,089	.70
Craftsmen, Production Process and Related Workers	44,055	16.6	58,597	19.7
Laborers	12,256	4.6	17,565	5.9
Not Stated	356	.13	2,302	.8
Total of all Occupations	264,944	(100)[1]	298,034	(100)
Saskatchewan				
Managerial	17.550	5.6	22.798	7.6
Technical and Professional	16,458	5.2	19,149	6.3
Clerical	11,959	3.8	19,801	6.6
Sales	9,259	2.9	12,515	4.1
Service & Recreation	27,402	8.7	22,917	7.6
Transportation and Communication	9,646	3.1	13,463	4.5
Farmers and Farm Workers	187,137	59.3	147,261	48.8
Loggers and Related Workers	920	.29	590	.20
Fishermen, Trappers and Hunters	2,675	.85	1,367	.45
Miners, Quarrymen and Related Workers	825	.26	846	.28
Craftsmen, Production Process and Related Workers	23,071	7.3	30,365	10.1
Laborers	8,180	2.6	8,992	3.0
Not Stated	476	.15	1,581	.52
Total of all Occupations	315,504	(100)	301,645	(100)

TABLE 5: CONTINUED

Prairie Labor Force 15 Years and Over By Occupational Division: 1941-1971

	1941		1951	
Alberta				
Managerial	16,047	5.6	28,350	8.0
Technical and Professional	16,541	5.7	23,874	6.8
Clerical	14,214	4.9	30,361	8.6
Sales	10,387	3.6	18,496	5.2
Service and Recreation	25,547	8.9	34,895	9.9
Transportation and Recreation	11,409	4.0	19,829	5.6
Farmers and Farm Workers	141,052	49.0	114,926	32.5
Loggers and Related Workers	938	.33	1,345	.38
Fishermen, Trappers and Hunters	3,004	1.0	958	.27
Miners, Quarrymen and Related Workers	7,540	2.6	7,469	2.1
Craftsmen, Production Process and Related Workers	30,471	10.6	54,177	15.3
Laborers	10,273	3.6	16,771	4.7
Not Stated	408	.14	2,046	.58
Total of All Occupations	287,831	(100)	353,497	(100)

Sources: Stats Canada CS94-6716, 1-3, 1-4, 1-7, 1-8.

Footnotes: [1]percentage totals may not equal 100 due to rounding
[2]discrepancy between individual sums and 1971 total appear in
Stats Canada Table indicated, This appears for all 3
provinces.

TABLE 5: CONTINUED
Prairie Labor Force 15 Years and Over By Occupational Division: 1941-1971

	1961		1971	
	#		#	
Manitoba				
Managerial	25,663	7.5	33,930	8.1
Technical and Professional	29,328	8.6	47,553	11.4
Clerical	45,288	13.2	52,466	12.5
Sales	20,928	6.1	25,510	6.1
Service & Recreation	45,392	13.2	53,952	12.9
Transportation and Communication	19,926	5.8	25,251	6.0
Farmers and Farm Workers	59,924	17.5	48,817	11.7
Loggers and Related Workers	876	.26		
Fishermen, Trappers and Hunters	1,253	.37		
Miners, Quarrymen and Related Workers	2,807	.82	3,686	.88
Craftsmen, Production Process and Related Workers	65,964	19.3	71,301	17.1
Laborers	17,290	5.0	20,104	4.8
Not Stated	8,003	2.3	33,290	8.0
Total of all Occupations	342,642	(100)	418,147	(100)[2]
Saskatchewan				
Managerial	23,318	7.2	27,489	7.5
Technical and Professional	27.858	8.6	35,985	9.8
Clerical	26,639	8.2	43,601	11.8
Sales	16,981	5.2	15,438	4.2
Service & Recreation	31,731	9.7	42,580	11.6
Transportation and Communication	14,796	4.5	12,492	3.4
Farmers and Farm Workers	119,580	36.7	98,319	26.7
Loggers and Related Workers	1,016	.31		
Fishermen, Trappers and Hunters	1,138	.35		
Miners, Quarrymen and Related Workers	2,014	.62	3,540	.96
Craftsmen, Production Process and Related Workers	41,887	12.9	46,277	12.6
Laborers	10,972	3.4	9,505	2.6
Not Stated	7,659	2.3	30,556	8.3
Total of all Occupations	325,589	100	368,125	100

TABLE 5: CONTINUED

Prairie Labor Force 15 Years and Over By Occupational Division: 1941-1971

1961

1971

Alberta				
Managerial	41.691	8.5	52,812	7.6
Technical and Professional	46,579	9.5	83,781	12.2
Clerical	55,317	11.3	90,376	13.2
Sales	31,629	6.5	44,705	6.5
Service and Recreation	59,055	12.1	86,983	12.7
Transportation and Recreation	28,261	5.8	31,155	4.5
Farmers and Farm Workers	104,162	21.3	88,347	12.9
Loggers and Related Workers	2,195	.45		
Fishermen, Trappers and Hunters	814	.17		
Miners, Quarrymen and Related Workers	5,291	1.1	5,331	.8
Craftsmen, Production Process and Related Workers	81,237	16.6	111,142	16.2
Laborers	21,827	4.4	29,177	4.2
Not Stated	11,453	2.3	60,894	8.9
Total of All Occupations	489,511	100	687,042	100

TABLE 6:

Tertiary and Agricultural Workers as Proportion of Prairie Workforce: 1941-1981

	1941 #	%	1951 #	%	1961 #	%	1971 #	%	1981 #	%
Manitoba										
Total Work Force	264944		298034		342642		418147		510885	
Tertiary sector	94849	35.80%	123264	41.36%	166599	48.62%	213411	51.04%	306705	60.03%
Agri. sector	91784	34.64%	73576	24.69%	59924	17.49%	48817	11.67%	42640	8.35%
Saskatchewan										
Total Work Force	315504		301645		325589		368125		461380	
Tertiary sector	82628	26.19%	97180	32.22%	126527	38.86%	165093	44.85%	248325	53.82%
Agri. sector	187137	59.31%	147261	48.82%	119580	36.73%	98319	26.71%	86055	18.65%
Alberta										
Total Work Force	287831		353497		489511		687042		1213705	
Tertiary sector	82736	28.74%	135976	38.47%	234271	47.86%	358657	52.20%	737720	60.78%
Agri. sector	141052	49.01%	114926	32.51%	104162	21.28%	83475	12.86%	83960	6.92%
Pr. Region										
Total	868279		953176		1157742		1473314		2185970	
Tertiary sector	260213	29.97%	356420	37.39%	527397	45.55%	737161	50.03%	1292750	59.14%
Agri. sector	419973	48.37%	335763	35.23%	283666	24.50%	235483	15.98%	212655	9.73%

Source: Stats Canada Estimates, Stats Canada CTE81B33

- 1981 Census Estimates, Stats Canada CS94-716, 1-3, 1-4, 1-7, 1-8

[1]Tertiary includes managerial, technical/professional, clerical, sales services and recreation for 1941 to 1971. The 1981 figure includes those occupied in natural sciences, social sciences and related fields, religion, teaching and related fields, medicine and health. The arts and related occupations, clerical, sales and service occupations.

[2]1981 figures based on Stats Canada estimates derived from 20% sample data.

TABLE 7:
Prairie Native Population: 1941-81

	1941	1951	1961	1971	1981
Manitoba					
Inuit	1	26	208	130	230
Status Indian	15473	21024	29219	21165	39710
Non. St. Indian					5855
Metis	8692	NA	NA	NA	20485
Total	24166	21050	29427	21295	66280
Saskatchewan					
Inuit	4	3	2	75	145
Status Indian	13384	22250	30628	40475	37470
Non. St. Indian					4135
Metis	9160	NA	NA	NA	17455
Total	22548	22253	30630	40550	59200
Alberta					
Inuit	4	47	85	135	510
Status Indian	12565	21163	28469	44545	35810
Non. St. Indian					8595
Metis	8808	NA	NA	NA	27135
Total	21377	21210	28554	44680	72050
Prairie Region					
Inuit	9	76	295	340	885
Status Indian	.41422	64437	88316	106185	112990
Non. St. Indian					18585
Metis	26660	NA	NA	NA	65075
Total	68091	64513	88611	106525	197535
Canada					
Inuit	7205	9733	11835	17550	25390
Status Indian	118316	155874	209286	295215	292700
Non. St. Indian					75110
Metis	35416	NA	NA	NA	98260
Total	160937[1]	165607[2]	220121[2]	313765[3]	491460[4]

Souces: Stats Canada Memorandum, Jan. 28, 1983, "Data on Native
Peoples" Tables 1 & 2.
- 1971 Census Vol I. Pt3 92-723 Table 2 "Ethnic Groups"
- 1961 Census Vol. I Pt2 92-545 Table 35 "Ethnic Groups"
- 1951 Census Vol. I   Table 32 "Origin"
- 1941 Census Vol. II   Table 30 "Population"

[1] Includes native Indian, Inuit & persons of mixed native and nonnative
ancestry traced on father's side.
[2] Includes native Indian, Inuit & some persons of mixed native and
nonnative ancestry
[3] Includes native Indian & Inuit only, traced on father's side
[4] Includes native Indian, Inuit and self reported métis, traced through
both parents.

TABLE 8:
Women in Prairie Workforce by Province: 1941-81

	1941	1951	1961	1971	1981
Manitoba					
Fem. Pop.	257,787	272,908	306,473	353,020	396,435
Fem. W/Force	49,764	66,135	96,444	136,421	207,355[1]
%	19.3	24.2	31.5	38.6	52.3
Sask					
Fem. Pop.	286,579	272,150	291,953	318,230	359,225
Fem. W/force	42,681	50,936	77,110	122,615	174,010[1]
%	14.9	18.7	26.4	38.5	48.4
Alberta					
Fem. Pop.	256,857	306,448	413,800	548,680	818,265
W/Force	40,375	62,566	127,550	246,633	476,240[1]
%	15.7	20.4	30.8	45.0	58.2
Pr. Reg					
Fem. Pop.	801,223	851,506	1,012,226	1,219,930	1,573,925
Fem. W/Force	132,820	179,637	301,104	505,669	857,605[1]
%	16.6	21.1	29.7	41.5	54.5
Canada					
Fem. Pop.	4,026,867	4,837,897	5,993,523	7,655,530	9,457,690
Fem. W/Force	831,129	1,162,232	1,763,862	2,960,098	4,898,890[1]
%	20.6	24.0	29.4	38.7	51.8

1 work force figures for 1981 based on 20% sample data

Source: 1971 Census Vol. III pt 2 CS94-716 Table 1
          1971 Census Vol. I pt 2 CS92-715 Table 1
Econ. Statistics 1981 Cen. — CTE81 B31 & CTE 81 B13

TABLE 9:

Some 'Prairie' Corporations on The Financial Post 500: Industrials, 1981
[in the Financial Post 500 (June 82), 65-95]

Rank by Sales		Sales or Operating Revenue	Company (Head Office)	Rank by
1981	1980	$000		Assets
1	1	12,336,266	Canadian Pacific Ltd. (Montreal)	3
12	10	4,172,442	Hudson's Bay Co. (Winnipeg) Jan. 82	20
13	15	3,404,897	Trans Canada Pipelines Ltd. (Calgary)	17
20	22	2,006,302[1]	Canada Safeway Ltd. (Winnipeg)	90
24	37	2,854,265[1]	Total Petroleum (North America) Ltd. (Calgary)	59
27	32	2,669,551	Nova Corp (Calgary)	15
28	64	2,646,365	Petro Canada (Calgary)	11
35	56	2,238,800	Dome Petroleum (Calgary)	5
38	28	2,145,922[4]	Genstar Ltd. (Vancouver)	27
40	39	1,941,433[4]	Saskatchewan Wheat Pool (Regina) July 81	85
53	68	1,390,978[4]	Alberta Wheat Pool (Calgary) July 81	120
54	49	1,374,576[4]	United Grain Growers Ltd. (Wpg) July 81	125
56	57	1,327,037	Federated Co-Operatives Ltd. (Sask) Oct. 81	140
59	55	1,276,851	Cargill Grain Co. (Winnipeg) May 81	177
65	63	1,204,141	James Richardson & Sons Ltd. (Winnipeg)	87
66	135	1,200,889	Atco Ltd. (Calgary) Mar. 81	40
67	58	1,200,000	Burns Foods Ltd. (Calgary)	n.a.
69	72	1,168,608	Westburne International Industries Ltd. (Calgary) Mar. 81	103
76	0	1,040,000	Nu-West Group Ltd. (Calgary)	32
80	69	988,012	Amoco Canada Petroleum Co. (Calgary)	50
81	0	977,177	Can West Capital Corp. (Winnipeg)	31
86	70	904,601	Mobil Oil Canada Ltd. (Canada)	66
90	99	838,547	PCL Construction (Edmonton)	169
122	134	566,397	Inter-City Gas Corp. (Winnipeg)	106
136	181	510,163	Cana Construction Co. (Calgary)	296
142	0	481,050	Carma Ltd. (Calgary)	57
143	161	478,954[4]	Bow Valley Industries Ltd. (Calgary)	71
151	120	454,304[4]	Manitoba Pool Elevators (Winnipeg) July 81	208
152	179	450,721	Trimac Ltd. (Calgary)	115
164	158	402,714	Trans Alta Utilities Corp. (Calgary)	35
167	189	393,846	Consolidated Natural Gas Ltd. (Calgary)	341
168	162	390,969	Acklands Ltd. (Winnipeg) Nov. 81	186
176	153	361,843	Manitoba Hydro-Electric Board (Winnipeg) Mar. 81	29
185	0	352,298	Canadian Superior Oil Ltd. (Calgary)	81
186	185	349,758	General Distributors of Canada Ltd. (Winnipeg) Jan. 82	213
190	214	343,057	Ocelot Industries Ltd. (Calgary) Mar. 81	107
198	182	315,656	Wardair International Ltd. (Edmonton)	139
200	212	313,348	Pacific Western Airlines Ltd. (Calgary)	124
208	201	294,533	Interprovincial Steel and Pipe Corp. (Regina) Aug. 81	161
213	210	285,100	Alberta Energy Co. (Edmonton)	74
223	198	264,372[1]	Canada-Cities Service (Calgary)	105
234	269	240,769[1,5]	Ranger Oil Ltd. (Calgary)	117
236	224	240,652	Manitoba Telephone System (Winnipeg)	101
238	232	236,274	Revelstoke Cos. (Calgary)	265
266	264	204,255[1]	Greyhound Lines of Canada Ltd. (Calgary)	248
277	329	200,000[3]	Banister Continental Ltd. (Edmonton) Mar. 82	n.a.
278	245	198,378	Canadian Occidental Petroleum Ltd. (Calgary)	146
284	0	195,000	Qualico Developments Ltd. (Winnipeg)	127
286	276	192,690	Federal Industries Ltd. (Winnipeg)	202
291	206	187,421	Dome Mines Ltd. (Toronto)	98
313	294	167,260	L-K Resources Ltd. (Calgary) Sept. 81	325
323	300	160,008	Agra Industries Ltd. (Saskatoon) July 81	289
332	0	152,118	Associated Grocers Ltd. (Calgary) Sept. 81	354
336	366	147,000	Peter Bawden Drilling Ltd. (Calgary)	191
337	309	146,546	Murphy Oil Co. (Calgary)	192
339	327	144,051	N.M. Paterson & Sons Ltd. (Thunder Bay) Mar. 81	342
365	.	124,199	Central Alberta Dairy Pool (Red Deer)	371
345	303	140,850	Nowsco Well Service Ltd. (Calgary)	242
386	378	108,793	Canadian Motorways Ltd. (Winnipeg)	351
391	346	106,952	Union Oil Co. of Canada (Calgary)	190

FOOTNOTES FOR INDUSTRIALS

1. converted from US $
3. estimate
4. sales include grain purchased for the account and delivered to the Canadian Wheat Board; assets
    include grain held for the account of the CWB.
5. fiscal February 1982 figures unavailable; sales based on 12 month period ended November, 1981.
13. each owns 20.2%
n.a. *Not available/not applicable

Assets $000	Employees	Foreign Owner-ship %	Major Shareholders
4,586,300	129,223	28	Power Corp. of Canada 11%
16,330,185	47,000		Woodbridge Co. (Thomson Family) 73%
3,895,185	1,856	1	Dome Petroleum Ltd. 46%
830,832	24,539	96	Safeway Stores Inc. Oakland, Calif.
1,302,613	1,893	78	Compagne Francais des Petroles France 53%
5,003,919	10,000		Wide Distribution
6,612,533	5,801		Federal Government 100%
10,208,700	9,500	43[3]	Dome Mines Ltd. 27%
2,858,794	20,225	45	Societe Generale De Belgique 15% Directly/Indirectly
910,244	4,200		Co-op Members
488,585	2,112		Co-op Members
441,299	2,028		Co-op Members
391,838	2,426		Co-op Members
264,785	1,495	100	Cargill Inc. Minneapolis
895,928	n.a.		Richardson Family
1,948,584	8,400		Southern Family 51%
n.a.	8,500		R.H. Webster 61%; A.J.E. Child 25%; Officers 14%
655,793	7,000		J.M. Scrymgeour 13%; W.H. Atkinson Estate 14%
2,518,000	2,500		R.T. Scurfield 22%; C.J. McConnell 20%
1,580,600	1,986	100	Standard Oil Co. (Indiana), Chicago
2,543,824	8,570		Institutions 55%, Private 45%
1,164,251	1,228	100	Mobil Oil Corp New York
284,691			PCL Employees 85%, Great-West Life 15%
648,960	3,680	30	Wide Distribution
98,604	3,000		J.L. Simpson 80%; H.I. Thomas 20%
1,373,382	1,301		Nu-West Group Ltd. 48%
1,061,869	3,036		Seaman Brothers 17%; Cemp Investments 12%
191,365	1,170		Co-op Members
507,349	5,300	4	McCaig Family 37%
2,369,958	2,500		Nu-West 20%
66,986	19	100	Internorth Inc. Omaha, Neb.
239,760	3,200		Mindy's Ltd. 18%; Wolinsky Estate 16%; N. Starr 15%
2,649,841	3,634		Manitoba Government 100%
950,100	699	100	Superior Oil Co., Houston
183,187	5,800		Cohen Family 75%
624,541	1,500		J.V. Lyons
396,451	2,513		M.W. Ward 72%
449,389	3,791		Alberta Government 100%
307,279	2,289	2	Sask, Crown Invest; Alberta Steel; Slater Steel[13]
1,036,900	396		Alberta Government 50%
651,642	n.a.	100	Cities Service Co., Tulsa Okla.
502,424	230		Wide Distribution
702,241	4,620		Manitoba Government 100%
115,704	1,805		Venture Funding Corp. 45%
131,603	3,200	62	Greyhound Lines Inc., Phoenix
n.a.	2,000		R.K. Banister 27%; Trimac Ltd. 16%
371,670	605	84	Occidental Petroleum Corp, Los Angeles 80%
428,000	n.a.		Privately Owned
206,304	1,493		C.L. and S.A. Searle 15% Directly/Indirectly
718,605	1,674	39	Dome Petroleum Ltd. 39%
74,743	500		McKinnon Family 60%
101,388	2,200	1	B.B. Torchnisky 21%; Crown Investments of Sask. 16%
53,017	750		Owned by Members
220,000	n.a.		Directors & Officers
219,494	276	77	Murphy Oil Corp., Eldorado, Ark.
66,786	500		Paterson Family
136,433	1,020	62	Big Three Industries Inc., Houston
36,509	673		Co-op Members
55,161	n.a.	100	British Electric Traction Co., Britain
227,761	316	100	Union Oil Co. of California, Los Angeles

TABLE 10:

Some 'Prairie' Firms among the 50 Big Subsidiaries 1981 [from the *Financial Post* 500 (June 82) 98]

SALES OR REVENUES $'000	COMPANY	ASSETS $'000	NET INCOME $'000	PARENT COMPANY	OWNERSHIP %
8,558,759	Canadian Pacific Enterprises Ltd.	11,241,120	404,600	Canadian Pacific Ltd.	71
2,070,977	CP Rail	2,526,640	127,168	Canadian Pacific Ltd.	100
1,509,591	Husky Oil Ltd.	2,074,839	43,582	Nova Corp.	68
1,426,434	Algoma Steel Corp.	608,581	164,970	Canadian Pacific Enterprises Ltd.	58
1,416,904	Cominco Ltd.	2,027,824	64,710	Canadian Pacific Enterprises Ltd.	54
1,342,000	CIP Inc.	n.a.	n.a.	Canadian Pacific Enterprises Ltd.	100
1,024,564	Canadian Utilities Ltd.	1,602,740	81,437	Atco Ltd.	58
827,572	CP Air	844,749	(22,781)	Canadian Pacific Ltd.	100
726,400	Hudson's Bay Oil & Gas Ltd.	2,019,100	71,700	Dome Petroleum Ltd.	53
621,496	PanCanadian Petroleum Ltd.	1,604,047	203,737	Canadian Pacific Enterprises Ltd.	87
568,594	Great Lakes Forest Products Ltd.	586,016	77,774	Canadian Pacific Enterprises Ltd.	54
525,342	Saskatchewan Power Corp.	1,723,168	(2,325)	Crown Investments Corp. of Sask.	100
267,620	Saskatchewan Telecommunications	765,480	24,309	Crown Investments Corp. of Sask.	100
226,989	Marathon Realty Co.	1,086,712	24,027	Canadian Pacific Enterprises	100
165,374	Greater Winnipeg Gas Co.	123,352	3,991	Northern and Central Gas Corp.	100
134,500	Markborough Properties Ltd.	573,435	10,000	Hudson's Bay Co.	100
99,782	White Pass & Yukon Corp.	71,895	3,059	Federal Industries Ltd.	100

TABLE 11:

Canada's 10 Largest Crown Corporations, 1981 Financial Post (June 82) 100.

Rank	Assets $'000	Name
1	20,730,000	Hydro-Québec
2	17,829,521	Ontario Hydro
3	6,911,727	British Columbia Hydro & Power Authority
4	6,612,533	Petro-Canada
5	6,140,167	Canadian National Railway
6	5,064,141	Crown Investments Corp. of Saskatchewan
7	2,649,841	Manitoba Hydro-Electric Board
8	2,377,648	New Brunswick Power Commission
9	2,072,162	Alberta Government Telephones
10	1,869,928	Air Canada

TABLE 12:

Some 'Prairie' Firms among the 75 BANKS/FINANCIAL INSTITUTIONS, 1981 [from the *Financial Post* 500 (June 1982) 106-7].

RANK BY ASSETS	COMPANY	ASSETS** $'000 OLD	ASSETS** $'000 NEW	NET INCOME $'000	FIVE-YEAR GROWTH RATE PER ANNUM %
26	Province of Alberta Treasury Branches (Edmonton)	2,355,486		18,108	9.0
34	Investors Group (Winnipeg)	1,391,546		60,523	28.3
37	Alberta Home Mortgage Corp. (Edmonton)	1,277,062		(12,358)	n.a.
45	Fidelity Trust (Edmonton)	975,000		11,480	56.0
58	Co-operative Trust Co. of Canada (Saskatoon)	607,620		446	-19.2
61	North West Trust Co. (Edmonton)	534,847		6,505	37.7
62	Northland Bank (Calgary)	517,370	514,186	4,242	n.a.
74	Edmonton Savings & Credit Union (Edmonton)	330,491		48,463	35.8
75	Sherwood Credit Union (Regina)	292,984		(840,000)	n.a.

FOOTNOTES TO BANKS/FINANCIAL INSTITUTIONS

** Banks have been ranked according to assets at year end Oct. 31, 1981, under old accounting rules, with the exception of Continental Bank of Canada which because of its amalgamation with IAC Ltd., prepared no information under these rules. New accounting rules apply to fiscal 1982, and some banks have restated 1981 figures according to them.

TABLE 13:

Canada's 10 Largest Co-operatives. 1981 Financial Post 500 (June 1982) 100

Rank	Sales $'000	Name
1	1,941,433[1]	Saskatchewan Wheat Pool
2	1,390,978[1]	Alberta Wheat Pool
3	1,374,576[1]	United Grain Growers
4	1,327,037	Federated Co-operatives
5	1,075,873	Co-opérative Fédérée de Québec
6	604,047	United Co-operatives
7	526,935	Agropur, Co-opérative Agro Alimentaire[3]
8	454,304	Manitoba Pool Elevators
9	254,025	Fraser Valley Milk Producers' Association
10	196,193	Co-op Atlantic

[1] Sales include grain purchased for the account and delivered to the Canadian Wheat Board.

[2] Name has been changed from Co-operative Agricole de Granby.

TABLE 14:
Credit Unions and Caisses Populaires, Western Provinces and Canada 1982

	Members	Number of C.U. & C.P.	Number of Branches	Savings $000	Loans $000	Assets $000
Man.	318,814	137	203	1,365	1,051	1,394
Sask.	594,140	225	303	2,874	2,093	3,113
Alta.	507,000	137	272	2,183	1,871	2,438
B.C.	930,000	142	340	4,826	3,904	5,266
Canada	9,529,383		4,245	31,124	23,497	33,701

Source: (i)Canadian Cooperative(/i) Credit Society Limited, (i)Annual Report(/i) 1982 p. 20.

TABLE 15:
Number of Divorces, Prairie Provinces: 1921-81

Year	Alberta	Saskatchewan	Manitoba
1921	89	59	122
1931	157	55	94
1941	311	146	242
1951	589	226	361
1961	1039	251	312
1971	3656	813	1370
1981	8418	1932	2399

Source: Stats Canada 84-205 (i)Vital Statistics(/i) II (i)Marriages and Divorces

TABLE 16:
Personal Income per person and as % of National Average by Province 1954-1981

	1954		1961		1971		1981	
Manitoba	1126	93.44%	1557	94.3%	3231	94.1%	10806	93.8%
Saskatchewan	927	76.93%	1172	71.0%	2759	80.3%	11583	100.5%
Alberta	1239	102.82%	1651	100%	3399	99.0%	12799	111.1%
Prairie Region Average	1097	91.05%	1460	88.4%	3130	91.1%	11729	101.8%
Canada	1205	(100)	1651	(100)	3435	(100)	11520	(100)

Sources: CS 13-201, Table 36, Table 29

TABLE 17:
Life Expectancy at Birth, By Sex, Alberta and Saskatchewan: 1931-71

	1931		1941		1951		1961		1971	
	M	F	M	F	M	F	M	F	M	F
Alberta	60	62.1	63	66.3	66.3	72.5	68.4	74.2	70.4	77.3
Saskatchewan	63.5	65.5	65.4	68.2	68.4	72.3	69.8	75.7	71.1	77.3

POLITICAL CHANGE IN THE "NEW WEST"

Roger Gibbins

Coming to grips with political change in a regional society over a span of almost forty years is a difficult task. In essence, one must weave together a great many strands of social and political change, and then determine to what extent the resulting tapestry takes on any pattern or coherence. In so doing, one encounters a daunting set of problems.

First, neither social nor political change is unidirectional. Societies seldom move in a straight line from point A to point B; they are more prone to move off in a number of quite different directions at the same time, or to experience random oscillations rather than patterned change over time. If we ask, for example, whether the Canadian society is becoming more liberal or more conservative over time, evidence of change in both directions can easily be found. Analytically, then, one must take into account the broad array of changes through which a society moves over time, weigh the importance of each, and determine the extent and direction of any net change. This process is contentious, as we will all attach differing weights to different types of change.

Second, in the case of the Canadian West neither social nor political change have been uniform across the four western provinces. The rate and intensity of change, the scope of social and political disruption flowing from change, and in some cases, the direction of change itself have all varied. Divorce rates soar in Alberta while remaining low in Saskatchewan; the NDP wilts in British Columbia, is thrown out of the office in Saskatchewan, and sweeps back into office in Manitoba. Thus any conclusions about change in "the Canadian West" are subject to continual provincial qualifications. Even the nomenclature causes a problem; to what extent is there a Canadian West that is more than the sum of four quite different provincial societies?[1]

Third, the linkages between social and political change are far from clear. While it is generally assumed that social change fosters political change, that the political system reflects its changing social environment, it is also true that the political system can itself affect the rate and direction of social change. Provincial governments in the western provinces have not been passive ledgers for the social transformation of the western society but have played a major role in that transformation. "Province-building" strategies have had a marked impact on the postwar western Canadian society; without their monuments—the Alberta Heritage Savings and Trust Fund, BCRIC, B.C. Rail and countless others—the western landscape would seem barren indeed.[2]

Fourth, there is a normative dimension to change which can distort what may purport to be a descriptive enterprise. If, for example, the small prairie community has been the casualty of social change, should we lament its passing? Or should we welcome a more metropolitan and perhaps more cosmopolitan prairie community? Certainly analytical indifference to the postwar transformation of the Canadian West is a difficult stance to maintain.

These problems serve as a prelude and caveat to the essay on the Canadian West which follows, the term "essay" implying a search for general patterns rather than the documentation of specific details. Two questions inform and guide that search: how has the western Canadian society been transformed since the end of World War II, and in what way has that transformation altered the political relationship between the Canadian West and the Canadian nation?

The Paradox of Change

It is difficult not to be struck by the postwar transformation of the Canadian West.[3] On the prairies in particular, a very different society emerged from World War II and the dustbowl of the 1930s. Agriculture had entered a period of relative decline that has continued to this day; its proportionate contribution to the western and national economies declined, the percentage of the western Canadian population living on farms fell as did the absolute size of the prairie farm population, and the number of prairie farms decreased even as the absolute output of agricultural producers increased over time. Prairie society became increasingly urbanized as new metropolitan skylines came to dominate the prairie landscape and psyche just as the grain elevator had in the past. The base of the western economy gradually broadened to include oil, natural gas, potash, uranium and coal. Contact with the rest of the Canadian society became progressively easier; Toronto was only four hours by air from Vancouver, three from Calgary or Edmonton, less than two from Winnipeg. Apart from dialing an extra four numbers, Ottawa and Montreal were as close by telephone as the neighbour down the street.

In what came to be known as the "New West" of the 1970s, rising prices for western natural resources fueled a dramatic economic boom. With new wealth came an influx of new westerners as across the country Canadians packed their belongings into the U-hauls and headed off for the end of the resource rainbow in the West, seeking not a quarter-section of land as in the past but a piece of what appeared to be an ever-growing natural resource pie. Boosterism gripped the region, and westerners saw themselves at the cutting edge of the Canadian society. The West was where things were happening, where the future was being unveiled today. To an extent this image was shared by Canadians across the country although it often generated resentment and a degree of hostility toward the brash and aggressive "New West."

While the changes that swept across the western Canadian society were not unidirectional in character, on balance they produced a western society increasingly similar to other parts of Canada. Postwar social change eroded the regional distinctiveness of the West; western Canadians came more and more to resemble their compatriots in Toronto, Ottawa and the Atlantic coast, just as Canadians at large were coming more and more to resemble Americans to the south. The typical Calgarian, for example, came no closer to a field of wheat than his breakfast cereal and no closer to cattle than a steak in a nationally-franchised steak house. Calgarians lived in a suburban environment little different from suburban environments elsewhere in Canada or North America, drove Japanese cars, listened to American and British pop music on a Japanese stereo set, went out to American movies or stayed at home to watch Monday Night Football or Johnny Carson on cable television, read *People Magazine* and *National Enquirer*, ate out at Burger King or McDonalds, and travelled south in the winter to Hawaii, Mexico, Florida or Phoenix. For better or for worse, then, western

Canadians had entered the Canadian and North American mainstream. The distinctive elements that had set the West apart in the past were submerged, a transformation that was assisted by an influx of new westerners who had no roots in the West's agrarian past.

Yet in this tide of national integration, a perplexing paradox emerged; the "New West" was no more at home in the national political community than the old West had been. Indeed, the 1970s witnessed an alarming spread and intensification of western alienation. Largely unrepresented within a series of Liberal national governments, western Canadians found those governments to be at best indifferent and at worst hostile to the concerns, interests and aspirations of the West. The deteriorating political climate throughout the 1970s culminated with the February, 1980 federal election in which Joe Clark's minority Progressive Conservative government was defeated despite massive support in the West, only to be replaced by a Pierre Trudeau-led Liberal government holding but two seats in western Canada and no seats west of the Manitoba-Saskatchewan border. Following the 1980 election a significant separatist movement arose for the first time in the West. Combined with this came intensified intergovernmental and regional conflict in the wake of the National Energy Program and federal initiatives to patriate the constitution. Thus the paradox: the social integration of the West came hand-in-glove with the progressive political estrangement of the West from the national political community.

To explain this paradox of intensifying regional alienation despite countervailing social change rendering the West more and more like the broader Canadian and North American societies, it is useful to compare the "New West" with the "Old West" which came into full blossom in the decades preceding the Great Depression and World War II.

Points of Comparison: The Old and New Wests

Although in a social sense the West of the last decade bears only a slight resemblance to the West of the 1900s, 1910s and 1920s, there are some underlying constants in western life that stand out from the backdrop of social change sketched in above. It is these constants which form the principal pillars of western Canadian political discontent.

Both the old and new Wests were associated with important demographic shifts in the regional composition of the national population. While in 1901 the four western provinces contained only 11.1 percent of the Canadian population, this proportion grew to 23.9 percent in 1911, 28.2 percent in 1921 and 29.4 percent in 1931. Then the devastating impact of the Depression trimmed the region's share of the national population to 28.2 percent in 1941 and 26.5 percent in 1951, the first census year following the war. In 1961 the West's share dropped marginally to 26.4 percent and then rose to 26.6 percent in 1971, 27.2 percent in 1976, and to 28.7 percent in 1981. The West was again on the move. The intraregional distribution of the western population, however, was very different in 1981 than it was in 1931. In 1931 the two western provinces, Alberta and British Columbia, contained slightly less than 47 percent of the region's population; by 1981 this had grown dramatically to over 71 percent. In the 1970s, then, Canada's population appeared to the shifting westward, and westward within the West, although it was not generally recognized that *by 1981 the*

West's share of the national population was still well short of what it had been prior to the onset of the Depression.

Both the old and new Wests were heavily dependent upon staple-based economies that were open to the fluctuations of world trade. In the old West, of course, the economic base came from wheat, and the trade collapse and climatic disasters of the 1930s demonstrated just how fragile that base could be. The new West enjoyed a broader economic base, but it was still dependent upon the extraction of natural resources and consequently on unstable world markets for oil, natural gas, potash, wheat, coal, lumber, copper and uranium. It was a crisis in the Middle East, for example, that set off the Alberta oil-boom in the early 1970s and which left the province's economy more resource-dependent at the end of the decade than it had been at the start, despite governmental attempts to spur economic diversification.

In both cases the health of the western economy was tied to the public policies of the national government. For the wheat economy the critical policies were those relating to tariffs, freight rates, rail expansion, immigration and the regulation of the grain trade. For the resource-based economy of the 1970s, federal policies relating to transportation, resource taxation, foreign investment, export trade and regional economic development continued to be of critical importance. No better example of the dependency of the West on national policies can be found than the impact of the National Energy Program in 1980.

Economic growth in the West has frequently been the cause of economic tension, and thus political tension, within the broader Canadian community. In the past, such tensions were moderated by the substantial economic spin-offs that western economic growth produced elsewhere in Canada. Western expansion fueled the national economy as the East supplied the goods, services and credit essentially to the agrarian frontier.[4] In the 1970s, however, escalating resource revenues in the West were the source of much sharper regional disputes in which the federal government was seen by Westerners not as an umpire, but as one of the opposing players. Whereas the profits of the wheat boom had flowed largely into private hands, be they of farmers in the West or of transportation and financial interests in the East, the energy windfall of the 1970s was largely claimed by the public treasury. The result was an intense taxation dispute between the federal and provincial treasuries, the principal battleground being the National Energy Program and the Alberta-Ottawa oil-pricing agreements.

Both the old and the new Wests faced parliamentary institutions which impaired effective regional representation within the national government and legislative process, and which thereby fostered alienation within the West. The unhappy Canadian marriage between British parliamentary institutions and the American innovation of federalism has left Canada without any effective regional counterweight to national legislative majorities.[5] Although the British North America Act of 1867 established a federal system through the constitutional division of legislative powers, the federal principle was not built into the institutions of the new national government. An appointed Senate rapidly proved to be an impotent forum for regional interests, and rigid party discipline with the House forced Members of Parliament to place the interests of their party above those of their regional constituents, should the two clash. Effective regional representation may be possible within cabinet and, to a lesser extent, within caucus, but in both cases it is obscured by a cloak of secrecy. If cabinet announces a policy that runs counter to regional interests we have no way of knowing whether our cabinet representative fought the good fight but lost; whether he traded off a loss today for gains tomorrow; whether he was convinced that on other grounds the policy had to be supported; whether he was asleep at the switch, or whether he sold us out. In short, then, the parliamentary system is such that western Canadians have been unable to see regional representation at work, and the general cast of national policies gives little evidence that such representation is being carried on effectively behind closed doors.

Lacking an effective voice within the national government, western Canadians have turned to their provincial governments as their regional champions in national affairs, thereby inflating the role of provincial governments. The result has been intensified intergovernmental conflict across a broad range of issues and the further estrangement of the West from the national political community. This conflict has in turn distorted electoral politics within the provinces. Provincial governments are able to use ''Ottawa-bashing'' in order to ward off any damaging discussion of purely provincial issues; campaigns take on an adversarial atmosphere which places opposition parties in the awkward position of appearing to side with either the provincial or federal government.

The institutional flaws within the Canadian political system would be less serious if the national political parties were able to knit together the disparate regional components of the Canadian community. Unfortunately, this has seldom been the case. The parties, themselves impaled upon parliamentary institutions, have been less than successful vehicles for national integration. Not unreasonably, the parties have paid closest attention to those regions which could yield the greatest number of parliamentary seats, and this has meant Quebec and Ontario rather than the West. (Ontario has been of particular importance, not only due to its number of seats, but also because of the sudden changes in the mood of its electorate, a volatility not shared by voters in the West or Quebec).

In recent years the West has suffered chronic weakness within government ranks, with only two western MPs sitting on the government side of the House after the 1980 general election. It has been the Liberal party which has fared the worst in the West, and to a large degree the party has been the author of its own misfortune.[6] The Liberals, however, have suffered under an electoral system which fails to translate a reasonable popular vote in the West (averaging close to 25 percent over the last four elections) into a reasonable number of western seats. More importantly, the Liberal failure in the West left that party's grip on national power unimpaired, while at the same time overwhelming Conservative strength in the West failed to propel that party into national office. The party system has thus exacerbated rather than moderated regional conflict between the West and the nation. The parties have come to be seen as part of the problem rather than as part of the solution.

Throughout this century, western Canadians have shared a general consensus that the political system is flawed, that it discriminates against the legitimate interests and aspirations of the West, that it fails to provide western Canadians with their rightful place in the national sun. That consensus is the core of western alienation. Yet while they agree that the West fails to find effective regional representation within national parliamentary institutions, there has been no consensus on a cure. Some have sought only to replace Liberal with Conservative governments or, more rarely, Conservative with Liberal governments. Others have supported regionally-based third parties. Still others have supported House elections based on proportional representation, an elected Senate, or a devolution of the federal system so as to provide more power to provincial governments lying within western control. A small, but at times significant, handful has even supported the extremity of separatism. Still others, such as John Diefenbaker and to a degree Joe Clark, emerged as forceful defenders of the very parliamentary institutions which lay at the root of western disenfranchisement.

While the above configuration of factors does not provide a complete explanation of western alienation, it does help account for the continuity of this discontent throughout most of this century. Yet, despite its continuity and, at times, its intensity, western alienation has at best affected the margins of the Canadian political system. No fundamental institutional change has resulted from western political discontent, no boundaries have been redrawn, and the Conservative and Liberal parties continue to dominate national political life as they did prior to the turn of the century. It is to an explanation of why western discontent has had such little impact that we now turn.

Conditions for Political Reform

Western Canadians have been caught on the horns of a persistent political dilemma. On the one side, they have been strong nationalists, proud of the country that they have done so much to build. The strength of this nationalism has never been in doubt, even though at times it took on a flavor that other Canadians found offensive. For example, while the "one-Canada" nationalism of John Diefenbaker may have grated upon French Canadians, it was nonetheless a legitimate if unrealistic Canadian vision. Canada, after all, is a land of many and conflicting national visions. On the other side, western Canadians believed, and were given ample reason to believe, that the national political system was stacked against them, that too often the "national interest" failed to reflect the interests, concerns and aspirations of the West. This tension between nationalism and regional discontent with national political institutions provides much of the underlying continuity of western political life.

If western Canadians were to remove themselves from the horns of this dilemma, they could pursue one of two options. The first would be to withdraw from the national community and go it alone. Western separatism, however, has never enjoyed the support of more than a radical fringe. Most western Canadians are Canadians first, and separatism holds little appeal.[7] Indeed, even among separatist supporters nationalist sentiment remains high; it is not uncommon to hear separatists argue that they are the true Canadians, that it is the East which has abandoned Canadian ideals and values. The second option, and in many ways the only option, is to seek the reform of national political institutions so as to ensure more effective political representation for the West.

Three basic conditions must be met if reform is to be achieved. The first is that there must be widespread discontent with the political status quo, discontent that goes beyond the party in power to the institutional structures of the Canadian state. There is little doubt that this condition has been met. The long history of political radicalism in the West and the current manifestations of western alienation provide the evidence.

The second condition is some consensus on the specific reforms required. Political discontent may provide the pressure for reform, but to be effective that pressure must be focused. This condition has not been met. As mentioned above, western Canadians have pursued a multitude of alternatives to the status quo including replacing the party in power, creating new parties, rejecting the party system altogether as was done in the 1921 Progressive revolt, giving more power to the provinces, reforming the electoral system, or reforming the Senate. The key point, however, is that western Canadians and their provincial governments have not yet come together behind a single vision of political reform.[8] Thus the second condition for reform has not been met. The third condition if reform is to be achieved is that the region must carry sufficient demographic, economic or political clout to impose change in the face of opposition from supporters of the status quo. This power has eluded the West although, in both the old and new Wests, western Canadians have come very close. Lacking alliances with other segments of discontent within the political community, western Canadians have been unsuccessful in their unfocused pursuit of institutional reform.

In the old West the potential for change was blown away in the dust clouds of the 1930s. This is not to say that political radicalism and experimentation died in the West, for they did not. What was lost was the region's capacity to impose any fundamental reform on the national political system. By the end of World War II a number of disturbing trends were apparent. First, the West's demographic punch was lost as the region's share of the national population began a long-term slide. Second, and related to the first point, postwar immigrants were generally avoiding the prairie West, in part because the open land was gone and the new, capital-intensive prairie agriculture was too expensive for immigrants to enter, in part because the Depression-scarred image of the West discouraged new settlement, and in part because postwar immigrants possessed occupational skills more suited to industrial cities than to the still largely-agrarian West. Third, the West's agricultural contribution to the national economy was on the wane. Lastly, the West was no longer the cutting edge of the Canadian nation-building enterprise. The symbols of that enterprise were now the new skylines of Toronto and Montreal rather than the line of combines silhouetted against the prairie sky.

Given that the old West had been unable to place any distinctive stamp on Canadian political institutions, and given that postwar social change was bringing the West increasingly into the national mainstream, it might well be thought that integration into the political mainstream would also follow. For a time it looked as though this would be the case, and that the unlikely vehicle would be the national Progressive Conservative party under the leadership of prairie populist John Diefenbaker.[9] In 1957, Diefenbaker won a minority victory on the basis of strong support in Ontario (61 of 85 seats) and lukewarm support in the West (21 of 70 seats). In 1958, he swept to the greatest victory in Canadian history, capturing 65 of the 70 seats in the West, 67 of the 85 Ontario seats, 50 of the 75 Quebec seats, and 25 of the 33 seats in Atlantic Canada. This unprecedented national landslide led western Canada into the fold of one of the national parties and all but destroyed the regionally-based Social Credit and C.C.F. parties. Diefenbaker's passionate support for British parliamentary institutions once again bound the West to national institutions that had been rejected in the past. For a short time a truly western national vision, Diefenbaker's "One Canada," held sway in Ottawa.

The Diefenbaker years, however, turned out to be but a brief interlude in the national reign of the federal Liberal party. In 1963 Diefenbaker was defeated, and the federal Conservative party retreated to its newly-won western periphery. Ironically, just as the Conservative party had brought the West into the national mainstream in 1958, the West's continued allegiance to the Conservatives after Diefenbaker's defeat drove the West back into the political wilderness. Conservative loyalties during two decades of almost unbroken Liberal rule extracted a heavy regional price; chronic weakness in, and at times near exclusion from, Canada's governing party.

By the 1970s political unrest was running high in the West. Now, though, the West's economic boom and the regional in-migration that resulted meant that the West had growing economic and demographic clout in the Canadian union. Once again it appeared that the West might be strong enough to impose some reform on national institutions. Commentators began to ask "What does the West want?" just as they had asked "What does Quebec want?" in the 1960s. Even though social change had brought the West into line with the national society, political unrest was again rampant. The western premiers waded into battle with the federal dragon, waving the standards of western alienation and emboldened by the conviction that it would be the West that would lead Canada into the twenty-first century. It was the federal government's efforts to patriate and reform the Canadian constitution that provided the principal battleground for the premiers, and the testing ground for the political ascendancy of the "New West."

Now that the constitutional fray is behind us and the 1982 Constitution Act is in place, we are in a position to assess the impact of the "New West" on Canadian political life. After more than a decade of constitutional, intergovernmental and partisan warfare, what has changed? The short answer is, very little. The constitution has not been reformed so as to provide greater powers to western provincial governments. Indeed, the Constitution Act did not alter the federal division of powers in any significant way. The Senate has not been reformed, although the issue of Senate reform clings to the political agenda. The bonds of party discipline in the House have not been weakened; western MPs still act first as party tokens and at best second as regional representatives. Intergovernmental conflict between Ottawa and the provinces continues unabated, although the acrimonious energy conflict of 1980/81 is temporarily behind us. The West has no greater role in the federal regulatory agencies, such as the Canadian Transport Commission and the National Energy Board, which play such a major role in western economic development. In short, the institutional impairments to effective regional representation within the national government and national legislative process remain intact. Nothing has been done to strengthen the place of the West in the national political community, and nothing has been done to weaken the institutional underpinnings of western alienation.

So little was accomplished largely because western Canadians and their provincial governments were unable to reach any consensus on an alternative vision of the Canadian federal state. Thus the western economic and demographic upsurge of the 1970s did not resolve in any effective manner the political problems which have confronted the West in the nation since the turn of the century. In this sense an opportunity has been tragically lost, for the political power that the West gained in the 1970s is already beginning to fade. The western economy has softened dramatically since 1982, and it no longer appears that the West will lead the country into the next century. The population tide that followed and fed the western economic boom in the 1970s is beginning to ebb as people repack their U-hauls and head back East. (In the last half of 1982 more people moved out of Alberta than moved in, and during the same year Calgary's population fell for the first time ever). While the western economic downturn of the mid-1980s is not to be compared to the Depression of the 1930s, the West appears once again to be losing its ability to impose political change, with a purchase that it possessed, but was unable to use only a few short years ago.

Conclusion

What, then, can be said about political change in the Canadian West since the end of World War II?

In the first place, political change has not been in step with the postwar social change that has transformed the West. Social change has brought western Canadians into the national mainstream, eroding the distinctive features of the Canadian West. The changes have been profound, sweeping and, in most cases, irreversible. Yet on the political scene the prewar legacy of discontent and alienation has been extenuated, not left behind. While the forms of western discontent have changed considerably from the prewar West, the substance of that discontent remains much the same. The root of western alienation still lies in the apparent disenfranchisement of the region within the national government and the national legislative process.

Thus, while much has changed socially, far less has changed politically. The institutional underpinnings of political discontent in the "Old West" are still in place today; the Senate remains impotent, party discipline chokes off effective regional representation within the House, secrecy cloaks whatever regional representation may take place within caucus or cabinet, and the national parties remain beholden to the more populous central Canadian electorate. Canadian parliamentary institutions are not designed to provide effective regional representation. The West has sought to alter those institutions, but it has lacked sufficient power to do so. It has also lacked a strongly articulated regional consensus on the solution to rather than the cause of western alienation, on some alternative institution vision that would strengthen the place of the West in Canada. Twice, when the West was riding the crest of economic and demographic growth, a sudden deterioration of the western economy crippled the pursuit of political reform.

Because the West remains so locked with parliamentary institutions that it is unable to exploit or to reform, alienation has been a constant landmark on the western political landscape. While its strength may wax and wane over time, western alienation never disappears. Nor is it likely to do so in the absence of fundamental institutional reform, the prospects of which are remote. Thus discontent and alienation are likely to be as characteristic of western political life in the future as they have been in the past.

It is essential, of course, that the burden of western alienation is not exaggerated. The region will persist, people will raise families and pursue productive lives in a fashion largely untouched by the cloud of western alienation. Yet, at the same time, the persistence of alienation signals a frustrating failure on the part of the Canadian political system. Western Canadians have served their country well. And in its spirit, its physical landscape and land mass, in the richness of its people and natural resources, in its promise for the future, the West is Canada. Yet the region has not been served well in return by national parliamentary institutions. Such is the political legacy and apparent future of the West.

Footnotes

1. For an expanded discussion of this problem, see Gibbins, *Prairie Politics and Society: Regionalism in Decline* (Toronto: Butterworths, 1980).

2. For a discussion of province-building, see Alan C. Cairns, "The Governments and Societies of Canadian Federalism," *Canadian Journal of Political Science* 10 (December, 1977), pp.395-726, and John Richards and Larry Pratt, *Prairie Capitalism: Power and Influence in the New West* (Toronto: McClelland and Stewart, 1979).

3. While World War II was a watershed in the evolution of the western society, it is important to note that the major changes have roots deep within the prewar society. In many ways the Great Depression had the largest impact; the end of World War II marked the culmination of massive social and economic changes set in motion by the onslaught of the Depression. For further details, see Gibbins, *Prairie Politics and Society*, chapters 2-4.

4. See J.R. Mallory, *Social Credit and the Federal Power in Canada* (Toronto: University of Toronto Press, 1953), p.39. For a more general discussion of this point, see Vernon C. Fowke, *The National Policy and the Wheat Economy* (Toronto: University of Toronto Press, 1957).

5. For an elaboration of this argument, see Gibbins, *Regionalism: Territorial Politics in Canada and the United States* (Toronto: Butterworths, 1982), chapter 3.

6. David Smith, *The Regional Decline of a National Party: Liberals on the Prairies* (Toronto: University of Toronto Press, 1981).

7. In December, 1980 the Carleton School of Journalism conducted a national telephone survey in which the following question was asked: "Where does your first loyalty lie—with Canada or with the province in which you live?" Across Canada, 74 percent of the respondents chose Canada and 26 percent chose their province, while in the West alone 80 percent chose Canada compared to only 20 percent who chose their province.

8. For an expanded discussion of this point in reference to the constitutional negotiations of the early 1980s, see Gibbins, "Constitutional Politics and the West," in *And No One Cheered: Federalism, Democracy and the Constitution Act*, edited by Keith Banting and Richard Simeon (Toronto: Methuen, 1983), pp.119-32.

9. Prior to 1957, Conservative support in the West was generally no more than a fraction of that garnered by the Liberal party. In the 1953 national election, for example, the Liberals captured 25 seats in the West with 35 percent of the popular vote while the Conservatives captured only 9 seats with 16 percent of the vote.

CONTEMPORARY WESTERN ALIENATION: AN OPINION PROFILE

David K. Elton

Introduction

Western alienation is a concept that refers to an attitude held by many western Canadians regarding the Canadian political system. This attitude has two principle elements: (1) a sense that western Canadians are essentially powerless in national political life, and (2) national policies are at best indifferent to western concerns and at worst exploit the human and natural resources of western Canada. This sense of powerlessness and the belief that Ottawa is at best insensitive or even exploitative of the West have led to a profound sense of regional estrangement from the national political community. For many, although by no means all western Canadians, the Government of Canada is no longer seen as a truly national government but rather as one that reflects the narrower regional interests of central Canada.

Many western Canadians often cite lists of grievances concerning programs and policies of past or present national governments such as western transportation policy, trade policy, the national energy policy, and the like.[1] Whether these grievances are real or imaginary is not at issue. What is of concern is the extent to which western Canadians hold and share this sense of alienation from their national government. The purpose of this presentation is not to comment upon the costs and benefits to western Canada of government programs and policies, but rather to provide an overview of the public opinion research which has been accumulated over the past ten to fifteen years to indicate the breadth and depth of the mind-set we call western alienation.

The Data Base

Public opinion polling on the attitudes of western Canadians towards government has taken place since the early 1940s. However, most of the research on western alienation has been undertaken only in the past fifteen years. The data used in this presentation was obtained from two sources: the Centre de Recherche Opinion Publique (CROP) periodic omnibus studies, and studies commissioned by the Canada West Foundation.[2]

Questions asked range from very general inquiries regarding people's satisfaction with the overall performance of the national and provincial governments, to specific questions regarding a particular policy. In some instances the population samples were limited to a specific city, province or region (e.g., the four western provinces), while in other instances national studies have included questions of relevance to this subject. Some of these studies utilized a face-to-face interviewing procedure, while in others the interviews were conducted over the telephone. All of the studies utilized in this presentation were conducted by professionally trained interviewers whose work has been verified. In each study a random-probability sampling procedure was used to ensure that the results obtained would accurately reflect, within acceptable confidence intervals, the opinion of the population from which the sample was drawn.

General Attitudes towards the National Government

One general measure of western disaffection is the extent to which western Canadians indicate more dissatisfaction with the general performance of their national government than with that of their provincial government. Figures 1 and 2 present data from fifteen public opinion surveys conducted over a four-year period in which respondents from across Canada were asked to indicate whether they were satisfied, somewhat dissatisfied, or very dissatisfied with their federal and provincial governments.

Figures 1 and 2 show that, in every instance, both in the West and across the other six provinces, more respondents were satisfied with the performance of their provincial government than with that of their federal government. This "satisfaction gap" between the two levels of government is wider in the West, where it averages 29 percent, than it is outside the West where the gap averages only 12 percent. This difference comes about not because provincial governments are more popular in the West, but because the federal government is markedly less popular in the West than elsewhere in Canada.

FIGURE 1

Differences in satisfaction levels between Federal and Provincial Governments -
The West.

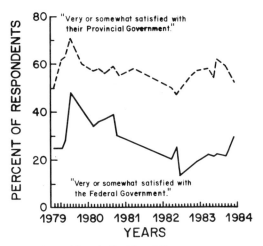

Source: Canada West Foundation.
Average sample size 650.

A more precise measure of the degree of disenchantment with the national government among western Canadians is evident from data obtained in a survey of 2000 western Canadians (i.e., residents of British Columbia, Alberta, Saskatchewan, Manitoba) conducted in 1980. Response patterns to questions

FIGURE 2

Differences in satisfaction levels between Federal and Provincial Governments -
Atlantic region, Quebec and Ontario, only.

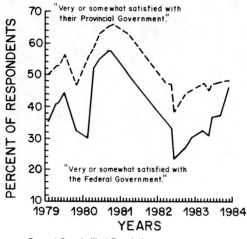

Source: Canada West Foundation.
Average sample size 1350.

regarding government frugality and the amount of trust in government (see Table 1), indicate that most western Canadians perceive their national government as being more wasteful and less trustworthy than their provincial governments. Opinion regarding wastefulness was constant right across the West with nearly ten times as many respondents identifying the national government as being more wasteful. There was somewhat greater variability in provincial response rates on the question of trust (i.e., 22 percent of British Columbia respondents as compared to 11 percent of Alberta respondents trusted the national government), but by far most respondents in all four provinces were more distrustful of the national government than of their respective provincial government.

In 1980 a nationwide survey asked respondents a series of three questions pertaining to their perceptions of the federal and provincial governments regarding confidence, deceit, and secrecy. These findings (see Table 2) further substantiate the extent of disenchantment among Westerners regarding their federal government. Confidence in or trust of the national government is a rarer commodity in the West than in the rest of Canada. For many Westerners the federal government is far more likely not only to be more secretive, but also to mislead or deceive them. While these sentiments are not evenly distributed across the West (i.e., British Columbia most closely approximates the national norm while Alberta represents the extreme edge of a much more disaffected prairie sentiment), there are substantial numbers of citizens in all four provinces who share this negative perception of their national government.

TABLE 1

PERCEPTIONS OF GOVERNMENT PERFORMANCE

% of Respondents

	West	B.C.	Alta.	Sask.	Man.
"Who wastes the most money?"					
Federal	57	55	56	57	62
Provincial	6	7	6	4	6
Both Equally	26	31	25	24	21
"Which Government Do You Trust the Most?"					
Federal	18	22	11	14	23
Provincial	49	41	63	51	44
Both Equally	8	8	5	13	6

Source: Canada West Foundation

TABLE 2

PERCEPTIONS OF CONFIDENCE—TRUST AND SECRECY

"THINKING FOR A MOMENT OF YOUR PROVINCIAL GOVERNMENT AND THE
FEDERAL GOVERNMENT, WHICH LEVEL OF GOVERNMENT WOULD YOU SAY
(1) YOU HAVE THE MOST CONFIDENCE IN (2) WOULD BE THE MOST
LIKELY TO MISLEAD OR DECEIVE YOU (3) IS THE MOST SECRETIVE?"

% OF RESPONDENTS

	Canada	B.C.	Alta.	Sask.	Man.	Ont.	Que.	Atlan.
1) YOU HAVE THE MOST CONFIDENCE IN:								
- FEDERAL	35	29	11	33	19	33	46	43
- PROVINCIAL	31	32	54	39	44	26	32	21
- BOTH THE SAME	32	36	32	26	32	39	20	34
2) WOULD BE MOST LIKELY TO MISLEAD OR DECEIVE YOU:								
- FEDERAL	34	30	57	56	43	33	29	24
- PROVINCIAL	26	28	11	19	14	18	40	32
- BOTH THE SAME	35	36	29	23	38	44	26	35
3) IS MOST SECRETIVE:								
- FEDERAL	44	54	61	63	53	45	30	45
- PROVINCIAL	18	11	5	9	10	11	36	21
- BOTH THE SAME	33	32	32	26	33	39	29	30
N =	1995	215	160	79	90	721	539	191

Source: CROP, June 1980

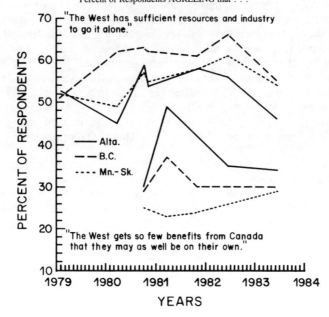

FIGURE 3

Provincial variations in Western alienation.
Percent of Respondents AGREEING that . . .

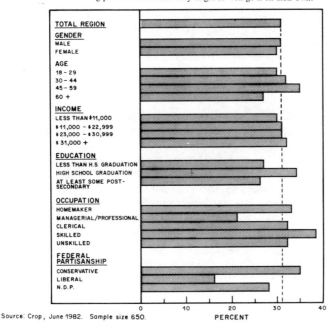

FIGURE 4

Socio-demographic variations in Western alienation.
Percent Respondents AGREEING that ''Western Canadians get so few benefits
from being part of Canada that they might as well go it on their own.''

Source: Crop, June 1982. Sample size 650.

Measuring Western Alienation

The first reported public opinion study which sought to measure the extent of western alienation was conducted among Albertans in 1969.[3] Respondents were asked to indicate their support of, or opposition to, a series of statements regarding the manner in which the national government dealt with western Canada. This study found that a majority of Albertans (55 to 60 percent) agreed with statements which mentioned the federal government's neglect of the West and suggested that federal policies benefited central Canada, often at the expense of Westerners. Since the 1969 study numerous surveys using a similar format have substantiated the widespread existence of the above mentioned perceptions not only among Albertans, but indeed among Canadians in all four western provinces.[4]

The most systematic research on western alienation has been conducted by the Canada West Foundation over the past four years.[5] These surveys have tracked the extent of western alienation within western Canada firstly by measuring the extent to which Westerners feel that their federal government ignores their problems and aspirations and, secondly, by seeking to identify the level of frustration with the existing political system. Figure 3 indicates that over the past four years there has been widespread agreement among nearly four of every five Westerners that the Canadian political system favors central Canada to the detriment of the West. Widespread recognition of the inequities within the Canadian political system throughout the West suggests that there is a consensus among western Canadians regarding their status as quasi second-class citizens within the Canadian federation.

A better measure of deep-seated alienation is provided in Figure 3 by the statement dealing with Westerners "going it on their own." Approximately one in every three western Canadians indicated that they are so frustrated with the present status of the West within confederation that they are willing to contemplate, if not actively support, substantive change to the existing political system. While this sentiment varies somewhat from province to province, the response patterns in Figure 3 suggest that this pervasive sense of alienation is widespread throughout the West.

The extent to which levels of alienation vary within specific socio-demographic groups across the West is illustrated in Figure 4. This figure indicates that the degree of support among particular segments of the population believing the West might just as well "go it on their own" deviated somewhat from the norm on the basis of age, education and occupation. The most striking difference in opinion is between supporters of the three national parties. Supporters of the Liberal party are much less estranged from the national government (16%) than are Conservative partisans (35%), while members of the NDP (28%) more closely approximate the population norm. This finding is not particularly surprising given that for Liberals the national government is in a sense "their government," while for Conservative and the NDP the partisan nature of the national government has given them even more reason to feel estranged.

Western Separatism

One of the most dramatic manifestations of western alienation in the past decade has been the recent development of a separatist movement. As shown in Figure 5, responses in studies conducted since 1979 to a question which asked respondents to indicate a preference for the West remaining part of Canada, joining the United States, or becoming independent, show that approximately nine of every ten Westerners in all four provinces and from all segments of the society would opt to remain Canadian.

FIGURE 5
Support for Western separatism.

"Would you prefer that the four provinces of Western Canada
(1) Combine to form an independent country   (2) Join the United States ?"

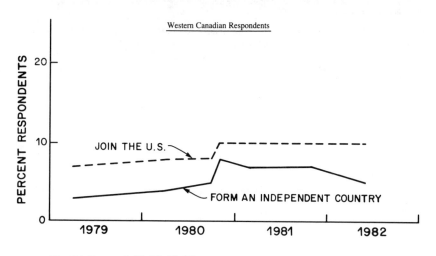

Source: Surveys 1, 21, 22, 23, 24.

The fact that relatively few Westerners support the independence option is not at odds with the earlier findings regarding the widespread negative perceptions of the federal government. Numerous studies have shown that the same western Canadians that feel alienated from their national government also see themselves as committed Canadians. Western alienation must not then be confused with a weak or absent national identity, but rather should be recognized as a regional political ideology of discontent.

In sum, for most Westerners alienation from their federal government represents a frustrated desire for fuller participation in the economic, social, and political mainstreams of Canadian life. The denial of this quest for national integration is at the roots of contemporary western alienation. For many Westerners, Canadian citizenship is an unrequited love affair.

Footnotes

1. For a detailed discussion of these policy areas see *Economic and Industrial Development Opportunities*, a background paper jointly presented by the four western provincial governments to the Government of Canada at the Western Economic Opportunities Conference, Calgary, Alberta, July 24-26, 1973; K.H. Norrie, ''Some Comments on Prairie Economic Alienation,'' *Canadian Public Policy* 2:2 (Spring 1976), and ''A Regional Economic Overview of the West Since 1945,'' in this volume.

2. The Canadian West Foundation is a public policy research institute whose research focuses on significant economic and social issues facing western Canada. All the data presented herein can be obtained from the Foundation's office at Suite 1123, 333 - 7 Avenue S.W., Calgary, Alberta, T2P 2Z1.

3. David Elton, ''Electoral Perception of Federalism: A Descriptive Analysis of the Alberta Electorate,'' in *One Prairie Province? Conference Proceedings and Selected Papers*, edited by David Elton (Lethbridge: *Lethbridge Herald*, 1970), pp. 143-46.

4. Roger Gibbins and David Elton, ''Western Alienation and Political Culture,'' in *The Canadian Political Process*, third edition, edited by Richard Schultz *et al.* (Toronto: Holt, Reinhart and Winston, 1979).

5. Since 1979 the Canada West Foundation has published quarterly reports entitled *Opinion Update*. For articles on western alienation see report numbers 1,4,7,9,12 and 16.

WESTERN ALIENATION: A BRITISH COLUMBIA PERSPECTIVE

Donald E. Blake

People complain and governments argue about their real and fancied grievance, but nothing in sight at present is going to change the belief that despite the problems that arise from time to time, this is the best of all possible worlds.[1] In one of his periodic attempts to win the hearts and minds of British Columbians, Prime Minister Pierre Trudeau likened residents of the province to those who reside at the foot of the mountain but never climb to the top. Whether wittingly or not, his comment implied that British Columbians have chosen to cut themselves off from other western Canadians and not just from central Canada, a point to ponder as we attempt to come to grips with the concept of "western alienation." It is not clear that British Columbia should be lumped together with Alberta, Saskatchewan and Manitoba even assuming that differences among those three provinces can be ignored. Alienation exists in British Columbia, and it is linked to beliefs that Ontario and Quebec have too much influence in national affairs, that the federal government is out of touch with provincial aspirations, and that the province pays a premium for participation in confederation which is not commensurate with the benefits it derives from the federal connection. But alienation in British Columbia, however similar its symptoms, has a different historical and structural basis.

The province's struggles with Ottawa are episodic rather than continuous, in part because the economic well being of the province is not so directly dependent on federal government policies regarding resource taxation, transportation, energy exports, and agriculture. Its economic self-interest sometimes set it apart from its neighboring provinces. For example, it is in competition with Alberta for the lucrative Japanese coal market and stands to benefit from abolition of the "Crow rate," which have long been a rallying cry on the prairies.

Look Back For Anger

It may come as a surprise to an audience in Alberta that the epithet "spoilt child of Confederation" was first applied to British Columbia, not Alberta, and by the British Colonial Secretary, not Pierre Trudeau. The description was employed during one of the many appeals from B.C. for adjustment of the terms of union or, as in this particular case, for financial compensation given the failure of the federal government to complete the transcontinental railway within the promised time period.[2] British Columbia even anticipated René Lévesque by nearly a century with a series of secession resolutions during the 1870s.

Many of the province's grievances will sound familiar to students of prairie politics. The province complained that its citizens bore an unfair share of the burdens of confederation because so many of its manufactured goods had to be imported either from abroad or from central Canada thus incurring extra costs from tariffs and freight charges. The added costs of building roads, railways and other communications links associated with the province's difficult terrain were cited as justification for additional federal subsidies and for adjustment of federal contributions to shared-cost programs when they became a prominent form of public finance. Federal strategies regarding industrial development and location were seen to focus on central manufacturing industries rather than the industrial potential of the province's resource industries. This emphasis was also reflected in the lending practices of central Canadian financial institutions. Some grievances were unique to British Columbia and now represent an historical embarrassment, namely those critical of federal interference with provincial desires to exclude Asians from certain occupations, from the rights of citizenship, and even from the province itself.

Some of British Columbia's problems with the federal system can be traced to a situation which it did not share with the other western provinces. Provincial jurisdiction over natural resources and public lands came with entry into confederation limiting any appeal to a quasi-colonial past. However, this jurisdictional advantage led to a preoccupation with questions of economic development among all governments of the province and to the early existence of a "province-building" mentality. When funds for provincial development schemes ran short, pressures on Ottawa increased.

Jurisdictional questions did not arise in a significant way until the 1920s, when Premier John Oliver complained about the federal presence in the personal income tax field.[3] In fact, Richard McBride, the premier associated with the railway boom at the turn of the century, was even persuaded to surrender jurisdiction over freight rates on the Canadian Northern Railway (the forerunner of the Canadian National Railway) to the federal regulatory agency in return for federal subsidies to ensure its completion.[4] The most serious jurisdictional battle resulted in Premier T. Dufferin Pattullo joining Aberhart of Alberta and Hepburn of Ontario to wreck the dominion-provincial conference of 1940 called to consider the centralizing recommendations of the Rowell-Sirois report. Pattullo's behavior stunned the province's economic establishment, was strongly attacked by the press and alienated many of his own supporters. With hindsight it appears he was defending an expanded role for provincial government. That, together with a philosophical justification for increased state responsibility for individual well-being, economic planning and regulation of business in the public interest, which he had developed as a response to the depression, placed the provincial Liberal party well to the left of its federal counterpart.[5]

The province's most famous "fed-basher" was undoubtedly W.A.C. Bennett. His development schemes only grudgingly acknowledged the existence of the federal government when financial support was required or when the exercise of federal constitutional authority was necessary, for example, to authorize power exports to the United States. Gratitude was not one of Bennett's reactions to support from Ottawa. When federal funds for maintenance of the Trans-Canada highway ran out, he ordered that highway signs be changed to identify it as "BC-1." He brooked little interference with his plans, and took a limited role in federal-provincial relations, except to bemoan the folly of the equalization grant program (whose constitutionality his government threatened to challenge), or to present his ideas for redrawing the map of Canada to recognize his view of the importance of British Columbia.

While this review of the historical record has been necessarily brief, certain tentative conclusions can be offered. First of all, conflict with Ottawa has been primarily conflict involving governments and particularly strong-minded premiers.

There have been no successful federal third party or protest movements in the province except the CCF, which in B.C. did not have the agrarian protest character of its prairie counterparts. Federal Social Credit support peaked at 26 percent in the 1953 election and did not survive the Diefenbaker landslide. Secondly, the federal government has never been credibly portrayed as a threat to the province's livelihood. Ottawa's alleged preoccupation with the economy of central Canada has not called for major sacrifices from B.C. or prevented it from becoming rich. The province's current list of official grievances is a chronicle of annoying federal practices rather than nonnegotiable demands. Thirdly, there is little evidence that the mass of the population has ever been particularly exercised about the inequities of the federal system as opposed to the policies of particular incumbents in Ottawa. Pattullo, for example, resigned after electoral losses which were widely attributed to his behavior at the 1940 dominion-provincial conference. The provincial fortunes of the federal Liberal and Conservative parties in the province were unaffected by Bennett's attacks on the federal power. Analysis of the current state of public opinion in the British Columbia confirms the impression that provincial and federal politics represent two different worlds for B.C. voters and that the concerns of federalism have a limited place on their provincial agendas.

Contrasts With The Prairies

On the surface British Columbia shares several characteristics with its immediate neighbours which are relevant to the degree of disaffection from the center: both regions have resource-based economies, and crucial decisions affecting those economies fall under federal jurisdiction over tariffs, and interprovincial and international trade. The federal party systems of Alberta, Saskatchewan and British Columbia, at least at their inception, represented artificial replicas of the party divisions of eastern Canada without the social and historical divisions which sustained them there. They share the frustration of limited influence in national affairs associated with small populations, and the suspicion and resentment of "special treatment" for Quebec which goes with the Britishness of their populations. Liberal weakness and Conservative strength characterize all the western provinces.

Despite these similarities, there seem to be fewer historical episodes and longstanding grievances to which B.C. governments can point as evidence of federal government unresponsiveness or injustice. British Columbia's major resource industries are based on forestry, mining and fishing, and the federal government has rarely expressed an interest in the first two. The province seems to have acquiesced to predominant federal jurisdiction in the fishery, perhaps because of its declining significance for provincial wealth or the fact that its needs often conflicted with the more lucrative and politically powerful forest industry. I suspect, although I am not aware of any research on the subject, that British Columbia's interests have been served by the similarity between its resource base and that of Ontario. Ontario seems to have won battles with the federal government on trade-related issues such as provincial legislation restricting the export of raw logs and requiring at least some domestic processing of forest and mineral products.[6] British Columbia also benefits from the different standards applied by the federal government to exports of energy in the form of hydro-electricity as compared to oil and natural gas. Without these victories, such issues could conceivably have served the same role for rallying opinion in British Columbia as federal interference with the export and pricing of oil and natural gas do in Alberta and Saskatchewan.

There are also more obstacles to the establishment of a feeling of community or shared interest vis-a-vis Ottawa. British Columbia's population has been constantly renewed by immigration from other parts of Canada and from abroad, partly as a response to the demands for labor in the resource industries of the province which could not be met from the small agrarian sector. These characteristics together with obstacles to communication within the province arguably inhibited the development of a "collective memory" of grievance based on the struggle for better terms or any of the other battles with the federal government.[7]

The State of Public Opinion

The perception of British Columbia's connection to national politics tends to be affected by the longevity of the Social Credit regime of W.A.C. Bennett which for twenty years maintained a studied aloofness from federal politics except when provincial interests were directly at stake. It was Bennett whom Pierre Trudeau described as the bigot who happened to be premier of a province in response to Bennett's remarks about the wisdom of "subsidizing" inefficient Quebec governments through equalization payments, and it was Bennett who fought major battles with Ottawa over the Columbia River Treaty and creation of the Bank of British Columbia. His rise to power coincided with the virtual elimination of the Liberal and Conservative parties from provincial politics.

Yet we would do well to remember that Bennett's conversion to Social Credit and his careful cultivation of the party as the best guarantee against a CCF victory was based on a belief developed during his experience as a coalition backbencher that provincial politics should be free of the entanglements of federal partisan differences. While the federal government provided a convenient target for his populist rhetoric from time to time, it is difficult to find any evidence that provincial voting habits were particularly affected. The fortunes of the federal Liberal and Conservative parties fluctuated independently of the level of support for their provincial counterparts, and the weakness of the latter can be traced to the impact of coalition on provincial party organization and the virtual takeover of provincial Conservative riding associations by Social Credit. While the current unpopularity of the federal Liberals may be preventing the revival of the provincial Liberal party, it was not responsible for its collapse.

After the Social Credit victory in 1952, the province developed two different party systems, a provincial system based on the clash between economic development strategies and different views of the economic and social role of the state and a federal system where similar questions became complicated by issues of jurisdiction, interregional equity, and (at least after 1960) cultural issues. Issues associated with federalism failed to unite electorates across federal and provincial party systems.

This separation persists at the present time despite the increased salience of federal-provincial conflict. My research on vote shifts between the provincial and federal elections of 1979 shows that federal Liberal and Conservative electorates are as internally divided on major questions dealing with the role of the state in economic and social policy as provincial New Democrat and Social Credit voters. Opponents in provincial politics are united by their degree of support or opposition to the cultural policy agenda and centralist thrust associated with the Liberals since Pierre Trudeau became Prime Minister. The level of support for the New Democratic party in federal politics is markedly less than its level of provincial support largely because highly alienated or ethnocentric (regarding French Canada) provincial supporters gravitate to the Conservatives in federal elections, despite that party's recent emphasis on its commitment to free enterprise. Religious divisions, which are irrelevant to provincial partisan choices, surface in federal politics in traditional ways.[8] Both major contestants in the 1983 provincial election campaign agreed that economic recovery was the major issue, but, unlike the case in the recent Alberta campaign, neither side claimed that the policies of the federal government are responsible for decline or constitute an obstacle to recovery.

From what has been said so far it should be clear that I have serious doubts about whether there is anything particularly "western" about western alienation. This position is supported by an analysis of alienation in the mass public contained in a recent article by David Elkins. His study suggests that alienation in British Columbia is more cultural and political than economic and "seems unrelated to the longstanding policy grievances of the west."[9]

Table 1 contains a list of the questions used in a survey of the British Columbia population conducted by David Elkins, Richard Johnston and myself following the 1979 provincial and federal elections in B.C. which form the basis of the alienation scale used in the Elkins study. The questions cover issues similar to those addressed by Roger Gibbins in his study of alienation in Alberta,[10] although with somewhat less emphasis on economic matters. They deal with the relative competence of the British Columbia and federal governments, the degree of affect for eastern Canadians, the sense of identification with other Canadians rather than with geographically closer Americans, the costs and benefits of Confederation, and evaluation of the amount of attention paid by Ottawa to local opinion and interests.

A glance at the responses reveals a variegated pattern of opinion. A majority of British Columbians (62 percent) feel that MPs are out of touch with local voters, but an even larger number (66 percent) do not feel that the province has been forgotten by the federal government. Nor does there seem to be strong support for the notion that the provincial level of government is more competent than the federal level, a finding which together with an analysis of views on major issues led Elkins to conclude that British Columbians do not reject a significant policy role for the federal government.[11] One of the well-worn questions in Canadian public opinion research asks voters to assess whether their province or region contributes more to Confederation than it receives in terms of benefits, certainly a favorite claim of W.A.C. Bennett. However, in the B.C. study, when respondents were forced to consider rejecting Confederation itself in order to agree with that crude cost/benefit assessment, most agreed instead that "on balance, B.C. is much better off in Confederation than out of it." In general it appears that residents of British Columbia shy away from endorsing statements which require a choice of British Columbia over Canada.

Alienation in Alberta seems to be associated with a monolithic conservatism, both in its links to support for the Conservative party in federal and provincial elections and to small "c" conservative attitudes. In British Columbia, alienation bears the expected relationship with federal voting. It is a source of strength for the federal Conservative, but it is utterly irrelevant to provincial partisanship.[12] Nor are philosophical conservatives more alienated than liberals. In fact, if anything, the reverse may be true as a weak relationship does exist between alienation and liberalism in B.C.[13] Alienation in Alberta has produced a consensus across social groupings in the population,[14] whereas in British Columbia the poorly educated or those in lower status occupations are more likely to exhibit alienated sentiments than well-educated or upper status residents.[15] Alienation is also related to populism,[16] which is itself more characteristic of the working class.

TABLE 1

B.C. ALIENATION: ITEMS, SCORING AND DISTRIBUTION OF RESPONSES
(alienated responses emphasized)

Item	%Agree	%Disagree	%DK/NA
1. Many things the federal government does, provincial governments would do a lot better.	**45**	47	8
2. I don't find people from eastern Canada very attractive.	**7**	85	8
3. The federal government has all but forgotten B.C.	**26**	66	7
4. In B.C., we have more in common with people in Washington than with people in Ontario.	**25**	*	
OR			5
I think of myself as a Canadian first and a British Columbian second.	**69**	*	
5. B.C. pays more into Confederation than she gets out of it.	**21**	*	
OR			9
On balance, B.C. is much better off in Confederation than out of it.	**70**	*	
6. Ottawa is so far away, our MPs lose touch with the people who elect them.	**62**	*	
OR			11
I sometimes feel that the federal government is more in touch with B.C. opinion than the provincial government is.	**27**	*	
7. Local questions just don't get the attention they deserve in Ottawa.	**47**	*	
OR			8
Frankly, I'm glad that the federal government resists certain kinds of local pressures.	**45**	*	

* Respondents were required to choose one of the two statements, rather than agreeing or disagreeing with each one separately.

Conclusion

The history of British Columbia yields many major battles between the province and the federal power. However, with the exception of the racial issue,[17] most of these battles involved the aspirations of politicians rather than the grievances of the mass public. The current level of alienation in British Columbia is a product of dissatisfaction with the image projected by the federal Liberal government and the definiton of the national political community associated with it, rather than evidence of a willingness to repudiate the federal connection. Nevertheless, large numbers of British Columbians have come to share the view that the federal government is unrepresentative of and insensitive to the needs and interests of the province.

The development of executive federalism is no doubt partly responsible. While advertised as a process by which provincial points of view could be accommodated at the center, it has also given provincial premiers a national platform and a virtual monopoly on expression of the "provincial" interest. Executive federalism in combination with cabinet dominance over parliament has undermined the purpose of that institution and contributed to the absurd notion that a province which returns no members of the governing party to the House of Commons is therefore unrepresented in Ottawa.

Despite the manifestation of symptoms similar to those which exist elsewhere in western Canada, alienation in British Columbia has weaker historical and social roots. While the distribution of opinion on the alienation dimension seems skewed in an alienated direction, it does not represent a provincial consensus. Even the prominence of the premiers Bennett in battles with Ottawa has not produced a body of supporters who are any more alienated as a group than NDP supporters. Alienation remains a factor dividing federal partisans, and has no place in provincial politics which remains a battleground between economic and social philosophies. This does not seem to have been realized by the erstwhile organizers of the Western Canada Concept. Their separatism has no place in provincial politics, the arena in which they chose to campaign, their conservatism faces stiff competition from Social Credit, and alienation is not related to conservatism in any event.

While the federal government may have neglected British Columbia's economic interests, it cannot be credibly portrayed, currently or historically, as pursuing policies fundamentally antithetical to those interests. This does not mean that alienation in B.C. can be ignored. The "National Unity" agenda pursued by the federal Liberals has been poorly explained and defended in British Columbia and, abetted by feelings of isolation and impotence in federal politics and the rhetoric of provincial premiers, has produced a serious loss of faith in the responsiveness of the federal system.

Footnotes

1. R.M. Burns, "British Columbia: Perceptions of a Split Personality," in *Must Canada Fail*, edited by Richard Simeon (Montreal: McGill-Queen's, 1977), p.72.

2. Attributed to Lord Kimberley, British Colonial Secretary in 1881 when called upon by Premier Amor de Cosmos to assist in obtaining compensation for failure of the federal government to adhere to the promised timetable for completion of the CPR. See Margaret Ormsby, *British Columbia: A History* (Toronto: Macmillian, 1971), p.283.

3. Norman Ruff, "British Columbia and Canadian Federalism," *The Reins of Power: Governing British Columbia*, J. Terence Morley *et al.* (Vancouver: Douglas and McIntyre, 1983), p.296.

4. Patricia E. Roy, "Progress, Prosperity and Politics: The Railway Policies of Richard McBride," *B.C. Studies* 47 (Autumn 1980), pp. 23-4.

5. See Margaret A. Ormsby, "T. Dufferin Pattullo and the Little New Deal," in *British Columbia: Historical Readings*, edited by W. Peter Ward and Robert A.J. McDonald (Vancouver: Douglas and McIntyre, 1981), pp.533-54.

6. See H.V. Nelles, *The Politics of Development: Forest Mines and Hydro-Electric Power in Ontario, 1849-1941* (Toronto: Macmillan, 1975), pp.172-5 and *passim*.

7. See W. Peter Ward, "Population Growth in Western Canada, 1901-1971," in *The Developing West: Essays in Honour of Lewis H. Thomas*, edited by J.E. Foster (Edmonton: University of Alberta Press, 1983), pp.155-78 for a similar argument about the implications of demographic differences between British Columbia and other western provinces.

8. Details are presented in my *Conflict in Context: Politics in British Columbia*, draft ms., University of British Columbia, chapter 7.

9. See David J. Elkins, "Allegiance and Discontent in British Columbia," *Ibid.*, p.111.

10. See his "Western Alienation and the Alberta Political Culture," in *Society and Politics in Alberta*, edited by Carlo Caldarola (Toronto: Methuen, 1979), Table 1, p.147.

11. Elkins, "Allegiance and Discontent," p.111. It should be noted that David Elton and Roger Gibbins report a similar finding for Alberta, namely that when asked to indicate which level of government should have jurisdiction in a variety of policy areas, majorities of Albertans supported a federal role in those areas which are already under its jurisdiction. See their "Western Alienation and Political Culture," in *The Canadian Political Process*, 3rd edition, edited by Richard Schultz, Orest M. Kruhlak and John C. Terry (Toronto: Holt, Rinehart and Winston, 1979), p.95.

12. Daniel Wong, "Western Alienation and Intra-Regional Variation: A Comparative Study of Regional Discontent in British Columbia and Alberta," (unpublished M.A. Thesis, University of British Columbia, 1982), Table 8, p.43.

13. *Ibid.*, Table 5, p.31.

14. Gibbins in Caldarola, pp.149-51.

15. Wong, "Western Alienation and Intra-Regional Variation," p.59.

16. Elkins, "Allegiance and Discontent," pp.110-11.

17. For a provocative argument to the effect that class pales beside race as a basis for social divisions in British Columbia prior to World War II see W. Peter Ward, "Class and Race in the Social Structure of British Columbia, 1870-1939," in Ward and McDonald, *British Columbia*, pp.581-99. The federal government made frequent use of its power of disallowance in the late nineteenth century to counter some of the excesses of British Columbia's official discrimination against Asians.

A REGIONAL ECONOMIC OVERVIEW OF THE WEST SINCE 1945

Kenneth H. Norrie

Introduction

The broad theme suggested for this paper would, if it included government policies in addition to narrowly defined economic events, be a truly staggering task. Consider the number of major economic and political developments since 1945. The period has witnessed, first of all, major structural changes in the key agricultural sector, with all that these have implied for the economies more generally. Fewer but larger farms, rail-line abandonment, the decline of small towns, net outmigration and even absolute population losses for Manitoba and Saskatchewan, and the diminishing political influence of the farm vote[1] are all direct or indirect consequences of increased mechanization. In addition, and still within this sector, there have been significant fluctuations in prosperity over the period, ranging from the near depression conditions for wheat in 1969/70 to the boom years of the mid-1970s.

The third major development has been the emergence of two new staple industries, oil and gas[2] in the three westernmost provinces and potash in Saskatchewan. The former event has obviously been the more dramatic, completely transforming the economic, social and political structure of Alberta and to a much lesser extent Saskatchewan and British Columbia. Edmonton and Calgary replaced Winnipeg as dominant growth points within the Prairies, as Alberta became the primary destination for labor displaced from agriculture in Manitoba and Saskatchewan. Potash has had a much less pronounced effect, although the construction spin-offs together with the government revenue it has provided have altered the economy somewhat. In many ways, the political controversies generated by this staple base, ranging from public versus private ownership debates to a Supreme Court challenge to provincial taxation and regulation powers, have been its most interesting legacy.

The fourth significant event in the postwar period has been the turbulent economic events occurring in the energy sector since 1971. The large increases in crude oil prices after this date were significant for western Canada in several respects. The conventional oil industry was directly affected, and natural gas prices and hence exploration activity soon followed suit. The perception that supplies of these conventional energy sources would soon be exhausted led to a frenzy of activity in substitutes such as oil from enhanced-recovery techniques, oil sands and heavy oil. Even further removed along the substitute continuum, there was renewed interest in coal and uranium, both of which the West possessed in abundance. Finally, and obviously, all of these developments were accompanied by serious and divisive political controversy, between public and private sectors, consuming and producing regions, and the various levels of government.

A fifth and often neglected event has been the accompanying boom in the other resource sectors of the region. The industrial expansion in the early years of that decade in the face of limited inventories of industrial raw materials meant that more than just grain, livestock and petroleum prices rose significantly.

Metallic minerals, potash, lumber and forest products all benefited as well. These upswings were of limited duration, relative to that for energy products, and had much less overall impact. They are, nevertheless, an important part of the economic history of the last decade.

The final two noteworthy events are political in nature, although they either stem in large part from economic developments or lead to them. First, the postwar period has seen the continuation, and even intensification, of the tradition of economic and political alienation in the West. The economic bases of this growing disenchantment are perhaps best exemplified in the position papers prepared for the Western Economic Opportunities Conference in 1973, where the traditional concerns over tariffs, freight rates, monetary policy, commercial bank behavior and central government purchasing policies were evident. To this list must be added the natural-resource jurisdictional disputes of the last decade. The oft-cited sense of political powerlessness relates to the long tenure of the Liberal party federally, to the virtual disappearance of direct western representation in that government, and to the extinction of the several provincial Liberal parties.

The other significant political-economic development has been the emergence, or more correctly perhaps the explicit articulation,[3] of province-building strategies. The motivation behind these is complex and varied, but it certainly includes some mixture of genuine provincial loyalties seeking a political outlet, a defensive response to the alienation discussed above, and the use of the apparatus of state by regional elites to advance their own economic and political interests. Whatever the basis, the result has been a host of economic policies designed to stimulate economic growth and diversification. Taxes, subsidies, infrastructure projects, regulatory powers, and nationalization have all been used to promote new activities and to expand the scale of existing ones.

Given the number of important developments, and the inherent complexity of each of them, it is not obvious how to structure this overview. One strategy would be to attempt to survey all of these developments in a general way. The resulting product, though, would be lengthy, descriptive and largely superficial. A second tactic would be to focus on one or two key developments. This is done to some extent in other papers in this collection, however, and it would miss the essential task of synthesizing postwar developments.

There is a third strategy which I intend to follow for the remainder of this paper, namely to provide a conceptual overview which attempts to link together these economic and political developments. The hypothesis advanced here is that the staple or export base theory of economic growth, appropriately applied to a regional economy where economic rents are appropriated in the first instance by the local government, and supplemented by a few simple concepts from public-choice theory, is both necessary and largely sufficient to understanding economic and political developments in western Canada since 1945.

The first part of the argument stressing the export-base approach to economic growth is not new, at least to those somewhat familiar with Canadian economic history. The full implications of using such an avowedly deterministic model in a regional context are not always fully appreciated, however, so it is worth drawing them out more fully. The concurrent focus on public sector rents, both as a development tool and as a key link between economic and political variables, is perhaps more novel.[4]

The following discussion is organized around two general issues in regional economics. First, how can one explain the structure of a specific regional economy at any given moment in time? Second, how will this economy, given this economic base, adjust over time to changes in its economic fortunes? The first question is static in nature, and is akin to stopping the action on an instant replay of a hockey game and explaining the positioning of the players. Some conceptual or "theoretical" points will be needed as well as some reference to the preceding action. The second query is dynamic, with the obvious analogy of letting the replay run again and explaining the subsequent action. Again "theory" will be needed, but now of a different type.

The following section takes up the first or static question with respect to the western economies as of 1971. The dynamic analysis, covering the decade of the 1970s through to the present, is contained in Section III. The year 1971 is used as a reference point because of the widely-held view that the West entered a new phase of political and economic development about that time—the westward-shift hypothesis to be precise. Section IV discusses the political economy of province-building in the West, while a final section makes some brief concluding comments.

The Economics of a Small, Resource-Rich, Regional Economy

The argument advanced in this section is that the economic status the West had achieved by 1971, after more than seven decades of extensive development, was largely a product of its geographical and institutional environment. The region throughout its history was a classic example of a small, resource-rich, regional economy. Each of these characteristics individually imposed a particular constraint on the type of economic growth that could occur, and collectively they forced the economy into the only development pattern that was feasible in the long run. To see this, it is necessary to consider each of these features in turn.

Looking at the appellation "resource-rich" first, the obvious implication is that a region endowed in this manner will have an initial comparative advantage in producing raw materials and semi-processed products for export. The economy will thus develop around the leading sector or sectors, at least initially, with ancillary or linked activities forming locally to the extent that location considerations are favorable. The condition that firms locate so as to minimize total costs typically means that service activities will be drawn to the region while manufacturing other than simple directly-linked industries will not. Construction, personal services, retail trade and the like must be consumed on site by definition. In this sense, they are like the primary resource sectors in that they use an industry *and* a geographically-specific factor of production, in this case urban land. Relatively large primary and tertiary activities together with relative underemployment of the manufacturing sector is, of course, an oft-cited feature of staple economies.

This much is just conventional staple or export-base theory, supplemented by classical location concepts.[5] Two points emerge immediately, however. The first is that this conceptual approach provides a remarkably complete explanation of the basic economic structures of the West *circa* 1971. Primary industries that export a large portion of their output did dominate each of the provincial economies;

service industries were relatively large; the manufacturing sector was noticeably small; and what industrial activities were present typically involved further processing of primary products prior to export or provision of specific inputs for the extractive sector.[6] On a cyclical basis the obvious link between agricultural, energy and timber profitability and the macroeconomic performance of the four western provinces further establishes the relevance of this classic export-base model.

The second point follows logically from the first. If economic and geographical determinism can explain industrial structure in the West adequately, there is no need to resort to more nebulous and ill-defined assertions such as the following recent statement (Sahir and Seaborne, 1982, 92), ''The failure of the prairie region to significantly diversify its economy is, in part, a reflection of its continued role as a hinterland economy and its domination by the national heartland.'' If ''hinterland economy'' and ''heartland'' are meant to distinguish between regions with a comparative advantage in primary and manufacturing activities respectively, this is simply a restatement of the export-base theory. If the term ''domination'' is to be the key one, however, the quotation ceases to have much meaning. Space limitations preclude more than an assertion that the basic industrial structure of the West has been very little affected by the mix of tariff, transportation, monetary, taxation and purchasing policies pursued by central governments over the decades.[7] The scale of the economies has undoubtedly been affected, and some of the policies have certainly reallocated income interregionally. But the basic point remains. The West is relatively dependent on primary industries because it has a strong comparative advantage in these, due to: favorable endowments together with a relatively late and sparse settlement, geographical remoteness, the prairies' lack of access to lake and ocean shipping, and harsh climate.

The two other characteristics that act to define the economies of the West are their smallness and the openness that stems from being a regional economy within a larger national one. To assert that an economy is small is to say that it is a price-taker on all items that are transportable. This applies to goods such as raw materials or processed products, some services such as finance or insurances, and factor inputs such as capital, labor and technology. In technical terms, Westerners face virtually perfectly elastic demand curves for exports, and horizontal supply curves for imported goods, services and factors of production. As with a basic resource orientation, this does not represent any failure or shortcoming within the region, or any perfidy on the part of the central government or eastern Canada. Rather it reflects the small size of the regional market, the number of close substitutes for most of its output, and the technical difficulty in effectively exploiting whatever small degree of market power it might potentially possess.

Openness refers to the ability of goods and factors to move into or out of an economy in response to any initial price differentials, and as such really only reinforces the characteristic of smallness discussed above. The latter establishes that there will be an exogenously determined world price for wheat to the region for example, while the former ensures that the local price will be equal to this world rate less shipping and handling charges. To give another example, the West has no influence over the going rate of return on an asset in any given risk class, while the free movement of capital ensures that the reward to investment locally cannot long deviate from this given rate.

For the West, the combination of small and open means that nearly all prices are set externally. Given that provincial governments cannot in principle establish migration or investment quotas, interregional migrations of capital and labor will determine local factor prices. Since the regional exchange rate is fixed at unity, there is no possibility of having local prices of traded products behave differently than those in other, larger economies. The only exception to these statements, an important one as it will turn out, is that with respect to non-traded outputs and the associated industrial and geographically-specific factor inputs. In these instances, prices are set by regional supply and demand by definition.

Recognizing the small, open nature of the western economies is important in several respects. The first is that the economic fortune of the region will lie largely beyond its control. Events in national and international markets will be paramount, with the region having no recourse but to adapt accordingly. While this dependency is an inevitable outcome of overall endowment, it does typically generate sentiments of economic and political alienation, including a tendency to associate periods of instability with perceived shortcomings in existing national and regional institutions. Hinterland economies are thus very often politically restive ones, always in search of an elusive "better system."

Secondly, real factor incomes in the region cannot deviate very much, or for very long, from those available elsewhere in the national economy. Thus aggregate real per capita income, once adjusted for industrial structure, will approximate the national average. Put another way, changes in the economic fortunes of the region, coming from whatever external stimulus, will be resolved by adjustments in extensive variables such as investment or labor migration rather than in intensive ones such as rates of return or real wages.

The exception to this statement is the one noted above; namely, that real returns to owners of geographically immobile assets such as urban land will vary directly with the extensive growth of the region. Economic booms will increase the demand for the output of non-tradeables, generating economic rent for the owners of the specific factor. The converse is true for downturns. These income flows become the residual payment in effect, adjusting to equalize, the variation in the differences between exogenously-given output and factor input prices. What this means, politically, is that this group of property owners will have a vested interest in promoting extensive growth internally. Since regional politicians and bureaucrats are also typically assumed to favor extensive growth, for by now familiar reasons,[8] the result is a powerful, political alliance motivated to use the powers and resources of government to direct the province's economy.

The argument to this point has been that the economic development of the West to 1971 is adequately explained by noting that the region is a classic example of a small, resource rich, regional economy. Falling within the general survey of the theory are: the key leading sector role played by a few primary industries; limited secondary manufacturing activity; relatively large service sector; a pattern of extensive rather than intensive growth in response to external stimuli; approximately national-average per capita incomes; tendencies toward regional dissent; and activist economic strategies by politically influential local elites. By extension then, one need not resort to vaguely defined notions of dependency or conspiratorial theories to explain the present economic structure of the region.

These considerations lead to hypotheses about the structures of the western economies at any given point in time. By extension though, they should also be useful in predicting the nature of the economic adjustment within the region to any exogenous disturbances. Specifically, they should provide a basis for analyzing the western response to the energy price shocks of the last decade. These events were seen by many, both within the West and outside it, as a vehicle for developing and diversifying the western economies, and thereby shifting economic and political power in Canada westward. Western political leaders clearly expected this at the outset, and they did create these expectations in the populace more generally. This raises an obvious question then, and an important corollary. Has there been structural change in the nature in the western economies over the last decade? If not, why not? These topics are taken up in the following section.

Energy and Regional Economic Adjustment

The reason for singling out the last decade for analysis is that these years have been among the most crucial and interesting in the entire history of the region. All the grand themes of western economic and political history—primary sector volatility, export-led growth resulting in large swings in investment and migration, a quest for economic diversification, and political and economic alienation— have all been present in pronounced fashion. These events should, therefore, provide a good test of whether the general themes introduced above carry over to this turbulent decade as well. The argument is that they do, once public-sector resource rents are brought into the picture.

There are three key facts to be kept in mind when looking at the economic and political history of the West over the past decade. First, the increase in energy prices in 1973/74 and again in 1979/80 represented a significant shift in intersectoral terms of trade. Left alone, a market economy will undergo a predictable response to this disturbance. In Canada, the fact that energy sources are located primarily in the West while the bulk of population and industrial capacity is in the East, means that the inevitable intersectoral reallocation of resources will at the same time be an interregional one. This complicates the simple mechanics of the adjustment slightly, and the politics of it immensely.

The second fact is that unlike the wheat boom seventy years earlier, much of the economic rent generated over the decade was appropriated in the first instance by provincial governments. This revenue, combined with regulatory control over energy resources, gave the provinces considerable scope to intervene in the economy to promote economic diversification. The final point is that these rents and powers came at a time when there was increased concern within the region about the long-term implications of remaining tied to the traditional economic base. The need to develop new economic bases to offset an expected decline in the conventional petroleum industries became the theme of Alberta's then Opposition Leader Peter Lougheed, for example.

The analysis of an adjustment to a shift in the intersectoral terms of trade in favor of energy within a closed economy (i.e., assuming a fixed supply of factor inputs) is straightforward. The potential for higher returns in petroleum and petroleum-related activities (including substitutes such as coal, uranium, synthetic fuels, etc.) means an increased demand for capital and labor inputs to these sectors. Prices for these factors start to rise as expanding sectors begin to bid for a larger share of the given supplies of productive inputs. Average costs of production increase and local firms begin to lose out to competing suppliers, both in export markets (e.g., forestry products) and through increased imports of manufactured products. The service sector is able to pass along cost increases in the form of higher prices, which together with an income elastic demand means it typically rises slightly overall.

The net result is a wealthier economy, but one even more specialized in energy and service activities. It is wealthier in the sense that one unit of petroleum output will now exchange for a significantly greater amount of other products than before; i.e., a greater consumption is possible from any given production effort. But it is more specialized in that this very increased value of petroleum has now induced a reallocation of the region's productive resources toward this sector, and away from other traded activities. If energy output is to expand, and there are fixed supplies of capital and labor, some other sectors must decline to release these factors. Since nonpetroleum exports and secondary-manufacturing products face highly elastic external demands and competing supplies respectively, it is they who perform this function. This establishes the important proposition that in the absence of offsetting factors the energy prices boom of the 1970s could have been expected to increase the economic specialization of the region, rather than to provide a once-in-a-lifetime opportunity to escape as it was often alleged. For the latter to be true there would need to be further, offsetting factors.

The first such qualification is provided by the fact, noted above, that the West as a small, regional economy faces a highly elastic supply of capital and labor from other jurisdictions. As excess demands for these factors appear due to expansion of the energy sector, they are met by increased supplies from outside rather than price adjustments within. The result is that the energy sector can expand without having to draw as much upon other, traded industries in the process. In the extreme, if all factors are perfectly mobile with respect to price incentives, there will be only extensive growth; rewards to mobile factors will not change at all. The regional economy will simply be larger by the amount of the expanded energy sector, plus whatever output growth it has induced in other, linked industries. Note again, however, that the economy will still appear more specialized, even in this limiting case. Energy production has increased absolutely as have service and more directly-linked manufacturing activities. The only difference now compared to the closed economy case is that the other activities have only declined relatively rather than absolutely.

This limiting case is too extreme even for a small regional economy such as the West, however. In point of fact, not all factors are perfectly mobile. Services require a geographically-specific input, the final output cannot be traded interregionally, and they are an important input to production and a key item in consumption. Thus as energy and other outputs rise, and labor moves in response to higher wages, the demand for services will rise. Since production is constrained to follow an upward-sloping supply curve because of a limited supply of the specific input, and imports are ruled out by definition, prices must rise. This means increased production costs for the traded sectors, causing them to lose sales to competitors as before. It also contributes to a higher regional cost of living, meaning that nominal wages will need to rise to continue to attract workers. Again, this puts upward pressure on production costs overall, and the consequent absolute decline of some activities.

This realistic case, intermediate between the extremes of a completely closed economy and a completely open one, predicts increased specialization in energy and its directly-related activities together with services. The point may be seen belabored, but it is an important one given the widespread view in the West and elsewhere during the 1970s that the energy boom *per se* would be the means whereby the West would escape its traditional dependence on primary activities.[9] In fact, exactly the opposite would be true, all else being equal. Natural market forces would operate to increase the region's relative[10] dependence on its now more valuable energy sector. This is the additional[11] constraint which regional policy makers faced over the decade in their quest to diversify the provincial economies.

The energy boom did provide some offsetting scope for economic diversification in two other important ways, however, and herein lies the interesting political economy of the decade. First, provincial governments have broad constitutional authority over natural resources. The western provinces have used this provision to guarantee supplies of feedstocks to locally-based processing firms, at the expense of exports if necessary. Thus in the early 1970s, when security of supplies of natural gas was a dominating locational consideration, the Alberta government managed to lure petrochemical firms to the province upon the promise of a guaranteed long-term supply of feedstock. Attractive feedstock prices also apparently played a role in this development, although no formal subsidy was ever acknowledged.[12]

By far the more significant factor, though, was the huge economic rent captured by the provincial governments, especially Alberta, after 1973. These revenues provided a unique opportunity to intervene to alter the basic structure of the economy. Normally, the ability of a regional government to tax factor incomes in excess of value of services provided in return is effectively precluded by the mobility feature. Hence there is little scope for offering subsidies to attract industrial activity to the area. Economic rent, by definition, is free of this problem. Intramarginal units of land and resources can be taxed without having their services withdraw, and the revenue used to provide fiscal incentives to attract capital and labor from other jursidictions. It is this feature more than any other which gives some substance to the claim that the energy boom provided a once-in-a-lifetime opportunity to reverse the staple orientation of the western economies.

This opportunity did not come without cost, however, both economic and political. Economically, the cost would be the dissipation of some or all of the potentially available natural resource rent. An industrial diversification beyond that already evident by 1971 would need to be subsidized and, because of the locational disadvantages discussed in Section II, this could be expected to be costly. In addition, as seen in this section, whatever natural disadvantages the region already possessed in this respect were magnified by the nature of the internal economic adjustment to the terms of trade shift. The political cost, at least in Alberta, was that the government was being forced to compromise its declared adherence to free-market principles in order to make good its economic promises. Diversification was only possible, if at all, through active intervention in the economy. Yet, the only western government in any real position to affect the basic allocation of resources significantly had constrained itself politically not to do so. It is to this complicated political economy of province-building that the paper now turns.

The Political Economy of Province-Building

The complete story of province-building efforts in the West over the last ten years has yet to be told.[13] There are two economic questions to ask in this respect. First, what in principle might a revenue-rich provincial government have done to promote industrialization and diversification, and to what effect? Second, what did they actually do in this regard, again to what effect? The interesting political question obviously is why did they choose the policies they did, or indeed any at all? This section takes up each of these issues in turn.

There are a variety of subsidy programs that a regional government can in principle employ to affect industrial structure, from the very specific to the very general. The former refers to grants directed to specific firms or industries with a view to offsetting natural disadvantages. Examples are: subsidized feedstock prices for petrochemical plants, performing research and development for private forms in certain areas, relocation or modernization grants, and low or no cost loans. These would be effective to the extent that the subsidy actually covered the extra costs of locating the activity within the province rather than its most preferred site. The cost would be relatively straightforward to compute, being equal to the value of the revenue expended in this manner.

There has been remarkably little recourse to industry or firm-specific subsidies, even in Alberta where the financial wherewithal certainly exists. Rather the typical procedure has been to funnel resource revenues through the existing taxation-expenditure system so as to provide a general subsidy to any capital and labor located within the province. Low corporate and personal taxation rates, special treatment of small business profits, the absence of a sales tax, and the recent mortgage subsidy schemes are examples of these policies. They all have the effect of increasing the real, after-tax return from any given nominal payment. As an example, an individual earning $20,000 per year in Alberta is better off in a real income sense than his identical counterpart in Ontario, since he will receive a much greater value of government services per tax dollar (net fiscal benefit) thanks to the subsidy provided by the resource revenue.

Higher real-after-tax returns in the West can be expected to attract capital and labor from other jursidictions for as long as the differential persists. This immi-gration proceeds, and drives down nominal returns in the West below those in the East, until the point where the net fiscal benefits expected are just equal to the private-sector real income foregone. At that point there will no longer be an incentive to relocate, and the interregional capital and labor markets will be in equilibrium. Note however that now costs of production within the region have fallen, due to the lower nominal factor payments. This allows all sectors to increase their hiring and expand output until these cost differentials are again eliminated. The final result is a regional economy that is bigger in the sense that Gross Provincial Product, the capital stock and the labor force are all larger than they would be in the absence of the general subsidies. The government has used its resource revenues to promote extensive growth, without resorting to specific subsidy schemes.

This policy of providing general locational incentives through the taxation-expenditure system has received considerable attention recently under the heading of fiscally-induced migration.[14] The reason for the interest is that a movement of capital and labor from higher to lower tax jurisdictions can be shown to be socially inefficient, even if privately rational. In essence, the notion is that too much capital and too many workers end up in the resource-rich region. The contribution each makes to total national output in the new location is less than that foregone by leaving the old one. For the individual migrant this is acceptable, even if it is reflected in a lower private-sector wage, since the difference in made up by the net additional fiscal benefits enjoyed. For the economy as a whole, however, there is a social cost in that total output is lower than if factors were allocated more properly across regions.

There was considerable concern over the last decade that the large fiscal surpluses enjoyed by the resource-rich western governments were causing this type of distortion within the Canadian economy.[15] If true, this would mean that the western economies are currently larger and more diversified than they would have been in the absence of this particular use of resource rents. Unfortunately, there is little firm evidence on this yet one way or the other. We (Norrie and Percy, 1982, 1983a, 1983b) have looked at the question in a more general way by developing a stylized model of a small, resource-rich regional economy, calibrating it roughly to Alberta data, and performing a series of experiments designed to simulate the economic adjustment to an energy-price increase under a variety of rent-disposition schemes. The basic conclusion that emerges from this work is that it is certainly possible to use resource rents to promote the growth of either specific activities or of industries more generally. The manner in which the public sector revenues are distributed turns out to be important; under some scenarios, for example, the main effect is an expansion of government activities and a partial crowding out of the other sectors. The extent of the induced diversification is also shown to depend crucially on a variety of technical parameters such as the sensitivities of export demands to price changes, the degree of responsiveness of migration to economic incentives, and so forth.

The next logical step in this type of research has not yet been done. That is we (Norrie and Percy) have simply simulated the implication of alternative, *possible* uses of natural resource rents. In acutal fact, the western governments have adopted a variety of rent disposition schemes, ranging from potash nationalization in Saskatchewan and tax relief in Alberta through specific industrial incentives and mortgage assistance to Heritage Savings Trust Funds. To date, no one to our knowledge has attempted to estimate the actual effect any of these has had on growth and economic structure in any given province. One suspects the impact has been marginal at best, for the reasons given above: viz, the region has a large natural disadvantage to begin with; the simple economics of the energy boom exacerbated this condition; and the key province, Alberta, has been notably recalcitrant to use much of its resources in this manner, until recently that is.

Supporting this conjecture is the evidence given in our report demonstrating no significant structural change to 1979 at least (Norrie and Percy, 1981).

What is clear from the existing research, however, is that each of these subsidy programs leads to a dissipation of economic rent to some degree. That this must be true can be seen by recognizing that the general object is to use resource revenues to make up the difference between (a) the maximum amount that industrial concerns will pay for factors and still locate in the West and (b) the total income these same inputs require to come to or remain in this region. The greater the disadvantage is in this sense, the higher the costs. Subsidizing specific projects is the least costly, but it has the least effect on overall extensive growth. More general subsidies through the taxation-expenditure system have a larger overall impact, but use up much more of the resource revenue.

Herein lies the fundamental political economy issue for the western provinces. Developments in world petroleum markets have given the current residents of the West an unanticipated real income gain. Under existing institutional arrangements much of this appears in the first instance as provincial government revenues. The government then has to decide how to allocate this windfall. The options run from distributing the proceeds as an equal per capita dividend payment to all current residents[16] to spending the entire amount on province-building activities. The former would maximize the gain to current residents, but leave the region increasingly specialized in its traditional activities. The latter option can introduce a measure of extensive growth into nonpetroleum sectors, but dilutes the real income gain to "pioneers." Measures in between the two extremes will have an element of both.

Why might a provincial government pursue province-building activities, if the cost is foregone real income gains to current residents? There are three possible, not necessarily mutually exclusive, answers to this question. The first is that the subsidy process will eventually produce an industrial and service sector which will be nationally and even internationally competitive in its own right. This is certainly the position that many in the Alberta government hold, for example. It would be credible if one could demonstrate that any of the following are true and important: national economic policies are largely responsible for the current lack of industrial development in the region such that a few key policy measures by the provincial government can offset these distortions; agglomeration economies exist, and the West is on the threshold of being able to exploit them significantly; locational considerations for the next generation of industrial development (e.g., high-technology industries) have shifted away from traditional centers, putting the West at less of a disadvantage now. A quick response to this would be that the first has already been discounted above, while the jury is still out on the second and third.

The second explanation is that these activities are costly and conceded to be so, that a diversified economic base is sought nonetheless for noneconomic reasons, and that this represents the expressed and considered will of the populace. Residents may equate a more diverse economy with greater economic stability, regional political power, or a greater choice of jobs, now or in the future. The society then "invests" its resource revenue in creating this economic structure.

A final explanation is suggested by a public-choice theoretical approach along the lines used to explain why protective tariffs, which are known to reduce real income, are nevertheless an almost universal policy. The basis of the explanation lies in recognizing that tariffs reallocate income from the population as a whole to specific groups within the economy. The gains in total are less than the losses, with the difference equal to the efficiency loss. But the fact that the gains are relatively concentrated, and hence appropriable by a specific group, makes them highly visible. Groups will be formed to lobby for the measures, and politicians will receive political credit for implementing them. The very diffuseness of the losses, on the other hand, makes political action against such measures unlikely. No one will take the time and effort to lobby against them, since the individual cost is so little relatively, and politicians will not lose much from being identified with them. Thus economically inefficient measures can still be popular policy options.

Province-building strategies based on resource rents seem to fit this model well. As shown above, there are groups that gain from extensive economic growth even in a small, regional economy; viz, the owners of geographically immobile factors in the service industries. This group, Richards's and Pratt's (1979) new urban elite, will thus have a strong incentive to lobby for policies which will draw additional capital and labor into the region. The costs, like those from tariffs, are borne by the population as a whole. Individuals already in the region may perceive that they are not sharing in the province's resource wealth to the extent they might, and that they do not appear to benefit much from the extensive growth that is occurring, but the incentive for taking political action is small.

The costs associated with using resource revenues are even more obscure than this, however. In the first place, they are not so much costs as foregone potential gains. That is, any revenues expended on province-building efforts do not come form direct taxation of the population, but from government resource royalties. Thus, no individual resident is actually worse off as a result of the policy; he or she simply does not receive the capital that would otherwise have accrued. Even further, however, few residents expect to receive any direct share of these resource revenues, due to the manner in which they have always been collected and utilized. In effect, provincial governments levy a 100 percent tax on each resident's share of royalty income. These same authorities then decide how much of this shall be saved, how much to provide government services at subsidized rates, and how much devoted to other objectives such as sponsoring extensive economic growth. Since this has always been the procedure, there was little awareness over the last decade that there was an individual cost to such policies. With benefits concentrated and appropriable, and with costs nebulous and diffuse, there is little wonder that province-building was a politically appealing policy over the last ten years.

Conclusion

The main arguments of this paper can be summarized very briefly. The post-war period has witnessed several significant economic and political developments within western Canada, but the basic structure of the region is unaltered.

The West was born a small, resource-rich economy, and it has remained so through to the present. This endowment has provided the region with average or above average living standards, and with a unique economic and political structure. Resources and linked sectors dominate the economy, with more traditional secondary manufacturing activities being relatively underdeveloped. The openness of the economy means there will be swings in extensive growth, with rewards to mobile factors never deviating much from national variables. This inevitable dependence on external conditions in both product and factor markets generates sentiments of economic alienation, while the small population and hence relative underrepresentation federally creates a feeling of political isolation. Geographically immobile factors and public-sector resource revenues are the key indigenous variables which provide a a degree of uniqueness to the regional political economy.

The intent of this paper has been to argue that these considerations explain both the economic structure of the West circa 1971 and the nature of the economic adjustment to the favorable terms of trade effect after that date. Before the disruptions in commodity markets some ten years ago, the economic history of the West in the postwar period was essentially one of adapting to labor-saving technological change in agriculture in the face of some rather severe swings in its profitability, and to the extensive economic growth resulting from the new staples. The economic structure of the region thus displayed every characteristic that one would expect of a richly endowed but small and geographically-remote regional economy.

Analysis of events since that date must necessarily focus on two conflicting tendencies: the increased returns in the energy sector pushed the western economies (primarily Alberta's) toward increased specialization in these industries; while at the same time the obvious volatility of the current structure provided the incentive, and with the revenue and regulatory powers the apparent means to achieve exactly the opposite outcome. The result was a series of policy measures destined to have little real impact on economic structure, but guaranteed to dissipate much of the real income gains potentially available. Compounding this conflict was the fact that such policies would, nevertheless be politically popular, given the concentrated and obvious nature of the benefits compared to the diffuse and nebulous perception of the costs. Indeed, the dynamics of western political economy over the last decade have revolved around this theme of perception versus reality.

Three brief comments which follow from the above are offered in conclusion. First, it must be stressed that western provincial governments have been admirably restrained in the use of natural resource revenues, at least until recently.[17] This is all the more commendable given the magnitude of the revenues they had to work with, and the political ease with which more ambitious development projects could have been pursued. Ironically, the Alberta government is currently bearing the wrath of editorial writers among others for not having followed a more activist policy in the last ten years. This paper has argued that province-building strategies, always costly because of natural economic disadvantages, would have been doubly so if pursued in the heat of the energy boom.

The second point concerns the phenomenon of regional economic alienation. The crux of what has been discussed above is that the basic economic structure of the western economies is effectively explained by geography, history and market forces. The implication is that federal economic policies, with the possible exception of the Crow rate distortion, have played little or no role in determining this structure. In particular, they have not made the West less industrialized or diversified than it might have been otherwise. This is not to say that some of these policies have not reallocated income among regions within Canada to the detriment of the West. Indeed they have done this, the National Energy Program being the most obvious instance. The point is, however, that the cause of good policy analysis would be well served if western spokesmen were to begin with a more rigorous appreciation of the binding constraints.

Finally, the considerations raised here support the view that, barring further major disruptions in energy markets, the long-term future for the western Canadian economies may well involve a slow and orderly reversal of the pattern of extensive growth.[18] This means GPP increases of less than the national average, net outmigration, and so forth. The process will be slow, because, contrary to current alarmist reports, the economic base will clearly not collapse. It will be orderly, because past experience has shown that product and factor markets in the West adapt rather efficiently to changes in relative returns. But it will mean that the West will not play the leading role in Canadian economic and political affairs that many inside and even outside the region had to come to expect.

Footnotes

1. Howard and Tamara Palmer (1983) argue that the relative decline of rural Alberta was a primary factor in the defeat of the Social Credit by the Lougheed Tories in 1971, for example.

2. There was an oil and gas industry in Alberta prior to 1947, of course, but of insignificant scale until the Leduc and subsequent discoveries.

3. Province-building strategies in one form or another are as old as the region. For a survey of earlier efforts see Owram (1982).

4. Much of the argument in this paper is based on work done by the present author in conjunction with my colleague Michael Percy (Norrie and Percy, 1981, 1982, 1983a,b,c).

5. The best reference to the staple theory are Watkins (1963) and Stabler (1968).

6. See Norrie-Percy (1981) for a discussion of the economic structure of the West in 1971 as it related to primary export industries.

7. This point is developed further in Norrie (1976, 1978). The Crow or Statutory Grain Rate distortions are a possible exception to this view. See Norrie-Percy (1983c) or Harvey (1980) for a discussion of the impact of these freight rates on prairie manufacturing.

8. See Cairns (1977) for a discussion of province-building and regional elites.

9. The possible exception to this pessimistic view is if the energy boom were to increase the absolute size of the economy sufficiently that agglomeration economies came to be important. Little is known about this phenomenon, however, theoretically or empirically. Norrie and Percy (1983a) do incorporate it in some simulation experiments.

10. There would almost certainly be absolute expansion of these sectors, it should be stressed. The discussion here is in terms of structure, not total output.

11. Additional to the existing natural disadvantages as discussed above, that is.

12. Natural gas is relatively expensive to transport, so there is a significant wedge between western and delivered eastern prices. The presence of long-term contracts at very low, preboom prices added to this advantage.

13. Indeed, much of it is yet to happen, given the concern over the current economic slump in the region and the consequent pressure to use Heritage Savings Trust Funds to bolster growth.

14. See Economic Council of Canada (1982) for a summary discussion of this literature.

15. Purvis and Flatters (1980).

16. See McMillan and Norrie (1980) for a discussion of this point.

17. The mortgage subsidy schemes introduced recently by both Saskatchewan and Alberta are examples of the worst possible use of public natural-resource wealth.

18. The paper by Schweitzer (1983) is the most recent example of this view.

References

Cairns, Alan C. "The Governments and Societies of Canadian Federalism." *Canadian Journal of Political Science* 10:4 (December 1977), pp. 695-725.

Economic Council of Canada. *Financing Confederation.* Ottawa: Supply and Services, 1982.

Harvey, David R. *Christmas Turkey or Prairie Vulture? An Economic Analysis of the Crow's Nest Pass Grain Rates.* Montreal: Institute for Research on Public Policy, 1980.

McMillan, M.L. and K.H. Norrie. "Province-Building vs. a Rentier Society." *Canadian Public Policy* 6 (Supplement 1980), pp. 211-24.

Norrie, K.H. "Western Economic Grievances: An Overview with Special Reference to Freight Rates." *Proceedings of the Workshop on the Political Economy of Confederation.* Institute of Intergovernmental Relations and Economic Council of Canada. Ottawa: Supply and Services, 1978, pp. 199-237.

Norrie, K.H. and M.B. Percy. "Westward Shift and Interregional Adjustment: A Preliminary Analysis." *Economic Council of Canada Discussion Paper No. 201,* 1981.

_____. "Energy Price Increases, Economic Rents, and Industrial Structure in a Small Regional Economy." *Economic Council of Canada Discussion Paper No. 220,* 1982.

_____. "Economic Rents, Province-Building and Interregional Adjustment: A Two Region General Equilibrium Analysis." *Economic Council of Canada Discussion Paper,* 1983a. (forthcoming).

_____. "Province-Building and Industrial Structure in a Small Open Economy." Prepared for the Second John Deutsch Roundtable on Economic Policy (Kingston: Queen's University, November 11-13, 1983b).

_____. "Freight Rate Reform and Regional Burden: A General Equilibrium Analysis of Western Freight Rate Proposals." *Canadian Journal of Economics* 16:2 (May 1983c), pp. 325-49.

Owram, D. "The Economic Development of Western Canada: An Historical Overview." *Economic Council of Canada Discussion Paper No. 219,* 1982.

Palmer, Howard and Tamara Palmer. "The Alberta Experience." *Journal of Canadian Studies* 17:3 (Fall 1983), pp. 20-34.

Purvis, Douglas D. and Frank R. Flatters. "Ontario: Policies and Problems of Adjustment in the Eighties." In *Development Abroad and the Domestic Economy.* Toronto: Ontario Economic Council, 1980, pp. 129-65.

Richards, John and Larry Pratt. *Prairie Capitalism: Power and Influence in the New West.* Toronto: McClelland and Stewart, 1979.

Sahir, A.H. and A.A. Seaborne. "Economic Diversification in the Canadian Prairies." *Prairie Forum* 7:1 (Spring 1982), pp. 91-4.

Schweitzer, Thomas. "Migration and a Small Long-Term Econometric Model of Alberta." *Economic Council of Canada Discussion Paper No. 221,* 1983.

Stabler, J.C. "Exports and Evolution: The Process of Regional Change." *Land Economics* 44 (1968), pp. 11-23.

Watkins, Melville H. "A Staple Theory of Economic Growth." *Canadian Journal of Economics and Political Science* 29:2 (May 1963), pp. 141-58.

THE ECONOMIC GEOGRAPHY OF PRAIRIE CANADA IN REGIONAL PERSPECTIVE

Brenton M. Barr

Intermezzo

Although the first hundred years of modern commercial development of the Canadian prairies have been marked by periods of euphoric expansion and traumatic retrenchment, the febrile expansion of commercial and industrial opportunity in the 1970s led many observers to believe that the future of this region was one of boundless expansion and to conclude that the traditional fetters on the prairie economy had been permanently removed. Forgetting that this region like many others had experienced optimistic periods of rapid growth followed by abrupt decline in earlier periods, many of us justifiably expected the prairie spatial economy of the 1980s finally to become the bountiful cornucopia denied our forbears. Maturation of the spatial economy, high urban and rural employment, rising per capita disposable incomes, buoyant resource-extractive small communities, and comprehensive diversification of metropolitan centers clearly presaged by the late 1970s a proud and creative future for the region and its inhabitants. These expectations were further justified by analyses based on itemized accounts of capital investment project (Semple, 1981), changing world demands for primary agricultural and industrial commodities (Barr and Lehr, 1982), or shifts of economic and human priorities within Canada (McCann, 1982b: 31).

All the expectations for a stable and fulfilling prairie future were explicitly or tacitly based on the assumptions that: (1) the demand and price for energy would continue to rise; (2) that traditional markets for prairie commodities would remain open and would continue to expand; and (3) that the locus of financial opportunity and provincial governmental political initiative would continue to shift toward western Canada. These assumptions have subsequently proved erroneous although they were fostered by prominent decision makers in commerce, finance, industry, politics and government administration, and widely accepted by analysts in the media, academe and numerous quinary enterprises (comprising the knowledge-creation sector of developed economies). Furthermore, however parochial and self-fulfilling they may have been for those within the region, the assumptions were clearly shared by those elsewhere in Canada and in world financial centers who expected significant economic gain by investing in prairie resources. Thus until the beginning of the 1980s, many regions of prairie Canada, particularly in Saskatchewan and Alberta, were elevated to levels of appeal unmatched since the enthusiastic period of land settlement and railway construction which preceded World War I.

At this point in the 1980s, the prairie agricultural and industrial economies are showing lackluster performance, disorientation and retrenchment. The spatial economy seems to be hovering between bare stability and shrinkage; the exciting projects of yesteryear are on "indefinite hold" or have been cancelled, and few new ventures will come on stream in the middle years of this decade. The economic bases of small communities have contracted, the viability of many single-activity communities is now questionable, and erstwhile confident metropoli, especially in Saskatchewan and Alberta, whose diversification appeared imminent in the 1970s, are struggling to accommodate functional dislocations caused by the unexpected malaise in their significant service components.

The strength of those international and national forces which generated so much anticipated economic return in the 1970s has declined almost beyond recognition. The OPEC cartel is nearly devoid of its previous ability to exert a concerted influence on the price and supply of petroleum. The economic recession generated in part by the inflationary and unpredictable rise in energy prices after 1973 has reduced the industrial world's demand for petroleum. Many additional sources of energy discovered and made economic by the high price of petroleum in the 1970s now undercut the international price of petroleum and reduce the inflationary demand for further exploration and production in the sedimentary districts of the prairie region. Furthermore, increases in domestic American supply of natural gas and surpluses of international crude oil available to that economy are seriously eroding the volume of petroleum exported from the prairies to the United States—the region's major foreign energy market. Recession in central Canada and falling costs of offshore energy available to it have caused domestic Canadian markets for prairie energy to decline and have brought further constraints to the region's activity.

Much of the malaise affecting the prairie region can be traced directly to changes in the extra-regional demand for petroleum and other forms of energy. Traditional markets for other major prairie primary commodities such as wheat, lumber, sulphur, potash and nonferrous metals have also declined due to worldwide recession, coupled with intense competition from other producers, and growing protectionism within such major markets as the United States and the European Economic Community. On many fronts, therefore, the opportunity for rapid economic growth and return on investment within the region has quickly been eroded, and the attendant shifts in population and anticipated western increases in political influence have stabilized or evaporated. The powerful levers represented by various provincial "heritage funds" in the 1970s have been cleverly negated or curtailed by federally-induced energy exploration and development in northern and eastern frontier regions. These now provide alternatives on federal or sympathetic provincial lands when Ottawa negotiates energy agreements with its western constituents.

Concurrent with diminished increments to these significant pools of provincial capital have come diminished provincial incomes from other sectors, necessitating deficit financing and diversion of funds otherwise intended for the heritage savings funds. In numerous economic sectors and political milieux, therefore, the financial prowess of the prairie region, epitomized by the buoyancy of its primary industries for nearly a decade, has now diminished in its apparent ability to accomplish spatial, economic, political or financial realignment within Canada. Diminished regional economic prosperity is affecting the very ability of many of its communities to survive, and is inhibiting the continued redistribution of financial and political power which had become so apparent by the end of the last decade. Contrary to earlier expectations, the prairie region has not significantly diversified its economy; this failure "is, in part, a reflection of its continued role as a hinterland economy and its domination by the national heartland" (Sahir and Seaborne, 1982:92).

Prospects

Regional perspectives thus suggest to the economic geographer that the prairie region should be assessed at this juncture through examination of those factors which could cause further growth in the region, sustain current levels of uncertainty and adjustment, or lead to fundamental decline and collapse of the spatial economy and its related settlement systems. Prediction of outcomes of any variety would be specious in view of world economic uncertainty and numerous structural problems inherent in its institutions. Too many unknowns and imponderables now affect the milieux in which the region exists for any analyst to do more than estimate some of the likely implications for the prairies if its future is expansionary, stable or contractive. The remainder of this analysis, therefore, seeks to evaluate the implications of various future paths for the locational and functional characteristics of the prairie spatial economy, and to draw analogies where possible with events which have occurred since the recent rebirth of the entire region following World War II.

Further Growth

The prairie regional economy during the 1970s was characterized as an upward-transitional hinterland region in which its previously narrow profile was diversifying and strengthening through the generation of interlinked productive, financial and political facilities. The region appeared to be on the threshold of taking command of key sectors of its economy and of being able to offset many of the previous obstacles to its prosperity. Prairie metropolitan centers grew and diversified, the volume and value of primary industrial and agricultural commodities increased, the friction of distance to world markets was reduced by rising values for regional products, and the long-neglected opportunities for trade with the Pacific Rim and the Communist world were realized (Barr and Lehr, 1982). Many of these changes exerted profound influences on the size and function of the region's settlements, particularly in Saskatchewan and Alberta.

The relative strength of metropolitan centers, however, is evident in all prairie provinces and attests to the urban-oriented nature of numerous activities in commerce, finance, administration and research which characterize modern regional economies. The full regional, agglomerative nature of such activities is somewhat constrained by the provincial legislative domains of each province, however, and the spatial metropolitan structure of the region shows the indelible influence of provincial spheres of authority. The rapid growth of regional metropolitan centers, particularly in the two decades preceding 1980, is also testimony to the growing influence and activity of provincial governmental power in Canada generated by profound changes in the expectations of government by individuals and politicians during the past quarter century. The growth of strong provincial centers of power throughout Canada has fostered the ability of regionalism to exert an influence on national events and economic development, once unprecedented outside traditional centers of influence in Quebec and Ontario. Metropolitan economic and political growth in prairie Canada, therefore, has set the stage for expectations that future regional development and prosperity could be significantly influenced from these new urban bastions.

The strong export performance by primary prairie producers since World War II has not only expanded the external and internal road, rail, pipe and air links of the region (Barr and Lehr, 1982: 286), but also has integrated numerous nonmetropolitan districts and centers into regional subsystems and the world trading environment (Thompson, 1977). Lacking an auspicious locational or comparative environment for manufacturing the prairies have not, except in localized instances, been characterized by intermediate-size urban places. Rather, the urban system outside of metropolitan centers has largely consisted of small communities whose economic bases rested with agriculture, energy, mining, forestry, recreation, transportation or government-sponsored activity. The growth of these communities throughout the different zones of the region has been facilitated by the ability of prairie producers to compete satisfactorily on world markets; the growth of many smaller communities has also been particularly pronounced during periods of rapidly increasing demand for the product of their economic base.

Regional prosperity has not caused the agricultural rural population to expand in recent decades, although its maintenance at existing levels is dependent on world trade, but it has generated the ability of many nonfarm rural environments to sustain processes of reverse urbanization or urban out-migration. In keeping with developed industrial economies and regions elsewhere in North America and in Europe, the prairies have reached a point in the late twentieth century where nonmetropolitan economic opportunity, regional transportation networks, and levels of disposable income permit a significant portion of the region's population to maintain high standards of living without having to reside in major urban places. Various individuals' own financial abilities to sustain rural, nonfarm, lifestyles are enhanced by the general financial abilities of local and provincial government to provide adequate levels of social and infrastructural services.

If the current economic malaise is viewed as a temporary aberration in this upward transitional regional development, then the 1980s and future decades could certainly witness the strengthening of many of the spatial developments achieved during the periods of rapid economic growth since 1945. If those shelved megaprojects which planned to extract and partially process energy and mineral resources should be forthcoming, then numerous small communities in Alberta and Saskatchewan will expand in the future. Then, the euphoria so confidently reported by Semple (1981) will likely be justified:

> The 1980s will be known as the good decade on the Prairies. Growth and prosperity will occur at higher levels than in the rest of the nation. Incomes will continue to increase above the national mean and hundreds of thousands of new arrivals will call the Prairies home for the first time. (Semple, 1981: 106)...

> Agricultural production will be surpassed not only by the value of petroleum production but by mining and manufacturing as well. The economies of the three provinces will become more mature and more technologically developed. (Semple, 1981: 106)...

> Economic development will continue at a feverish pace on the Prairies. More corporate headquarters will spring up especially in Calgary, Winnipeg and Saskatoon but the key political and economic decisions will continue to be made in the eastern metropolises of Toronto, Montreal and Ottawa. This will lead to a turbulent decade with western discontent at an all time high! Alberta will be the centre of growth and discontent. Saskatchewan will move forward cautiously within a tightly planned and governmentally orchestrated mode. Manitoba will prosper but slip behind its prairie neighbours. (Semple, 1981: 107)...

In general continued northern resource exploitation will ensure a decade of prosperity for the more southerly prairie communities. This continued expansion northward, however, will increasingly create tension unless the social and cultural integrity of the native population is preserved. (Semple, 1981: 107)

Given the exciting prospects of greater personal wealth which prevailed in much of the prairies by the late 1970s, Semple's remarks are quite justified and to many are probably highly restrained understatements of their own expectations for the region and for themselves. The key to understanding the enthusiastic expectations which so many people have for prairie Canada during times of rapid economic expansion probably lies in the anticipation of being able to overcome the traditional constraints to prosperity of marginal returns in this environmentally-harsh region, which for so long has denied continuing prosperity to its inhabitants. Many also feel that the large capital-and technology-intensive projects would assure prestigious jobs to the region and erase the sting of inferiority lingering since the prairie collapse of the 1930s. Above all, however, the dreams of ascendancy articulated by Semple presage a strong regional spatial economy capable of overcoming the traditional constraints of extra-regional control and perceived exploitation by central Canadian interests. Many of the sentiments expressed in Semple correspond to those of newly developing countries in the Pacific Islands. There, for example, beautiful and potentially bounteous peripheral economies generate flights of fancy among their population which are markedly at odds with the realities of the major international forces of economic activity.

Semple echoes many of these yearnings in his inspired vision of the prairies of the 1980s by noting that in the years following World War II, the prairie provinces

...began the long struggle toward economic and political maturity that would permit them to take their place beside their more diversified and mature eastern partners....For the first time the Prairies will begin to guide their own destinies within confederation. (Semple, 1981: 122)

Semple was not alone in his predictions and expectations. The present author and a colleague, drawing on many of the same events and trends as Semple, but emboldened with the authority of the heartland/hinterland paradigm, also expected the prairies of the 1980s to be fundamentally different from those of the past:

The heartland-hinterland paradigm, as applied to the Western Interior offers a classic example of peripheral dependence on developed core areas. Throughout much of its history, the Western Interior has been subordinate to central Canada, Great Britain, and the United States....The region came to depend on the importation of labour and capital from developed regions and to rely on the export of a limited range of raw commodities, or staples, to metropolitan markets. But now, a new era has dawned. The region is more in control of its development than ever before....In the 1980s, therefore, the Western Interior appears to have shaken off the yoke of perceived subordination and subservience to central Canada. Although the region still plays its major role at the beginning of the world's production chains, the attitude of the population and its politicians is one of self-confidence, optimism, and awareness of new found prowess. (Barr and Lehr, 1982: 288-9)

When these lines were written, contrary assessments of the region seemed completely devoid of imagination, expectation or truth. We should have foreseen, however, that the artificial circumstances of an international cartel, the rapid structural decay of western European and North American economies, and the significant changes being wrought upon the international economic order by Japan and Southeast Asia could not but portend ominously for this vision of uninterrupted prosperity in the prairie spatial economy.

Problem Hinterland

In the absence of rapid growth or abrupt decline, the most frequent condition of the prairie region seems to be one of accommodation to marginal hinterland status. Traditionally, at the spatial and economic margin, the prairies face uncertain markets for grain, livestock, timber, energy and minerals. The heartland/hinterland paradigm is, therefore, particularly useful for understanding this ongoing dilemma although categories of hinterland proposed by Friedmann (summarized in Berry, Conkling and Ray, 1976: 258-259) need modification. The region is neither just a special problem area nor a resource frontier. Because of its internal heterogeneity, it combines elements of these descriptions and probably should be termed, ''problem hinterland,'' for its economic bases and their attendant settlement system frequently face economic trauma.

Throughout much of the post-World War II period, particularly in the early 1970s, periodic world surpluses of grain and sulphur, extreme competition in, and federal restriction of, prairie petroleum markets, and more economic supplies of timber closer to markets kept the regional economy from expanding to its capacity. Many jurisdictions were characterized by out-migration, metropolitan diversification was restricted, and comprehensive transportation systems were minimal. Except for a few communities in the Canadian Shield associated with nonferrous mineral extraction, and some associated with petroleum exploration in the sedimentary regions of Alberta, the prairie spatial economy was marked by slow growth and limited expectation. Given the experience of regional inhabitants in the 1930s, the performance of the regional economy nevertheless was satisfying, particularly because so many employment opportunities drew more ambitious migrants to British Columbia, central Canada and the United States. Despite many encouraging signs of growth and maturation of the region's economic geography, the present author noted at the beginning of the 1970s (Barr, 1972) that uncertainty pervaded many dimensions of the region: ''The prairie region is in a state of flux arising largely from uncertainty about the strength of the continuing demand for its raw materials'' (Barr, 1972: 78); ''The fate of resource developments in the prairie provinces depends on the profitability of ventures in other world regions'' (Barr, 1972: 78); ''American decisions on oil import quotas, which have been pressed for by American producers who seek to exclude cheaper Canadian oil from their domestic markets, have been viewed with considerable apprehension in Alberta'' (Barr, 1972: 75); and Operation LIFT (Low Inventories for Tomorrow) 1969-1970 had just been carried out by the Federal Government to offer relief from the huge grain carryovers of the late 1960s.

The greatest problem facing this hinterland appears to be its ability to produce large quantities of primary commodities in excess of world demand and the consequent low return on investment caused by the lagging demand of markets to absorb excess capacity. Many components of the spatial economy, therefore, such as transportation, urban centers and size of plant and equipment are seldom able to operate fully. The compromise is to remain small, safe and undiversified, while many of the downstream benefits from processing continue to accrue to heartland regions in central Canada or abroad.

As in the period preceding the hyperactive regional economy of the 1970s, the prairies today have large stocks of unsold grain, only modest livestock markets, depressed timber activity, poor sales of minerals, and decreasing markets in North America for natural gas and crude oil. Many of the factors affecting these sectors and their communities in the 1960s have reappeared for regional producers, only with greater intensity as poor markets outside the region are compounded by the intervention of protectionist governments in setting tariffs and quotas or in subsidizing sales of their own producers. A large proportion of the prairie manufacturing economy has traditionally depended on sales within the region, but the markets for these items are generated by activity in the primary sectors. Unresolved penalties in transportation costs on shipping prairie manufactured goods to domestic and world markets also hinder the ability of the region to expand abroad and offset the limitations of depressed regional markets.

History suggests that the 1980s could witness the reappearance of significant out-migration, stagnant capital development and low utilization of human and economic capacity. A major difference, however, between earlier periods and the current situation is the lack of freedom to migrate easily internationally, and severe structural unemployment in central Canada. Consequently, regional levels of unemployment and per capita disposable income may be affected to a greater degree in the 1980s by poor economic conditions than in earlier more problematic eras.

Systemic Decline or Trauma?

If the region should stagnate and become a depressed or downward-transitional hinterland similar to the 1930s because of world economic and financial upheaval, then many of the dimensions characteristic of its economic geography since 1945 would cease to be significant. Most of the exploration, development and capacity expansion of the recent forty years has been predicated on modest or advanced optimism. Yet, as a hinterland, the prairies are particularly vulnerable to systemic traumas variously caused by: collapse of the international banking system; curtailment of world trade; closure of major commodity markets; capital outflows prompted by profound confusion and conflict between federal and provincial governments; and injurious institutional factors such as the National Energy Policy or, for many decades, the Crows-Nest Freight Rates. If these factors were to preponderate then the viability of numerous agricultural, extractive and recreational communities (the intra-regional hinterlands of the five metropolitan centers) will deteriorate beyond the point where even the welfare purses of government can provide effective sustenance.

The prairie region is currently operating in national milieu devoid of strategyor foresight, notwithstanding the promise represented by the Royal Commission on the Economic Union and Development Prospects for Canada. The federal government appears unable or unwilling to establish rigorous goals and programs for the nation and its regions which provide leadership and opportunity for employment and potential growth. The prairies, structurally unable to proceed alone, have always been complementary (discussed in Kaye and Moodie, 1973) to other Canadian regions, and have been historically manipulated to enhance the central Canadian spatial economy. By definition, hinterland regions are appendages to internally diversified heartland and are unable to take control of their political or economic destinies. Provincial governments are not independent entities and at best serve through their own programs to facilitate regional productive sectors when economic conditions in extra-regional markets are at least potentially accessible. The prairies have developed, however, because national tariffs guaranteed them basic internal markets which would provide minimal levels of development for the spatial economy when international markets were lacking in strength or periodically inoperative. The region is a contrived, somewhat protected, economic system that appears to thrive only when markets are artificially stimulated or cyclically hyperactive.

Although a modern regional economy with a highly developed infrastructure, the prairies are in excess of 1000 kilometers from ice-free tidewater and the region's primary commodities face stiff competition from regions and nations closer to markets and less restricted in adjusting prices to accommodate demand. Prices for petroleum, coal, nonferrous minerals, timber, sulphur and grain, for example, are set internationally and defy any influence by this region. Furthermore, currency-exchange rates are used predatorily by many nations whose major interests are associated with the regional products exported from the prairies. Lacking the ability to adjust the value at which the Canadian dollar is traded, the region is further hampered in its ability to develop enduring stability and international viability.

Comment

The prairie region in many respects resembles a third-world country in its dependence on primary industrial production and world markets, yet it possesses the infrastructure and human skills of a developed nation. Furthermore, it is a constituent part of an erstwhile developed nation which has not yet come to accept its own deindustrialization (Britton and Gilmour, 1978). Like many nonindustrial nations, however, the prairies (and Canada) probably suffer adversely from multinational firms and impeded entry into European, Japanese and American markets. Lacking coherent industrial strategies, and victimized by internecine political strife, Canada and its regions, even those with recognized potential like the prairies, face the prospect of economic uncertainty and unstability in their spatial economy. Not only are investment cycles sporadic and unpredictable, but the troughs between high employment generated by construction and primary production also create uncertainty throughout the system and stagnation or decline of marginal entities located in the ecumene.

While this analysis cannot adequately assess the present economic geography of the region on the basis of sectoral development or individual capital investments, it does suggest instead that the diverse factors influencing the region in the 1980s fit into different components of the heartland/hinterland paradigm. Should any of the forces outlined in this assessment prevail, then the economic geography of prairie Canada could in the forthcoming decade be better understood as a recurrent variation on the major recurrent themes of the region's spatial economic history.

References

Barr, M., "Reorganization of the Economy since 1945." In *The Prairie Provinces*, edited by P.J. Smith. Toronto: University of Toronto Press, 1972, pp. 65-82.

B.M. Barr, and J.C. Lehr, "The Western Interior: The Transformation of a Hinterland Region." In *A Geography of Canada: Heartland and Hinterland*, edited by L.D. McMann. Scarborough: Prentice-Hall, 1982, pp. 250-93.

Berry, G.J.L., E.C. Conkling, and D.M. Ray, *The Geography of Economic Systems*. Englewood Cliffs: Prentice-Hall, 1976.

Britton, J.N.H., and J.M. Gilmour, *The Weakest Link. A Technological Perspective on Canadian Industrial Underdevelopment*. Ottawa: Background Study 43, Science Council of Canada, 1978.

Kaye, B., and D.W. Moodie, "Geographical Perspectives on the Canadian Plains." In *A Region of the Mind: Interpreting the Western Canadian Plains*, edited by R. Allen. Regina: Canadian Plains Studies 1, Canadian Plains Research Center, The University of Regina, 1973, pp. 17-46.

McCann, L.D., (ed.). *A Geography of Canada: Heartland and Hinterland*. Scarborough: Prentice-Hall, 1982.

Sahir, A.H., and A.A. Seaborne, "Economic Diversification in the Canadian Prairies: Myth or Reality?" *Prairie Forum* 7:1, pp.91-4.

Semple, J.K. "A Geographical Perspective of the Prairies: the 1980s." In *The Prairies and Plains: Prospects for the 80s*, edited by J. Rogge. Winnipeg: Manitoba Geographical Studies 7, Department of Geography, The University of Manitoba, 1981, pp. 106-23.

Thompson, R. "Commodity Flows and Urban Structure: A Case Study in the Prairie Provinces." Unpublished Doctoral Dissertation, The University of Calgary, 1977.

TRANSFORMATION OF THE WEST FROM INDUSTRIAL TO POST-INDUSTRIAL SOCIETY

Walter G. Hardwick

At the end of World War II, the economy of Alberta and Saskatchewan was predominantly agrarian while British Columbia could be characterized more as industrial and commercial. In the census of 1941, 60 percent of those gainfully employed in Saskatchewan and 54 percent in Alberta were in agriculture and only 24 percent and 29 percent respectively were in those service jobs that enabled business and government to function, and that provided personal services including health and education. Although nearly 40 percent of the Manitoba labor force was in agriculture, another 30 percent was employed in fields like manufacturing, laboring and construction. Similar percentages were recorded for the latter in British Columbia. There, those in the extractive industries (12 percent) compensated for a much smaller agrarian labor force. British Columbia alone had a large service sector (43 percent), characteristic of more metropolitan and industrial regions.

In contrast, forty years later in 1981 only 4.1 percent of Canadians are engaged in agriculture. In prairie Alberta it is 7 percent, and in British Columbia all extractive industries including agriculture account for 5.2 percent of those gainfully employed. In all provinces over 60 percent are now in the service sector.

In highlighting the transformation of the occupational structure since World War II it is not to suggest that the economies of the West have become as independent of the cultivation, extraction and distribution of natural resources as the employment numbers suggest. They are still important. But the agriculture and extractive sectors have benefited tremendously from the substitution of technology for labor and posted productivity gains exceeding most industrial and service sectors. These traditional activities have been augmented by several new types of production, many based upon human resources. In the process, economies are much more diversified now than they were forty years ago.

This forty-year contrast in the mix of work is striking and the transformation has important ramifications for where people live and work, for the nature of social and interpersonal relationships, and for people's attitudes toward communities, society and political institutions.

In many ways, this transformation in the West mirrors major structural changes in economic activity that characterize all western economies. A way to gain understanding of the western case is to be aware of the broader situation.

One of the most elegant and comprehensive analyses of these changes has come from the American sociologist, Daniel Bell, who terms the transformation the emergence of post-industrial society. It is one in which theoretical knowledge supercedes capital as an "axial principle" in society. It is characterized by a trend from goods to a service-based economy, highlighted by the growth of a knowledge class, changes in the character of work, the growth of information-based activities and technology, and a concentration of people in cities.[1] Although in broad outline the salient characteristics of economy and society as outlined by Bell are evident in the West, his schema assumes a staged development from preindustrial through industrial to post-industrial, a model that does not corre-spond too well to the western Canadian case. Few western cities and towns were industrial in the sense of Hamilton, Pittsburgh, or Manchester.

Eric Trist, the British organization behavioralist presented in 1970 a similar schema describing in a Table of Comparative Salience the changes between the 1930s and 1960s.[2] He described power shifting from industrialists to scientists and professionals, changing levels and styles of education, types of organization, cultural and ecological values. Both Trist and Bell saw the transformation as an irreversible "drift," not a revolution.

Bell's metropolitan world was directed by industrial and merchant interests with factories, railroads, warehouses, merchant banking and modern retailing meeting growing corporate and consumer demand. Surplus people from rural America as well as immigrants were absorbed into cities whose industry became larger and more prosperous. Large cities became the magnets of growth. In those years, rural areas grew much more slowly and residents often felt cut off from the rising power of the centers.

Western Canada differed in two ways from the regions of metropolitan dominance. In large measure it avoided the industrial phase, yet it was a producer society. Secondly, rapid urbanization commenced rather later and was collapsed into a relatively short period. Under these circumstances one could ask if the emergent society of western cities differs from those from which Daniel Bell's idea flow? Also, what happens to communities, economies and social institutions when rapid growth is concentrated into a very few years?

In Canada's West in the 1940s and 1960s the post-industrial transformation was muted, being recognized primarily in Vancouver and in the intellectual enclaves in other provinces. The dominance of agriculture and extractive indus-try as economic propellants and major sources of employment contributed to a perception of regional stability. If change took place it was a product of cyclical forces of economy and nature. During these decades of apparent continuity of life, structural change of course was underway.

Few recall that a high-tech revolution permitted the enormous expansion in the output of the farms in North America with inputs from fewer and fewer farmers. Research and development in the land-grant universities produced drought resis-tant hybrids, larger animals, improved fertilizers both chemical and natural, and new consumer products such as modern bread. Commercial agriculture took advantage of emergent rail and ocean transportation technology to expand its market to the world. The result is that North American farms are a bread basket of the world. They can even afford to warehouse land in 1983 to limit production. The demographic impact of these innovations was enormous. Rural and small town populations shrank with the consequential impact on rural life. The process was acutely recorded in the 1950s Royal Commission on Agriculture and Rural Life in Saskatchewan.[3]

Upon reflection it can be argued that those engaged in commercial agricultural production behave much like their industrial urban contemporaries. Farm and city dweller alike became caught up in a materialistic society where consumer goods purchased from catalogue, coop or shopping center absorbed a large proportion of household income. Farmers purchase of combines and cultivators paralleled the industrialists' purchase of capital goods. Material goods sought by corporation, farmer, or household were mirrored in the public sector with demands for paved roads, public facilities, utilities and other infrastructure. The postwar mechanization of agriculture was the prairie's first industrial phase. Petroleum and mining was the second.

The Goods Sector

The increases in demand for consumer and corporate goods expanded throughout this century culminating in a great crescendo in the early 1950s. Then, those who felt deprived by depression and wartime were on a materialistic binge which benefited goods production and distribution. It is not surprising that the goods sectors, including agriculture, employed a majority of Canadians in 1951. But by 1961, the curve trended down to 44 percent and in the past two decades the shift has been increasingly to the service sector as measured in employment or value added.

In hindsight it is evident that in North America many corporations made strategic choices toward promotion of cosmetic change in style and models, and planned obsolescence as a means to fuel the industrial enterprise—and for a while it worked. Goods producers and merchandisers continued to thrive. However, the seeds of the undoing of this strategy were already sown at home and abroad. At home better educated and more discriminating households were rejecting, in part, the material hype—allocating a greater proportion of disposable income to the purchase of services, and if I may make an important distinction, of experiences. Abroad, newly industrializing nations entered direct competition with domestic production, sometimes managed by foreign nationals, in others by American-based supranational corporations. Some foreign companies in countries like Japan and Sweden not only engaged in price competition, they went a quality route, and the results were that Toyota and Volvo pricked the balloon of planned obsolescence of GM and Chrysler.

The economic buoyance of the 1970s camouflaged the importance of these shifts. Now that markets have shrunk and profits are down the goods producing sector is accelerating productivity adopting automation through computers and robotics. Both union and companies officials agree, as an example, that out of this recession, the numbers employed in the forest industry in British Columbia will never reach earlier levels. The same story comes from the automobile industry in Ontario, farm machinery in Winnipeg and garments in Montreal. In those years in which agriculture went through its major transformation, industry and trade compensated in the sense that its expansion absorbed surplus labor. One issue before us in 1983 is: will a post-industrial sector do for the goods sector what industry did earlier for agriculture?

The Service Sector

A service sector has always been present providing administrative, financial services, personal and social services and education. The number involved were relatively small, and to many the sector was perceived as parasitic to the goods sector.

The shift to a dominant service sector as measured in employment or value added started in the core metropolises and has gradually diffused to other cities. In doing so, a much more homogeneous pattern of economic activities has emerged by 1981 from three decades earlier. Using census data from employment and roughly classifying occupations as goods- or services-oriented, the point can be illustrated.

Western Canada
Ratio Production to Service Employment (P/S)[4]

	Canada	Manitoba	Sask.	Alta.	B.C.
1911	75/25	70/30	84/16	80/20	73/27
1941	57/36	60/36	72/25	67/30	58/42
1981	32/68	32/68	40/60	33/67	31/69

* Figures do not always total 100 percent because of ambiguous census classification.

From 1911 through the end of the War, Alberta and Saskatchewan were to an extraordinary degree producer provinces. Early in the century, Saskatchewan with its extensive agriculture had the largest population of any western province. British Columbia and Manitoba had ratios more similar to the country as a whole. By 1981, the ratio of production to services employment was similar in all provinces, with the service sector preeminent. The demographic conditions for post-industrial society are in place.

Services may produce new wealth. Although it is difficult for many economists and policy makers to grasp it, an artist who gives pleasure to thousands and a surgeon who restores health are both key producers. For those who see mechanization as a key to increasing productivity, and private sector activity as the sole source of new wealth it may not be obvious that clerical and computer workers are engaged in production of services and information. The value added of producer services in the United States now equals the value added of all manufacturing.

Perhaps Bell's industrial stage for our purposes might be better described as the "goods stage," a term that encompasses commercial agricultural as well as industry and commerce. In the goods sector a majority of gainfully employed in one way or another handle goods through manufacturing, transportation, wholesale or retail trade. The location of these activities was accounted for by classical location theory. Those interests that controlled land, resources, and transportation and distribution systems were powerful. Services, largely consumer services of that era, were dispersed more or less in proportion to population.

With the emergence of post-industrial society functions which have always been present, but employed a miniscule number of people, have expanded in numbers to a remarkable degree. One subset is an "enabling" group which plays a catalytic role in the development and management of new activities. A second group caters to experiences. A century ago a catalytic person might have been a tinkerer working in a garage or an owner-entrepreneur with a vision of a good or service to market. They were few in number and depended upon intuitive knowledge to succeed. Now the need for marketing information, and the need for elaborate management skills have drawn thousands into teams that parallel in function the isolated individual of a century past.

The largest increases in employment in the West in absolute and relative terms are managers, professionals and technicians from natural and social sciences and clerical occupations. Between 1971-81 these occupations have accounted for 50 percent of all new jobs. This percentage does not include other services or sales, health, education, artistic, religious or other white-collar occupations. Percentage-wise the increases were generally highest in Calgary, but in all occupations but natural sciences, Vancouver recorded the largest absolute increase. Winnipeg trailed.

Absolute and Percent Increases — 1971-1981[5]

	Managers	Nat. Sci.	Soc. Sci.	Clerical	All Occup.%
Vancouver	31,775 (151)	10,975 (77)	7,280 (133)	54,590 (161)	(45)
Calgary	23,705 (231)	17,160 (189)	4,165 (213)	40,065 (114)	(97)
Edmonton	21,645 (216)	9,945 (127)	3,860 (151)	37,385 (90)	(72)
Winnipeg	10,846 (86)	3,252 (45)	3,375 (54)	16,715 (33)	(28)
Saskatoon	3,822 (171)	1,525 (89)	1,150 (186)	6,240 (67)	(58)
Regina	3,780 (106)	1,225 (56)	1,110 (110)	6,596 (98)	(42)
Victoria	4,970 (179)	2,280 (90)	1,600 (193)	9,470 (68)	(44)

Unfortunately 1961 data is not comparable for most occupations. However, clerical occupations provide a longitudinal trend. Vancouver increased 84 percent between 1961-71 adding 40,731 to a 48,731 base. The next decade it was 161 percent. Calgary increased 75 percent adding 15,000 to a 20,000 base and Winnipeg increased 30 percent adding 11,500 jobs to a 38,325 base. There were higher proportions than growth of the labor force as a whole. Vancouver had a head start on the Alberta cities, if the clerical sector is representative of the other categories.

For analysis of the impact of post-industrialism on the pace of city development it is useful to categorize the service sector among: (a) those who provide and market consumer services; (b) those who enable goods and services to be produced; (c) those who maintain and regulate the system; (d) those providing experiences.

Those who produce and market consumer services have a pattern of location quite like retailing. Shopping centers, community centers, health centers and schools are all market-oriented. Their scale of enterprise and location is closely related to the distribution of population.

A portion of the managerial, natural and social science and artistic occupations are the driving force of a post-industrial economy. These activities are not located in equal proportion in every town or city. These key human resources are rarely located in centers of raw material production nor manufacturing. These occupations are the driving force in the growth of Vancouver, Edmonton and Calgary, and for the agricultural sector, Saskatoon. They are less prevalent in smaller centers.

Some other managerial, clerical and service occupations can be classed as "systems maintenance" in the sense that they are not catalytic in creating new products or services. In contrast they monitor, control, regulate and maintain balance in an economy. Many of these occupations are in government but a considerable number are in large private business. Capital cities as well as metropolises attract these functions.

Post-industrial activities have emerged in various regions of North America in a symbiotic relationship with the regional economy, but have often taken on a life of their own. Teams of people, a human resource, assembled to deal with local industry may later provide a region with intangible exports of intelligence. They spawn as well auxiliary goods industries, while dependent upon the locale for an initial market, and later export goods across the world. Examples of the first are engineering firms in British Columbia like Swan Wooster (ports) and Sandwell and Company (forestry), and in Alberta, consulting geologists. An example of the latter would be the prefab builder, ATCO Industries.

If these teams can be maintained, even after a resource phase slows, a city can have a life of its own and draw the regional economy along. The cultivation of this sector should be a high priority of western people. Parenthetically, Dr. John Warkentin in his study of Winnipeg argues that the slaughter of the best young minds of that city in World War I set the stage for that city's relative decline.

The "experiential" sector should gain attention of those concerned with regional growth in the West. The hotel in which this conference is housed, the Banff Springs, is a symbol of the importance of special places to world tourism. When this hotel opened tourism was the preserve of an aristocratic and moneyed elite described by Veblen. Today as discretionary income for a majority has increased, millions are engaged in touring, and ordinary people from across the continent, Japan and Europe are appropriately mobile. On another front, a generation ago only Toronto and Montreal could support major league sports, an experience industry, even though passive. Who in 1945 could have predicted that the Oilers would be right up there? Memories of the Rockies, an exhilarating downhill ski, are intangible exports, so are the Oilers!

Uniqueness is a crucial variable if experiences are to be an intangible export. Those cities and regions which identify those cultural and physical amenities that are unique and capitalize on them have enduring assets that fuel a post-industrial economy. Those that do will benefit from an economic multiplier.

Some consumer services when specialized can become economic stimulants. A growth sector in the United States is in health, fitness and nutrition. Well-being is an intangible, but it is a sector to which an increasing portion of consumer discretionary income is directed as clearly demonstrated by European spas, the Houston Medical Centre and Esalen. Our region has been slow to capitalize on these strengths, in part, because these services have been predominantly provided by the public sector, one not noted for entrepreneurship. Yet the Positron Emission Tomography Scanner at UBC recently unveiled by the Queen and other ventures could provide the basis of new activities.

One of the aspects of a post-industrial sector that the West is just beginning to share in is merchant banking (in contrast to consumer banking). In the United States, the federal reserve system and banking legislation have promoted regional banking. For too long the control of banks has been in the East. The strengthening of western financial institutions is essential for sustained regional growth.

The growth in real income of households over the past forty years has been important in explaining the growth of demand for personal services and experiences.

There is an additional aspect as well. In British Columbia, 9.1 percent of federal taxpayers report "investments" as their primary source of income. Another 7.3 percent report pensions. These folks are found disproportionately in Victoria and the Okanagan Valley. This phenomenon parallels the move to the sunbelt in the United States. Another form of income transfers, unemployment insurance and welfare, seem to have different patterns, and do not contribute to growth centers.

Post-Industrial Urban Culture

Vancouver was the first city in the West to adopt the character of a post-industrial city.[6] Leaders held attitudes about city life and a perception of what is important that differs from agriculture or industrial interests. Although in Calgary and Winnipeg an old managerial and professional elite created for themselves quality neighborhoods, on the west coast as funds became available a park system and cultural amenities suitable for a metropolis were developed. Both quality private and public environments were enhanced copying both aristocats and social reformers of Britain and the United States.

In early Vancouver elegant private space and neighborhoods contrasted with the vernacular of working persons' neighborhoods. Individualistic and upwardly mobile, the latter were concerned more with their own condition than the community at large. But over the decades as socially and territorially mobile groups moved to the west coast they joined a coalition with an old elite to challenge the commercial and working groups for power. In the process they advanced a quality public environment with views and vistas, planning controls, cultural and recreational facilities. When the most rapid population growth came to Vancouver urban development was controlled. This provides an interesting contrast with Calgary and Edmonton, both unicities, where it might be argued that the newcomers swamped the older elite and permitted a glass, concrete and blacktop public environment of commerce. Maybe in Calgary a hobby farm and escape to the Rockies are the experiential world suitable for those entrepreneurs, scientists and technologists with a cowboy complex.

In conclusion, I have argued that there has been a transformation in the West best described in terms of changing occupations, value added and urban concentration. Following an agrarian and extractive phase the West went through a goods phase, but now the occupational structure suggests a post-industrial society. The goods phase was concentrated in a few years of mechanization of agriculture, expansion of mining and processing and the growth of trade. Although cities quickly evolved a service-oriented urban economy, the staple industries continued to dominate public awareness. Somehow our perception of the region prevented an appreciation that the viability of our cities and our region are now more dependent upon the human resources. The perception must change. The post-industrial sector with intangible exports of expertise, and sharing our region with visitors from abroad are now critical elements in our future. The maintenance and enhancement of our cities as excellent places to live attract individuals with catalytic roles to play and those with investment income. They are the human resources which exceed natural resources as propellants of the West. Continued population expansion in our cities provide a significant multiplier. These factors are far removed from those of the beginning of the modern West in

1945. They must be understood and capitalized upon if the West is to continue to be the region of opportunity.

Footnotes

1. Daniel Bell, *The Coming of Post Industrial Society* (New York: Basic Books, 1976).

2. Erik Trist, ''Urban North America: The Next Thirty Years,'' *Plan Canada* 10:3, pp.4-20.

3. Saskatchewan. *Royal Commission on Agriculture and Rural Life*, 12 vols., (Regina: The Commission, 1955-57).

4. ''The Labour Force and the Gainfully Occupied,'' in Historical Statistics of Canada (Toronto: MacMillan and Co. and Census of Canada 1981: Occupation, 1965).

5. *Census of Canada, 1981*, Labour Force and Occupation Trends 1971-81, Cat 92-920 and other reports.

6. See Walter Hardwick, *Vancouver* (Toronto: Collier MacMillan, 1974).

THE IMPACT OF OIL ON ALBERTA: RETROSPECT AND PROSPECT

John J. Barr

Introduction

Oil has changed Alberta dramatically. The big question is whether the changes will prove to be spectacular, superficial and transitory—as they were in East Texas early in this century—or quiet, profound and enduring.

The first thing to be noted about the "oil era" is what a small part of Alberta's human history it represents. The first humans are thought to have trudged warily into our forests and onto our grasslands around 8,000 B.C., and for the next 9,700 years of our history we were a province roamed by small bands of nomadic hunters, a land scarcely touched by man. Somewhere in the next 150 years we see the development of fur trapping, a strange economic symbiosis between the white man and the native which results in a few small, ramshackle white settlements— the first—and the beginnings of a process which "pins down" the natives into more or less definable territories. Only late in the 1800s do we see the first sod being broken and the beginnings of agriculture and permanent settlement. Manufacturing did not start at a significant level until the 1900s, and the first oil and gas was not discovered, at Turner Valley, until 1914.

Oil and gas are finite, nonrenewable resources. Once discovered, they enjoy a predictable life cycle which follows a bell-shaped pattern called Hubbard's Curve. All the major fields discovered in Alberta from Leduc until the present day, with the exception of the last one, are now either at the peak of the Curve, or well past the peak and on the downhill slide. A good part of the province is "gas-prone" which is a reservoir condition, not a digestive ailment. What it means is, we have much more gas than oil and we'll have gas surpluses long after the oil is gone. By the way, when I say "oil," I mean of course conventional oil produced by wells, and neither heavy oil nor oil sands, which are quite different resources. More about that later.

Alberta never was a big or even a medium-sized producer in the world oil picture; and the way our oil is now depleting, within ten to fifteen years we won't even be the major force in Canadian conventional production. What this means is that the oil era will be quite a short one in our history, probably ending—at least as far as significant conventional production is concerned—by the end of this century. Gas will last a little longer, perhaps to 2050, and coal to the end of the twenty-first century. In other words the era of liquid, gaseous and solid hydrocarbons in Alberta is destined to last perhaps 150 years out of our total history, or about 1.5 percent of the time which man has occupied this province.

Now, heavy oil and oil sands have the capability of giving us a "second wind" in this economic race, but that will not happen automatically. Heavy oil and oil sands are quite a different type of industry, economically, technically and psychologically from conventional oil and gas, a realization which not even all oilmen have really yet appreciated.

The important point to remember, by way of introduction, is that the end of the era of conventional oil and gas is already in sight, if not for us, then at least for our children, at most, our grandchildren. After them, it won't matter all that much, and the memories of the great days of the fifties, sixties and seventies in Alberta will join those faded daguerrotypes of Dingman No. 1 and Spindletop we see in today's history books.

Early Effects of Oil in Alberta

Let's take Leduc as our starting point. I realize Turner Valley was an interesting and significant oil development, but Alberta didn't really enter the ranks of significant oil and gas producers until Leduc No. 1 blew in on 13 February 1947.

It came in at a remarkably propitious time. E.J. Hanson points out in his book *Dynamic Decade* that Alberta had been losing people steadily since 1931 and unless something dramatic happened, we were due for a further outflow after the war. It's estimated about 80,000 people left the province between 1936 and 1946, leaving us with a population of 803,000; Hanson says it would have dropped as low as 750,000 by the early 1950s if oil had not injected new life into Alberta. In fact, he argues, until the discovery of oil the likeliest scenario after the war was the steady decline of the prairie economy until we became Canada's second permanently depressed region, alongside the Maritimes.

The discovery of oil touched off a boom that added up to 600,000 people to the western provinces along with huge amounts of capital and economic opportunity. The impact on population was dramatic. Instead of declining, Alberta's population grew 40 percent between 1946 and 1956, faster than any other province. The labor force was changed radically. Oil created a demand for people with university or technical training in everything from engineering, geology, geophysics and the hard sciences through to a wide variety of skilled trades. Suddenly we had a need for whole new occupations, a new source of demand for university graduates, and the sudden emergence of a much more sophisticated labor force.

The oil industry generated a tremendous number of direct and indirect jobs. Twenty-two thousand direct new jobs were created between 1946 and 1956 in oil exploration and production, plus a vastly larger number in associated trades, construction, manufacturing, services, government and so forth. In this decade we saw the emergence of the modern Alberta economy. The best evidence is that employment in agriculture dropped from 40 percent of the labour force to 26 percent in the decade after 1946. In 1947, oil and gas generated five percent of Albertans' personal income, ten years later, it was 45 percent. And during the same period, income from farming dropped from 78 percent of Albertans' total personal income to 41 percent.

Let me inject a personal impressionistic note on this decade of growth. I grew up in Alberta and was becoming conscious of the world about the time the Leduc discovery's impact was really starting to be felt in Edmonton, which is to say the early to mid-1950s. Prior to this time, Edmonton was a backwater. If you wanted to see a really big city, you drove all the way to the "Big Apple"—Spokane. If you wanted to go out for dinner—and in those days, nobody ever went out for dinner, except to their sister's place—you either went to the MacDonald Hotel or the local Chinese cafe. There quite literally wasn't anywhere else to go. The modern restaurant industry was still a gleam in the restaurateur's eye. The highest building in Edmonton was the selfsame MacDonald Hotel, at a lofty eighteen storeys. Before 1954, television was only something you heard about from your glamorous American relatives (unless you vacationed in Spokane, of course) and Sundays were dead (it didn't matter, you were expected to be in church anyway). If you wanted to amount to anything in virtually any field, whether business, journalism, academia or government, you had to move to Toronto, or Vancouver if you could not quite make it in Toronto. Premier Manning would be Premier for the rest of the century and Dr. Praisegod Barebones of the Edmonton Police Morality Squad ensured the peace, order and good government of the city by periodically busting up card games in the back rooms of cafes.

Oil cracked this tight little world and let in dazzling rays of change. Suddenly, on the streets of Edmonton, there were all those swaggering, superconfident Marlborough Men with Oklahoma or Texas accents who winked at the girls, drove big cars, and came from a different world. The Edmonton Eskimos hired a coach who later returned to the States and came to symbolize big-time college football. His name was Darrel Royal, and he lived down the street from me. He was handsome, he had a beautiful blonde wife who used to be a cheerleader and he called his little girl "Sugar." He symbolized the beginning of a different kind of Alberta.

It was "Americanization," and we loved every minute of it. America was big-time. The big-league. Suddenly we were somebody, we were somewhere, and we were getting a piece of the action. Deep down, no Albertan who grew up in the 1950s could ever be truly anti-American. The Americans introduced us to the big-time. The made it possible to be first-class Canadians for the first time, instead of just the dumb hicks from the West.

But I'm getting ahead of myself. Let's talk about the medium-term economic and social effects of the oil revolution.

Medium-Term Effects

If you haven't looked lately at an analysis of the contributions made to the Alberta economy by the various sectors, it's an interesting exercise.

In no way do I mean to disparage the importance of farming and farmers to our economy. But in 1980, the contribution of agriculture to our Gross Domestic Product was...5 percent. The contribution of what Statistics Canada calls "Mining" (which in Alberta is mainly oil and gas) was 23 percent. If you look at the percentage share of Goods Producing Value Added, the contribution of mining is 55 percent and of agriculture is 6 percent. Construction adds 24 percent, manufacturing 13 percent.

Fine, but what about the contribution made by other sectors, like tourism? Well, in 1981 the total cash receipts from tourism were around $850 million (and of that, almost half came from internal tourism, that is, Albertans visiting other parts of Alberta, taking in each other's wash, as it were). The value of mineral production was over $17 billion. The total cash receipts from all forms of agriculture including crops, livestock and other products, were a little over $3.5

billion. So if we ever entertained the thought that once the oil industry is gone, we'll still be able to live well off agriculture and tourism, we may have to re-think that option.

The medium-term effect of this bonanza of cash, under both the Social Credit government, and later the Conservatives, has been to finance the building of a very impressive and high-quality infrastructure of physical and social services. The Socreds laid the groundwork with a first-class province-wide highways system, rural electrification, fundamental social services including medical care, hospitals, and of course a very large and expensive educational establishment. During this period of 1947 to 1971 the Province created two new universities, two institutes of technology, a province-wide colleges system, the upgrading of teacher training, and laid the foundations for cultural facilities like the Northern and Southern Alberta Jubilee Auditoria.

The good news was that, thanks to high government cash receipts generated by conventional oil and gas exploration and production, we financed all this on a "pay as you go" basis without creating massive debt—the nemesis of earlier Alberta governments, especially in the first thirty years of the century, which financed growth with borrowed money and accumulated huge debts which, during the Depression, became insupportable. So, the oil boom left us with a superior physical and social infrastructure, which came without a massive, crippling debt.

The bad news was that the operating cost of this infrastructure, especially the social part such as medical, educational and welfare services, was very high. As taxpayers, Albertans have been insulated from this cost by the government's high oil revenues. Take away those revenues, and we face the prospect of either massive tax increases, or highly controversial attempts to roll back the services. Either way, a very tumultuous prospect politically for the 1980s, the first tremors of which we are feeling already in the government's attempts to control education, hospital and civil service salary costs.

These improvements to infrastructure have unquestionably left individual Albertans better clothed, housed, educated, transported and cared-for-when-ill, than ever before in our collective history. Most of us live a very good life; and to the extent that comfort, knowledge, leisure and the "fine things of life" are good in themselves and contribute to human happiness, we should recognize and salute this fact.

I should not go further without mentioning the most important demographic change brought about by oil-induced development, namely urbanization. After Leduc, virtually all our population growth took place in our cities. Alberta doubled its population between 1946 and 1971. In 1941, 68 percent of our people lived on farms, thirty years later, 73 percent of Albertans lived in cities. Edmonton and Calgary became the fastest growing cities in the country, Medicine Hat, Red Deer and Grande Prairie experienced major growth almost totally due to oil and gas, and several new communities came into being exclusively because of oil and gas.

From my perspective, the importance of urbanization was the change it brought in the area of social and political attitudes. The rise of an urban middle class, well educated and strongly managerial in bent, undermined the political base of

Social Credit and led to its collapse in 1971. This same middle class has a strong interest in economic diversification and growth and provides the political foundation of the current government. It is also the dominant element in the shaping of Alberta's cultural and social consciousness.

If you wish to visualize the impact of oil-induced prosperity, I have created the following intellectual image-game. Close your eyes and imagine Edmonton and Calgary today and all that is therein. Now let's make disappear, one by one, all of the things that we owe directly or indirectly to oil and gas prosperity. Ready? You're in Edmonton first. Half of the University of Alberta. Most of the downtown, certainly all high-rise office buildings and apartments built since the mid-1950s; Commonwealth Stadium; the Coliseum; the Edmonton Oilers, the Jubilee Auditorium; two-thirds of our 300 restaurants; cable television and pay-TV; the Northern Alberta Institute of Technology; three-quarters of our residential subdivisions; The Walter MacKenzie Medical Centre; the Space Sciences Centre; the Convention Centre, and the Light Rapid Transit system. Now let's go to Calgary. The Saddledome; the Calgary Tower; most of the major corporate headquarters, starting with the Petro-Canada Tower, the Esso Resources Building, the Dome Tower and the Bank of Montreal Building. The Devonian Gardens, Palliser Square, Home Oil, Nova Corporation; and McMahon Stadium. Reduce the University of Calgary to a satellite of the University of Alberta. Most of Foothills Hospital, and three-quarters of all the new suburbs and the freeway access to them. Most of the restaurants, night clubs, theatres, boutiques, crafts stores, art galleries and museums, including the Glenbow.

Had enough? Now it's true that we would also lose some aspects of modern Alberta life which some would not miss. Tabloid journalism, high divorce rates, metropolitan crime which puts us into the big leagues. High rates of drug abuse, suicide, and urban despair. Pollution, especially in the city centers. Urban sprawl and the gobbling-up of good agricultural land, and so forth. Nothing comes without a price, and at times the price seems steep. I concede this, but on the whole, I doubt that many people today would not accept the trade-off.

Thomas Jefferson said you cannot do something *for* a people without also doing something *to* them. The oil revolution did a lot for us: it made us richer, better educated, more mobile, more aware of the potentialities of life. I dare say it has made us a great deal more tolerant as well. Without denying the existence of currents of thought that are still troubling—anti-semitism, chauvinism, intolerance— there is no question that today's Alberta is a vastly more accommodating and tolerant-of-diversity place today than it was before oil. Edmonton in the 1940s and early to mid-1950s was a city much compartmentalized by religious divisions, ethnic dislikes, and redneck values. One group of journalists were sternly coached by their bosses on the menace of too much Roman Catholic economic and financial power; WASPS and "ethnics" viewed each other with considerable suspicion across invisible but very real fences. We have become true North Americans—secularized, atomized, hedonized and homogenized. We are freer, if not happier, and we can thank the oil revolution for most of that. But, are we collectively freer, as well as individually? To essay that question, I would like to turn to the last issue.

The Future

As you could deduce from my brief recounting of our economic history, Alberta's future, once we exhaust our conventional oil and gas, is, to put it mildly, cloudy. The focus of conventional oil exploration is slowly but irrevocably shifting away from Alberta toward the far north and the Maritimes, and the declining production of our existing fields is well documented. Oil production in Alberta slipped 16 percent between 1979 and 1982, and Hubbard's Curve is not mocked: these declines, once they begin, are irreversible. The recent study by economist Thomas Schweitzer for the Economic Council of Canada, predicts a decline of per capita labor income in the late 1980s and a peaking of our provincial product by 1992, followed by a slow but steady decline of output. That is, unless we begin, as he says, a massive program of oil sands plant development.

Whether Schweitzer is accurate on the precise date of the decline is not the point; he is almost certainly right in his general prediction, which is that Alberta's economic star is beginning to dim, and if we do not want to see it go out altogether, we must begin immediate implementation of a long-term corrective strategy. It is not a refutation of this argument to point out that we will still be producing *some* oil from conventional fields into the next century; of course we will, but the amount will not be significant. Ontario is still an oil-producing province, from old wells around Petrolia, but its output is measured not in barrels, but in pails.

It is to Premier Lougheed's undying credit that he was the first provincial politician in Alberta to look down this road, as long ago as 1965, and see where it was pointing. And he was the first to argue the urgent necessity to develop and diversify our economy to prepare ourselves for the inevitable end of the oil era. The government's carrying out of this vision has much to commend it. One thinks of their support for the Prince Rupert Port, rail car purchases for grain movement, agricultural processing plants, the Heritage Fund itself. This is not to mention AOSTRA and their direct investment in Syncrude, which played a valuable role in maintaining the momentum of oil sand development in the 1970s. This was leadership, and as someone who worked for the last Social Credit government, at a time when Mr. Lougheed was knocking at the door, I believe it is time we acknowledged that he was the only provincial politician of that era who had sufficient foresight to put the future on his party's agenda.

But has it all been enough? There is broad room for doubt. We now see that, despite that euphoric visions of the late 1970s, Canada economic center of gravity has not really tipped west. The cooling ardor of our eastern-based financial institutions, and the shift of oil exploration away from Alberta are proof of that. The real question is whether our economic planners have really appreciated the magnitude of the investment that will be needed to create a new economic foundation anywhere near the size of conventional oil and gas.

There is nothing wrong, fundamentally, with trying to build a post-oil economic foundation on such foundations as tourism, agricultural processing, medical research, and silicon except that it is clear that even taken together, these industries are not even remotely capable of supporting our current population at anything like our current level of income. I am afraid there is only one resource left which has anything like that potential, and that is, the heavy oil and oil sands.

I say this personally, and not as a corporate spokesman, because I simply don't see what other conclusion one could draw from the evidence. No, that's not true actually—there is one other scenario. We *could* build an economic foundation based upon agriculture, agricultural processing, tourism, medical research, silicon, some coal and forestry, and simply take our lumps from a population and living standards point of view. In other words, treat the province like an overweight corporation and simple set out to "shed" a quarter or a third of our population until we reach a level our resources can comfortably sustain.

This is a perfectly rational economic plan, but it suffers from several drawbacks. I doubt that any sane politician would be willing to espouse it; it would lead to the rapid eclipse of whatever federal-provincial bargaining power Alberta has managed to accumulate in the last fifteen years, so that we would soon become what E.J. Hanson feared in the fifties—western mendicants, living off the federal dole; and finally, it would lead to a drastic decline in our standard of living in virtually all spheres of life. But it is true that it is a rational alternative to what I am proposing.

Albertans are very fortunate to have a choice. Unlike other jurisdictions that have built prosperity purely on conventional oil and gas, and have nothing else to sustain them when the well literally runs dry, Alberta at least has the heavy oil and oil sands. They are a very rich and large resource, larger actually than the conventional reserves by many orders of magnitude. And they do form a potential foundation for a new economy that could endure into the next century. How to bring that resource into production is another subject for another time.

Suffice to say, it makes sense to me that the basis of Alberta's medium-term economic planning should be the exploitation of what it does well, and has a lot of. I hope we will soon see an informed public dialogue on the issue of our economic future, a dialogue which begins by involving Albertans from all walks of live in a very sober examination of their actual and potential strengths and weaknesses as we enter the economy of the twenty-first century. While we contemplate the future, I believe it is worthwhile and healthy, to look back on where we have been. It is clear that over the last fifty years oil and gas have changed Alberta deeply, and mainly for the better. Those of us who were lucky enough to be alive at this time have been uniquely privileged. It has been a great ride.

———

THE IRONY OF OIL: THE ALBERTA CASE

R.W. Wright

The objective of this paper is to discuss the legacy that the prosperity of the seventies has left to the Province of Alberta. Some of the consequences are obvious: an overextended economy, an entrenched conservative administration and a mood of hostility toward the central government. However, these are just the more visible manifestations of a set of underlying social forces and it is these latter components of the system that I wish to examine. The paper is organized around six concepts: ideology, irony, efficiency, anxiety, addiction and illusion. Initially, each concept is defined and its relevance to conditions in the seventies is identified. Then their interrelationships are discussed, and it is suggested that they all constitute part of an ironic illusion which will shape political and economic policies during the eighties.

The Concepts

Ideology

Our heritage is such that our ideology[1] is capitalistic, a system based on democratic political institutions and decentralized markets. Of the many subcategories of capitalism,[2] two are particularly relevant: classical and managerial. The former is based on private property and markets and the minimization of government involvement except insofar as it preserves competition and corrects for disequilibrium. In managerial capitalism, the power and responsibility of the managerial class is elevated so that they become the trustees for *consumers* as well as workers and shareholders. Accordingly, a primary role of government is to maintain stability so that firms can plan, innovate and invest with a minimum of uncertainty.

The Alberta brand of capitalism is a hybrid of the classical and managerial strains. Judging from the political rhetoric one might conclude that the former dominates because there are continual references to the positive role of small business, individual initiative and entrepreneurship. However, these elements are emphasized primarily to convince the agricultural and middle-class interest groups that they have control over their own destinies. In reality, recent provincial policy fits more comfortably under the rubric of managerial capitalism because the government unquestionably supported the shift to corporatism and the captains of industry as the emergent urban elite.

There are other dimensions of the Alberta ideology which are well documented and worth noting: it is entrenched and virtually unopposed; it places the blame for dysfunction on external forces while proclaiming its own virtue as the cause of success; it eschews income redistribution while providing shelter for industry during periods of adversity. It is thus monistic, self-righteous and asymmetrical. Finally, it describes itself as "free-enterprise," a phrase which evokes more positive imagery than the coarser term "capitalism."

Irony

Irony can be defined as a situation in which the consequences of an action are contrary to its original intention and a significant part of the discrepancy between intention and outcome can be attributed to the disposition and perceptions of the actor. This is a Niebuhrian definition and is different from both rhetorical irony (a literary mode) and the deterministic idea associated with phrases such as "the irony of fate."[3]

There is an ironic element to most nontrivial human activity and many dimensions of the concept are of intellectual interest. Philosophers discuss irony with a concern about the boundaries of personal responsibility. Historians use it as an explanatory tool as, for example, when they show that individualism in an age of complexity invariably leads to ironic situations. I expect that political scientists could use the ironic paradigm and explain federal government policy as a series of actions to correct the unintended consequences of previous actions. Strangely enough, economists rarely conceptualize events in terms of their ironic consequences in spite of the fact that it is a ubiquitous force among the phenomena we study.[4]

However, the aspect of irony which I wish to explore is the nature of the *response* once an awareness of its existence surfaces. That is, what does a society or a community do when it realizes that its expectations are *not* being realized? Here Niebuhr's interpretation of recent American history and ideology provides insights. He argues that Americans are afflicted with an exaggerated perception of their own wisdom and worthiness and hence see prosperity as earned and deserved rather than recognizing "the fortuitous and providential element of their own good fortune." Given this view, Americans become disoriented when apparently noble behavior (e.g., individualism and initiative) leads to unexpected and undesirable consequences (e.g., recession and international criticism). Niebuhr argues that their responses to these ironies tend to be dominated by irrational searches for scapegoats and reactionary adjustments to reinforce the sanctity of the "American way."[5]

This analogy suggests that if an ideology is monistic and entrenched, as in the United States, the response to irony is likely to be reactionary. I will develop this point in the context of contemporary Alberta in a later section.

Efficiency

The term "efficient" as used in economics refers to the creation of the maximum value of output using a given quantity of resource inputs. It occurs when all resources are allocated in such a way that, at the margin, their productivities are identical in all technically feasible uses (the Lerner rule), and the output is distributed in such a way that society is on its highest feasible indifference curve. A rigorous theory has been developed to demonstrate that given certain strong assumptions about technology, preferences and motivations, this efficient condition is attainable in a system to decentralize competitive markets with private property. This theory is the primary economic argument used by proponents of classical capitalism. Managerial capitalism can be justified if it can be shown that a combination of benevolent stewardship, scale economies and greater incentive to innovate can lead to an even higher indifference curve.

However, the elegance of the underlying classical theory exceeds its realism (although probably not its influence). There are several reasons for this: the idealized assumptions cannot be achieved; it is not possible to attain efficiency in a subset of an imperfect market system; our societal arrangement is such that markets are penetrated by a system of rights.[6] Nevertheless, no one has been able to argue convincingly that there is an alternative method of production and exchange which is more efficient than the competitive system, so the theory and the system itself have survived as ideals.

Unfortunately, there are major problems associated with operationalizing the notion of efficiency in that deviations of actual performance from the idealized state cannot be measured with any degree of precision. Even in a relatively static environment, production and consumption units have different time-horizons and different strategies to counteract uncertainty and there is no way to make a definitive *ex ante* judgment about their eventual effectiveness. Furthermore, society's production possibility curves and indifference curves are continually shifting as finite resources are used up, new information is accumulated, physical and human capital ages, and income distribution and preferences change. The point of absolute efficiency is thus a moving target. When one adds to this the fact that during periods of instability, as at present, there are many otherwise latent variables activated, which in turn disturb traditional time-lag patterns and investment programs, it becomes apparent that the point of optimal efficiency is not only moving, but behaving in a unpredictable way. Thus one does not know whether a change in performance is moving the system toward or away from the optimal point.

Nevertheless, there were many reasons for Albertans to feel that their economy was performing efficiently during the seventies. Over the period 1971-80, personal income per capita rose from 99 percent to 109 percent of the national average and provincial GDP per capita rose even more dramatically from 108 percent to 156 percent of the national level.[7] Furthermore, there were many visible conditions which suggested that the economy was operating close to the production frontier and that the Lerner rule was being approximated: capital and modern technology were available, there was a high level of employment, labor was mobile and workers had the opportunity to develop and utilize their skills, business expansion encouraged initiative and entrepreneurial activities were continually acclaimed. In addition, the economy was growing rapidly and according to conventional wisdom, growth is a consequence of efficiency. Further comment on the validity of this line of reasoning will be given in a subsequent section.

Anxiety[8]

Anxiety can be defined as an unpleasant psychological and physiological response pattern (e.g., apprehension or fear) stemming from the anticipation of a threat. To an individual the nature of anxiety depends on his perceptions and his disposition and there is an analogous situation at the aggregate level where it depends upon the shared understanding about the nature of the threat (the perception) and the society's mores, values and decision-making processes (the disposition).[9]

Individual responses to the feeling of anxiety fall into three main categories: acceptance, avoidance and adjustment. Again, there are societal analogues. For example, a nation faced with declining import prices may submit to the possibility of balance of payments problems (acceptance), raise tariffs (avoidance) or seek to improve the productivity of competing domestic industries (adjustment).

Societal anxiety is a difficult variable to measure because of the inability to make meaningful interpersonal comparisons, and because many individuals repress their anxieties in order to create the impression that they are in control of their situations. Consequently one must rely on social indicators, voting patterns and insights provided by the more astute commentators. One of the most respected of these commentators is Robert Heilbroner who suggested in the early seventies that the United States faced three types of anxieties which he classified as "topical," "attitudinal" and "civilizational."[10] He correctly predicted that the responses would include a reemergence of patriotism and a swing to conservative economic policies.

Prosperity and parochialism seemed to insulate Alberta from these anxieties. If there was a concern, it seemed to focus on the federal government[11] which, during the seventies, sought to restrict the power of corporations and to take more initiative in plotting the course of national economic development. This rubbed against the grain of the province's free enterprise orientation and added one more stanza to the litany of grievances which had existed for decades. Yet, relative to regions in the rest of the countries which were not growing as rapidly, Alberta was comfortable and confident.

Addiction

Addiction refers to a situation in which a pleasurable stimulus generates weaker levels of satisfaction as it is repeated over time but in order to replicate the earlier positive sensations the individual seeks to increase his exposure to the stimulus. If that is not possible, anxiety ensues.

Solomon and Corbit[12] have developed a homeostatic theory to explain the phenomenon. The theory contains three elements. First, when an individual departs from equilibrium a physiological "opponent process" is triggered. This reaction is sluggish so that when the stimulus which caused the original departure is withdrawn, the opponent process dominates and causes an opposite affective state. For example, drinking champagne leads to a period of elation followed by its opponent process, a hangover. Second, if an individual is repeatedly exposed to stimuli designed to elicit a certain effect, the intensity of the effect will weaken and greater amounts of stimulation will be sought to replicate the original sensation or "rush."[13] For example, over time our imbiber will seek greater quantities of champagne to recapture the original level of elation. Third, if the original sensation was *very* pleasurable, the individual will not be satisfied with a return to the prestimulus equilibrium state. That is, our champagne drinker will not now be satisfied with *vin ordinaire*.

Thus, a sudden exposure to a pleasurable stimulus (champagne) makes a person vulnerable to triple jeopardy if it is withdrawn: the opponent process dominates (hangover), a dependency may have developed so that withdrawal symptoms are experienced and if the original sensation was particularly pleasurable, he may no longer be satisfied with a traditional substitute.

I believe that the addiction model can be used to explain some of the forces operating in contemporary Alberta. Prior to the seventies the province experienced a decade of satisfactory but not exceptional economic growth.[14] This equilibrium was shattered by a burst of prosperity which, like champagne, initiated a period of elation. Nor was the spirit confined to the energy industry alone: migration resulted in its diffusion into activities related to urbanization; high incomes expanded the demand for consumer services; boosterism attracted footloose industries. The euphoria became ubiquitous.

The unexpected collapse in the early eighties left the economy in a state of disarray and in fact, the local press had referred to it as a period of hangover in which the more enthusiastic revellers experienced the more painful traumas.[15] However, it is the longer run issue which is of interest: will the experience be imprinted on the collective psyche and make Albertans less than satisfied with a return to normalcy? Both the theory developed by Solomon and Corbit and the classic "... how are you going to keep them down on the farm..." would suggest that a residue of discontent will remain.

Illusion

The concept of illusion has been of interest to a number of social philosophers: for example, Marx and Mannheim spoke of false consciousness and mystification. However, rather than draw on these grand traditions I wish to use a contemporary example to demonstrate the relevance of the concept to the issue at hand. This example is taken from a book by the theologian, Harvey Cox, where he examines the manner in which eastern religions have penetrated the psyche of the American public in recent years. Cox was originally perplexed because these religions are spiritual and ennobling in their indigenous settings but on being transplanted to America become merely "interesting experiences" collected by unspiritual consumers seeking to whet their insatiable appetite for novelty. After analysing the issue, he explains this anomaly as follows:

> The problem with introducing Oriental spirituality into America today is that the cultural barrier which the light from the East must pass through functions as a thick prism. The prism consists of American consumer culture and psychological individualism. What emerges from the filtration process is something which has neither the impact of the genuine alternative vision nor the critical potential of biblical faith. Robbed by the prism of its color and sharpness, the new refracted Oriental light serves as one more support for the structure its original teachers had hoped it would undermine: the isolated, Western competitive ego.[16]

It is this metaphor of the cultural prism which I wish to borrow here. In Alberta, the underlying free-enterprise orientation has for decades distorted and deflected threatening ideas and facts until they are sufficiently deformed to be supportive of the local ethos. The most visible examples are in the political realm where government leaders from Aberhart to Lougheed have continually reinterpreted egalitarian federal initiatives to be threats to regional integrity and ideas advanced by local reformers and environmentalists to be subversive. The existence of these presumed threats has then been used to buttress the incumbents' positions of power.[17]

The cultural prism has created a situation in which Albertans invariably claim personal credit for positive outcomes but blame external forces for adversity. They have succumbed to the malady identified by Niebuhr and mentioned earlier for they see "prosperity as earned and deserved rather than recognizing the fortuitous and providential element of their own good fortune."

Given this perspective, Albertans treated the prosperity of the seventies as an internally-generated phenomenon. The prevailing attitude was as summarized in Statement A.

Statement A: *Free enterprise caused efficiency which in turn caused economic growth and led to a reduction in anxiety.*

On the surface there is a certain plausibility to this line of reasoning because all four conditions existed: the voting patterns left little doubt that the province embraced the free-enterprise ideology, the economic system appeared to be efficient, all indicators confirmed that the economy was growing rapidly and anxiety levels were not burdensome.

The problem, of course, is that Statement A is both naive[18] and false. A more accurate description of conditions in the seventies is as contained in Statements B and C.

Statement B: *Exogenously generated increases in energy prices led to apparent efficiency in the Alberta economy.*

Statement C: *Increase in energy prices caused economic growth and led to a reduction in anxiety.*

That is to say, efficiency, whether real or illusory, did not lead to economic growth; rather they were both consequences of the same exogenous cause. Further, the free-enterprise ideology had little to do with the prosperity the province experienced.

Nevertheless, Statement A identifies the illusion that Albertans carry into the eighties.

The Eighties

The rhetoric and the results of the recent provincial election provide evidence that the illusion about the relationship between free enterprise, efficiency and economic growth has survived the recent downturn. However, before speculating about its future stability, it is useful to inquire about the economic conditions that are likely to be experienced over the balance of the decade.

At the outset, it must be recognized that the province will have difficulty reestablishing its past momentum. The boom of the seventies was based on construction and migration and unless oil prices make another quantum leap, this is not likely to be repeated. Indeed there are at least three reasons why one might be very pessimistic about the medium-term prospects. First, there are no obvious candidate industries which can initiate growth by expanding exports and increasing their productive capacity.[19] Without these growth poles, the rates of migration will dampen and the opportunities for industries concerned with urban expansion and import substitution will be limited.

Second, there is no real evidence that the agglomeration economies which one might have hoped would emerge from the growth during the seventies have materialized.[20]

Third, the province's economic structure was distorted during the seventies and may lack sufficient resilience to react to the opportunities which will develop during periods of normal economic growth. For example, the petrochemical industry is unfavorably situated relative to world markets and the advantage of low feedstock prices which led to its original creation may disappear. If so, idle capacity will occur and remain because its technical systems and infrastructure are too specialized to convert to other activities. Other distortions occurred in the service sectors. Here, administrative systems which were enlarged to accommodate growth became redundant with the downturn and many firms are discovering that dismantling bureaucracies can be as difficult as dismantling petrochemical plants. In any case, the adaptive capacity of the Alberta economy is suspect.

If the Alberta economy does not grow the illusion will be strained: free enterprise may result in marginal improvements in efficiency but these improvements are unlikely to be sufficient to generate sustained growth. The critical question then becomes: what will be the fate of the illusion or, expressed another way, what will be the response when the anticipated expansion does not materialize and the irony of the situation becomes apparent? I have thought about this issue and offer the following predictions.

One possibility is that the illusion will be modified and that anxiety rates will not heighten even though growth rates are dampened. In my view, this is also unlikely to occur because the residue of addiction to the conditions of the seventies will persist and because the political rhetoric will have convinced the populace that high levels of performance are not only attainable but deserved. To recall the earlier metaphor, Albertans are unlikely to be satisfied with *vin ordinaire* after having sipped champagne.

Another possibility is that the illusion will become transparent, its fallacies recognized and its structure dismantled. Again, I believe that this is unlikely because too many opinion leaders in both the public and private sectors have vested interests in preserving the existing belief system.

I believe that the more likely scenario is that the provincial government will try to force growth by initiating or encouraging large-scale investment projects such as the interbasin transfer of water, the Slave River hydro scheme and oil sands development.[21] The advantages of such projects are that the investment boom is reactivated and the economy will grow over the short run. The disadvantages are that these types of projects must generate exportable outputs to be viable and there is no assurance that quality markets will exist for water, agricultural products from irrigated land, electricity or synthetic oil. The Canadian track record for forced growth is abysmal and marginal capital intensive projects can easily become an embarrassment and a financial burden to the sponsoring government.

A program of forced growth can thus have political consequences particularly if it falters. A possible indication of the nature of these consequences was revealed in the Niebuhrian insight identified earlier, that when an ideology is entrenched and monistic the response to an adverse irony is likely to be reactionary.

If this principle is transplanted into the Alberta situation it suggests that if growth cannot be sustained the present government may be challenged by a reactionary political movement advocating a return to classical capitalism.

Conclusion

The objective of this paper has been to discuss the impact that the boom of the seventies will have on Alberta as the province reacts to the economic environment of the eighties. It is argued that the juxtaposition of forces over the past decade has been such that Albertans developed the illusion that they were responsible for their own good fortune. This view became embedded in the belief that their free enterprise ideology had led to efficiency, economic growth and a reduction of anxiety levels.

The illusion persists into the eighties, and it is interesting to speculate about its durability should market forces lead to a situation in which economic growth continues to diminish in spite of local attempts to be efficient. It is likely that slow growth will cause anxiety because Albertans will carry a residue of addiction to the favorable circumstances which have existed in more prosperous times. There will thus be pressure on the provincial government to preserve the illusion by embarking on programs which force growth.

Should such programs falter one can anticipate that a reactionary political force will emerge to urge the return to the principles of classical capitalism. This would be the ultimate irony: that in order to preserve the illusion which made it so powerful, the provincial government might sow the seeds of its own downfall.

Footnotes

1. Ideology is defined as the set of values, ideas and priorities used to support a particular configuration of related political and economic institutions. This definition deliberately excludes the more pejorative connotation suggested by Mannheim in *Ideology and Utopia* (1936).

2. A taxonomy of capitalist systems is complicated by semantic imprecision, a confusion between positive and normative conceptualizations and by intersections between sub-categories. However, standard lists normally include the following: Kelso's idea of "people's capitalism" which is characterized by diffused property ownership and worker participation in management; Galbraith's suggestion of capitalism based on "countervailing power" and his concern that the dominant characteristic of the present American system is producer's sovereignty; Papandreou's notion of "paternalistic capitalism" which suggests that states have merely become support systems and protectors of corporations, many of which have international tenacles; Myrdal's proposals of "socialistic capitalism" where private ownership of the means of production is blended with fiscal intervention and a comprehensive welfare scheme; Daly's idea of "steady state capitalism" where economic growth is constrained by ecological considerations; Veblen's opinion, shared by some Marxians, that we must search for a "humane capitalism" where there is an end to mystification, where work is made satisfying and where the calculus of utilitarianism is replaced by the calculus of social concern. This is by no means an exhaustive list.

3. Niebuhrian irony can also be distinguished from paradox (where it is self-contradictory behavior which produces the unintended consequences), pathos (where the unanticipated is due to external events) and tragedy (which is the result of conscious actions taken with prior knowledge that some of the consequences may be adverse). See R. Reinitz, *Irony and Consciousness* (1980), chapter I.

4. For example, *laissez faire* leads to inequalities; technological efforts to protect ourselves against the hazards of nature may themselves become greater threats to survival than the original hazards; capitalist technology may create new desires faster than it creates new goods and hence may not contribute to human welfare; Canadian protection of the principle of freedom of information threatens the integrity of the national culture.

5. R. Niebuhr, *The Irony of American History* (1952).

6. See P.D. McClelland, *Causal Explanations and Model Building in History, Economics, and the New Economic History* (1975), p.121; R. Lipsey and K. Lancaster, "The General Theory of Second Best," *Review of Economic Studies* 24, p.11; F.M. Bator, "The Anatomy of Market Failure," *Quarterly Journal of Economics* (1958), p.351; and A.M. Okun, *Equality and Efficiency* (1975) for elaborations of these points.

7. *Alberta Statistical Review* (1981).

8. I have chosen to develop the argument in terms of "anxiety" rather than its converse, "utility" even though the latter concept is more commonly used in economics. This is not done to be perverse, but rather for methodological reasons which have their roots in ideas I attribute to Popper, von Hayek and Johnson, although there are undoubtedly other scholars with similar views. Popper has argued that minimizing anxiety is not just a negative formulation of maximizing utility because in logical terms they are not symmetrical. Further, von Hayek, as a member of the radical-subjectivist school, distrusted all economic statements that do not refer to something that is occurring in the minds of actual human actors and if as Harry Johnson suggested, "people are driven more by the fear of failure than by the challenge of accomplishment," it follows that the reduction of anxiety is a more pervasive motivator than the pursuit of pleasure. See B. Magee, *Popper* (1978), p.85; I. Kristol, "The Crisis in Economic Theory," *Dialogue* (1981), p.63; H. Johnson, *The Canadian Quandary* (1963), p.268.

9. It is useful to note that there is a synergetic element to societal anxiety. For example, disagreement about a particular response can make a threat appear more serious whereas solidarity (even if wrong-headed) can reduce its perceived significance. Also, some decision arrangements (e.g., a paternalistic government with a clear mandate) can generate social cohesion and instill confidence and hence lower anxiety at least over the short run.

10. Topical anxieties arose in response to a variety of confidence-shaking events which undermined the existing social ethos (e.g., the immorality of American aggression, the spread of the drug culture). Attitudinal anxiety was the fear that America had lost control over the course of future events. Civilizational anxiety was the realization that material improvement did not necessarily satisfy the human spirit. See R. Heilbroner, *An Inquiry Into the Human Prospect* (1975).

11. See the various opinion polls conducted by the Canada West Foundation.

12. See R.L. Solomon and J.D. Corbit, "An opponent-process theory of motivation," *Psychological Review* 81 (1974), pp. 119-45; R.L. Solomon, "The opponent-process theory of acquired motivation: The costs of pleasure and the benefits of pain," *American Psychologist* 35 (1980), pp. 691-712; and R.E. Franken, *Human Motivation* (1982).

13. It is useful to note that addictive behavior runs counter to the behavioral axioms normally included in mainstream economic analysis where the response to weaker level of satisfaction (i.e., decreasing marginal utility) is to reduce, rather than increase consumption.

14. See D. Owram, "The Economic Development of Western Canada: An Historical Overview," *Economic Council of Canada Discussion Paper No. 219*, 1982, p.43 for details of this period.

15. Corporate and individual names like Dome, Turbo, Nu-West, Pocklington and Skalbania come to mind.

16. H.G. Cox, *Turning East* (1977), p.136.

17. The illusion of the federal government as adversary has been reinforced by continually blaming it for economic hardship when in fact many of the problems (e.g., the absence of secondary industry, the excessive burden of transportation costs, the drain of savings from the hinterland to the industrial heartland) are conditions which one would expect to find in the normal course of events in a sparsely settled, isolated region of a capitalist economy. See K. Norrie, "Some Comments on Prairie Economic Alienation," *Canadian Public Policy* (1976), p.211.

18. Statement A represents conventional wisdom in our society but the terms and conditions must be carefully specified if it is to be valid. First "free enterprise" must be distinguished from "pro business" because the two do not necessarily coincide as, for example, when an existing industry is being protected or subsidized by government. Second, Statement A implicitly assumes that one is starting in an equilibrium position and under those circumstances it is reasonable to suggest that improved efficiency will lead to economic growth. However, if one starts in disequilibrium, a different sequence of events may occur. For example, if prosperity occurs in a region because of the rush to monetize a natural resource whose value has suddenly increased, the industrial system while fully employed, may not be efficient but merely active and scrambling to share the windfall rents. If efficiency is introduced into such a state of disequilibrium the result can be a reduction in employment, the closure of marginal firms and, at least in the short run, a *reduction* in the rates of economic growth. It is probable, although not certain, that this sequence of events occurred in Alberta in the early eighties although the efficiency was forced rather than voluntary. I would like to thank a colleague, W.A. Kerr, for drawing this point to my attention.

19. In the energy industry, expansion of export income will generate royalty income and corporate cash flow, but is unlikely to lead to substantial reinvestment or incremental employment because of gas surpluses and the fact that federal policy is deflecting exploration and development activity to other regions in the nation. Agriculture might blossom because of recent structural changes in the industry and the expansion of international markets but there is no visible sign of this occurring. The possibility of developing export-oriented manufacturing industries seems remote.

    It might also be noted that if unusual growth does occur it is more likely to be the result of favorable external forces than improvements in local productive efficiency.

20. See K.H. Norrie and M.B. Percy, "Energy Price Increases, Economic Rents and Industrial Structure in a Small Regional Economy," *Economic Council of Canada Discussion Paper No. 220,* 1982, p.86.

21. In effect, this would shift the ideological orientation to what Papandreou referred to as paternalistic capitalism.

CALGARY, CALGARIANS AND THE NORTHERN MOVEMENT OF THE OIL FRONTIER, 1950-70

Max Foran

The real beginnings of Canada's oil and natural gas industry date to 1947 with the major discoveries at Leduc near Edmonton, Alberta.[1] Before that date, Canada's oil production was restricted primarily to Turner Valley southwest of Calgary, and while Turner Valley wells pumped a record 9.7 million barrels in 1942, the field was known more for its inconsistency and unfulfilled dreams than it was as a major producer.[2] Following Leduc-Woodbend, the search for oil in Alberta accelerated dramatically, and during the 1950s the discovery of several prolific fields[3] consolidated the province's position in the forefront of a new and vibrant industry. Calgary shared in this prosperity by strengthening its role as the corporate headquarters for many exploration and consulting companies. In the 1960s the oil industry began a northern expansion into the muskeg country of northern Alberta and the North-West Territories, and beyond to the tundra and icy wastes of the high Arctic. It is interesting that the initiative for this northerly focus was provided not by big business, but by a small group of Calgary-based businessmen, entrepreneurs and visionaries. The accumulated knowledge of the geology of the Arctic; the drilling of the first wells in the Arctic Islands between 1961 and 1963; the formation of Panarctic Oils Ltd. in 1968; the impetus for offshore development in the Arctic Islands, and the advances in all-terrain vehicles and portable housing units were all examples of how Calgary local initiative responded to the challenges on the frontiers of a new and expanding industry.

The first petroleum development in the Canadian North was located on the Mackenzie River at Norman about a hundred miles south of the Arctic Circle. Tests of seepages taken in 1911 revealed a similarity to Pennsylvania Crude. A subsidiary of Imperial Oil Company drilled the first well in 1920 under the direction of renowned pioneer geologist, Dr. Theodore Link.[4] Oil was struck in August 1920, and the discovery well was subsequently deepened in 1923 to reach the reef reservoir of the Upper Devonian age. Even though at least one more potentially productive well had been found, Imperial attempted no commercial production.[5] Later the company built a refinery at Norman Wells to produce gasoline and diesel fuel for local use. But output was negligible until the development of the pitchblende deposits on Great Slave Lake, and the gold mines at Yellowknife in the mid-1930s increased demand. This expansion led Imperial to build a new refinery, and by the end of the decade, two additional wells were operating. Further impetus to Norman Wells production was provided by the CANOL Project during World War II. By 1956, Norman Wells had produced a total of five million barrels, one-sixth of the estimated recoverable reserves.[6]

The Norman Wells discovery, in combination with the presence of frequent seepages throughout the North contributed led to an enduring belief in the potential productivity of Arctic petroleum reserves. This view was further reinforced in 1947 when the Leduc discovery was also found in the Upper Devonian Reef. However, Norman Wells also illustrated the related logistical problems associated with oil exploration in high latitudes. Transportation was both difficult and costly, and this, combined with the lack of markets, kept northern exploration on the remote frontiers of commercial interest as late as 1950.

By the mid-1950s it was freely admitted that northern oil exploration, while potentially viable, was a low priority with the major companies. Successful exploratory efforts in Alberta continued to siphon off both interest and capital. Sales continued to be a problem, and by 1957 a tightening of world markets led to a 10 per cent reduction in development permits in Alberta.[7] With drilling time for northern wells two and one half times slower, and transportation costs up to eleven times greater than the average,[8] there was little incentive to probe the formidable barriers of Canada's northland.

The physical barriers were formidable indeed. Muskeg was the chief problem, being virtually impossible to traverse with conventional vehicles during the summer months. One operator had to build 24 bridges and 256 culverts to get to his drill site.[9] The remaining feasible alternative of aviation was prohibitively expensive. The journal, *Oil in Canada*, commented in 1955 that the major impediment to northern operations was the impossibility of developing an all-terrain vehicle with a payload of greater than 3,000 pounds.[10] Stories of privation and travail discouraged others. Living quarters were primitive and inadequate. Other hazards received exaggerated attention. One company advised its workers to carry hammers to ward off marauding timber wolves, while another warned against the prevalent danger to workers from rabid sled dogs.[11]

On the other hand, the development by the mid-1950s of the airplane as an exploratory vehicle had broken down the barriers posed by muskeg and ice. Using new air photographic techniques, and operating from airstrips at northern weather stations, geologists were able to indicate and verify the presence of varied thick sedimentary basins of several ages with very large folds and salt domes.[12] Several Geological Survey of Canada expeditions in the 1950s both showed promising stratigraphic sections, and vindicated the viability of small field parties supported by aircraft instead of the traditional canoe and dog sled. While the problems of large-scale overland transportation thus remained mainly unsolved, geologists were beginning to realize by the late 1950s the potential enormity of the North's oil and natural gas reserves.[13]

It was against this mixed background of promise and challenge that a handful of Calgary-based individuals initiated the activities which were to have such impact in the 1960s. Their vision, innovation and persistence in the fields of exploration, transportation and housing were heavily instrumental in helping roll back the northern frontiers of Canada's oil and gas industry.

The Work of Dr. John Campbell (Cam) Sproule

In 1970, less than a year after his untimely death, John Campbell Sproule was honoured by having a peninsula in the Arctic named after him.[14] During his dedication speech, the Hon. Jean Chrétien, Northern Affairs Minister, stated in part, ''As long as there are maps of Canada Cam Sproule's name will be inscribed as a tribute to his development of Canada's North.''[15] Chrétien went on to point out Sproule's role as the first to recognize the tremendous oil and gas potential of the Arctic Islands, and indicated his twenty-year crusade to bring the oil industry to the Canadian Arctic. Chretien was not understating Sproule's contribution to northern oil development which broadly manifested itself in three main areas. First, through his geological consulting firm, J.C. Sproule and Associates, Sproule laid the basis for Arctic exploration with a series of extensive and accurate geological surveys conducted during the 1950s and through the 1960s. Secondly, Sproule's infectious enthusiasm was instrumental in interesting several of his clients in northern oil plays. Finally, he was the driving force behind the formation of Panarctic Oils in 1968 as a group of investing industries, which together with the federal government combined to explore develop, produce, transport and market the oil and gas of the Arctic Islands.

John Campbell Sproule was born in Edmonton, Alberta in 1905.[16] He received his education in Grand Prairie and Edmonton, and graduated first with a B.Sc. from the University of Alberta in 1930, and later with his Ph.D in geology from the University of Toronto in 1935. Over the next fifteen years, Sproule took part in several Canadian surveys which took him from British Columbia to Nova Scotia. He also served as a senior geologist with the International Petroleum Company and Imperial Oil, where he became operations manager for Saskatchewan. In 1951, Sproule entered the consulting business with the formation of his own company, J.C. Sproule and Associates.

Sproule initially confined his survey work to the Mackenzie River basin. Partly as a result of his surveys, a total of twenty-nine wells and forty-one test holes were drilled in the southern parts of the Mackenzie Basin between 1951 and 1956.[17] In 1957 a Sproule client and Calgary company, Western Minerals, drilled the first well within the Arctic Circle. The logistics were impressive, and involved the haulage of 2,600 tons of equipment and supplies some 500 miles from Whitehorse to the wellsite at Eagle Plains.[18] Tractor trains, each with eight tractors and up to forty sleighs needed seven round trips to do the job. Though the first well was abandoned, a second was spudded and encountered oil and gas in the summer of 1959.[19] This success lent much credence to a statement made by Sproule in 1958 that "without much doubt we are dealing with a rich oil basin."[20]

By the late 1950s, Sproule's interest had shifted to the Arctic Islands as the most promising location for oil exploration. Not only were the prospective oil horizons favorable and varied, but there were economic advantages as well. According to Sproule, the total exploration and production costs would be less than similar expenditures on the mainland in the southern part of the Western Canada Sedimentary Basin.[21] Sproule based this opinion on the absence of muskeg, light precipitation and even the distance from potential markets.

By 1959 Sproule's enthusiasm was shared by several clients, namely Dan Bateman of Domex (Dominion Explorers), Bill Patterson of Trans-Western Oil Ltd., and Bryce Cameron of Round Valley.[22] This group, together with Sproule, who acted for several other clients, and a few multi-national companies applied to the Federal Government for regulatory permits covering exploration in the Arctic Islands. Caught unaware,[23] the government with its avowed interest in rolling back the northern frontier of Canadian resource development, responded favorably by allowing applicants to designate certain areas as having priority rights for permit award. Sproule's clients were quick to take advantage of carefully selected favorable acreage. They also utilized the interim period for consolidating their favorable position through further information-gathering surveys, and in a stepped-up publicity campaign to interest shareholders and potential investors in the potential of the Arctic "elephant sized fields" awaiting discovery. Further professional interest was stimulated by the International Symposium on Arctic Geology held in Calgary in January 1960. Six months later in June, 1960 regulations were promulgated, and forty million acres of permits in the Arctic Islands were issued, primarily to Canadian companies.[24]

Stipulations in the 1960 regulations militated against the multinational companies in favor of the small Canadian independents, thus reversing the earlier trend which had seen the multi-nationals dominate exploration in the Mackenzie Basin. Long-term leases of up to twelve and fourteen years necessitated only an initial annual expenditure of 5¢ per acre, but required 50 percent Canadianization by the time a well went into production.[25] Though definitive evidence is lacking respecting Sproule's personal influence in these stipulations, there can be little doubt that they were congruent with his thinking at the time. An ardent Canadian nationalist, Sproule entertained strong fears over the future of Canadian sovereignty over the Arctic Islands pending a major find by a foreign oil company.[26]

Between 1960 and 1963, Sproule easily spent his clients' required expenditures in several extensive field surveys.[27] In 1960, Sproule's large field parties worked in the central Queen Elizabeth Islands. A year later, Sproule consolidated this work with wide-ranging regional photo-mapping using up to seventeen aircraft. In 1962, Sproule parties mapped a number of oil sand deposits in northwestern Melville Island, as well as doing gravity work on Sabine Peninsula, King Christian and Lougheed Islands. This survey work conducted by Sproule in the late 1950s and early 1960s laid the basis for later systematic drilling, certainly so by Panarctic Oils Ltd. whose initial discoveries were in Sproule structures.[28]

Despite Sproule's unswerving optimism and extensive field work, commercial interest in the Arctic Islands was beginning to wane by the mid-1960s. Very simply put, the small Canadian companies were unable to marshall the funds necessary to pursue the more expensive phases of exploration. The larger companies, already deterred by the 1960 regulations, were by 1965 much more interested in developing oil plays at Rainbow Lake, Alberta, in the North Sea and offshore California. It was at this juncture that Sproule renewed his interest in the possibility of a consortium which was to find ultimate expression in the formation of Panarctic Oils in 1968. The idea was not new to Sproule. In 1962, when he was concentrating on the rich oil sands on Melville Island, he had put together a group of all leaseholders along the oil sands outcrops to undertake a substantial exploratory effort. A contemporary oilman termed it "a new industry practice"[29] and offered this description:

> One thing became clear to Sproule that it was uneconomic to work on isolated pieces of acreage purely according to the exigencies of client contracts. He therefore began to systematically explore the land between at his own expense. This led to negotiations with the Department of Indian and Northern Affairs and an arrangement whereby these overexpenditures would be accepted to earn acreage in as much that landholders could satisfy permit obligations by buying off-the-shelf information. Previously to have any work done for credit, permits had first to be obtained and then consultants assigned to a given programme.[30]

Under these arrangements, Sproule was able to take the initiative in securing the most promising acreage for chosen clients. Thus in 1964, amidst the lull in interest in the Arctic, it was not surprising to find the consortium idea again emerging in Sproule's thinking. The actual impetus was reportedly born in a casual conversation between Sproule and a colleague and client, Eric Connelly, of Pembina Pipelines. Connelly, a close friend of Dean Nesbitt of the brokerage house of Nesbitt Thompson, originally believed that he might be able to interest Nesbitt in putting together a $30 million package on the Canadian money market.[31]

Panarctic Oils Ltd. had a turbulent three-year embryonic period before its eventual birth in 1968[32] as a unique Canadian experiment involving government and private enterprise. The tribulations included complicated and volatile land negotiations, and the mammoth task of raising capital in an inhospitable Canadian money market. Sproule, however, persevered, doggedly following his scheme through frustration and disillusion. His own business suffered as he committed time, energy and a million dollars of his own money into what had become his personal dream. Dr. Gordon Jones, who was Sproule's chief agent in negotiating the complex land agreements, estimated that he devoted 95 percent of his professional time over three years to the Panarctic project.[33] Eventually the consortium necessitated twenty-three separate legal agreements with seventy-five different companies. Sproule's salesmanship was put to the ultimate test as he tried to raise the $15 million necessary to guarantee government involvement and the cooperation of Nesbitt Thompson. The majors viewed the whole project with jaundiced eyes, maintaining in those pre-Prudhoe days that feasible Arctic exploration was still a decade away. Canadian capital appeared uninterested, a fact which had long angered the volatile Sproule who once noted that, ''It is apparent and has been for some time that Canadian investors on the whole do not have either the vision or the intestinal fortitude to invest in their own country to the extent that they should or could.''[34] Twice he had $13.5 million committed only to see part of it slip away. He estimated that he lost $7 million of committed money alone to Rainbow Lake and North Sea plays, and once likened his task to that of trying to gather up an armful of wriggling snakes. Indeed, the project was enabled only by a reduction in scale from the original $30 million to $20 million, of which the federal government invested $9 million for a 45 percent equity.

There can be little doubt that government intervention saved the Panarctic project. While the precise reasons for this federal involvement in the oil industry can only be conjectured, at least one prominent oil authority sees a congruency between Sproule and the federal government over the sovereignty issue. Since 1965, when speaking about the activities of the French-controlled Petropar in the Canadian Arctic, Sproule warned, ''When French government controlled Petropar does find and produce oil and find a market for it, let me not hear any bleatings from Canadian politicos or others about foreign control.''[35] According to Carl Nickle, founder of the *Daily Oil Bulletin* and *Canadian Oil Register*, and a partner in the Panarctic project, the federal government was galvanized into action not by investor hesitancy, but by Charles de Gaulle's memorable utterance to Quebec in 1967.[36] Nickle asserts that with Petropar dominant in the Arctic the government viewed the remark as an implied threat to Canadian sovereignty, and hence its receptivity to the Panarctic project.

Panarctic Oils began to mobilize operations in the spring of 1968 with acreage holding of 47.6 million acres. Calgary's Dome Petroleum, a major participant, took over as interim operator pending the assemblage of a permanent staff. Drilling operations began in 1969 with success forthcoming quickly in the form of the Drake Point gasfield. Over the next three years more gas fields were located on East King Christian Island, at Kristoffer Bay on Ellef Ringnes, at Thor Island and in Hecla west of Drake Point. By the end of 1972, Panarctic Oils had drilled twenty-six wells in the Arctic Islands. Its impressive discovery ratio of one in five totalling gas reserves in excess of eight trillion cubic feet[37] affirmed in practical fashion the value of the geological data base it had inherited from the Sproule organization.

In terms of his own personal ambitions it is unfortunate that Cam Sproule did not figure more prominently in the operation and direction of the project he had worked so hard to bring to fruition. Though his company was retained as consultants for Panarctic, Sproule himself was passed over in the choice of top-echelon management positions. It is possible that Cominco Ltd. and Canadian Pacific Oil and Gas Ltd., the two major participants with a leading role in the organization of Panarctic, considered Sproule inappropriate. His boundless zeal and penchant for volatile spontaneity sometimes worried those of more reasonable and systematic corporate temper. For instance, his plans for immediate drilling following the organization of Panarctic were considered premature and even ill-advised. Fellow geologists sometimes winced at his sweeping generalizations and lack of preciseness, particularly with respect to geological extrapolations. In that sense, he might not have been considered the ideal of an infant company so politically sensitive as Panarctic. John Campbell Sproule was, however, a visionary with a dream that transcended the boundaries of his time. It was this vision and crusading zeal buttressed by thoroughgoing field work which has made Sproule easily the most important figure in the Canadian search for oil in the high Arctic.

The First Wells Drilled in the Arctic Islands 1961-63

Between 1961 and 1963 three test wells were drilled in the Arctic Islands, the first on Melville Island in 1961-62, the second just west of Resolute on Cornwallis Island, and the third on East Central Bathurst Island. Though all three were abandoned, they proved beyond doubt the feasibility of drilling in the high Arctic, not incidentally resumed until 1969.[38] The impetus for these frontier Arctic wildcats did not come from the large multi-nationals but from smaller Canadian-based enterprises, the most active of which were located in Calgary.

The historic first well in the Arctic Islands was drilled at Winter Harbour on Melville Island in the winter of 1961/62. While the project involved a consortium of some twenty mining and oil companies,[39] there were only two main participants. The operation was put together by Dome Petroleum Ltd., and the drilling component was planned and executed by Peter Bawden Drilling Company. Both were located in Calgary.

The individual impetus behind the Winter Harbour experiment was provided by J.P. (Jack) Gallagher of Dome Petroleum. There were many similarities between Gallagher and Sproule. Both were western Canadians, Gallagher being born in Winnipeg in 1916. Like Sproule, Gallagher was a geologist whose early employment experience included service with the Canadian Geological Survey, and with a major oil company (Shell and Standard). The parallel continued with Gallagher's formation of his own company (Dome) in 1951.[40] Though very different in temperament, the two men also shared common characteristics. They were both superb salesmen and Canadian nationalists. And most significantly, both were convinced of the vast oil potential of Canada's north.

When building Dome Petroleum in the 1950s, Gallagher concentrated on relatively safe step-out projects close to known oil fields with an occasional fling at a real wildcat.[41] His first speculative effort here was the unsuccessful Buckinghorse well in British Columbia. Given this strategy, and his own interest in the north, it was not surprising that Gallagher should look to the Arctic Islands for his second rank wildcat.

Gallagher's approach to the Winter Harbour project necessitated shared costs and government concessions. The latter were obtained through a relaxation in the 1960 regulations respecting Canadianization requirements. Participation in the Winter Harbour project was permitted even if Canadianization stipulations had not been met.[42] Furthermore, double credits were promised on the well regardless of final depth.[43] With these concessions secured, Gallagher was able to finance Winter Harbour[44] through farmouts to participating companies with Dome retaining a percentage net earned interest in the well and farmout acreage, in addition to direct involvement in the drilling costs. In all, some twenty mining and oil companies took part in the world's most northerly wildcat.[45] Yet is was throughout very much Jack Gallagher's personal experiment.

While Dome maintained a geologist and drilling supervisor at the site, the actual operations were carried out by Peter Bawden Drilling Company. Peter Bawden[46] was an Ontario farm-boy whose first job in the West was with a lumber company in the Peace River country. Here, he caught the excitement of the northern oil business and soon formed his own drilling company. He spudded his first well in 1952, and within seven years had become one of the major drilling operators in Canada. Like Sproule and Gallagher, Bawden was fascinated by the challenge of northern oil plays, and actually pioneered in the training and employment of Inuit as members of drilling crews.

Within ninety-six days of signing his contract with Dome, Bawden had moved 3,000 tons of supplies and equipment, and thirty-five men to Melville Island, and had begun drilling operations.[47] The equipment which included a 12,000 foot drilling rig (Rig 22), a million pounds of drilling mud, two ten-ton motorized landing craft, three tracked vehicles, two trucks and two camp buildings left Montreal on the Danish Polar ship "Thora Dan" and arrived at Winter Harbour on 20 August 1961. It took about two weeks to move the cargo to the wellsite. On 10 September, Winter Harbour No. I was spudded. By 31 October, the well was down 7,000 feet. On 1 December, it was decided to drill to 14,000 feet instead of the original target depth of 10,000 feet. On 7 April 1962, after 208 days and only minor gas shows, the well was abandoned at a depth of 12,543 feet. The total cost of the operation was $1 million.

Over the next two years, two more wells were drilled by small consortia involving twenty-three companies at a combined cost of $2 million. The second well at Resolute Bay was drilled by a group headed by Calgary based Round Valley (Lobitos Oilfields Canada Limited), itself a pioneer with Sproule in Arctic field work. The third well on Bathurst Island was spearheaded by another Sproule client, Domex (Dominion Explorers), and included six Calgary-based oil companies.[48] Both wells were unsuccessful, Resolute Bay being abandoned at

4,841 feet while operations on Bathurst Island were discontinued at a depth of over 10,000 feet.[49]

The experimental test holes in the Arctic Islands between 1961 and 1963 proved beyond doubt the feasibility of year-round drilling in very high latitudes. In this crucial test of men and equipment, the three wildcats helped break down the enduring myth of total Arctic inhospitability. The well-publicized operations[50] were unsuccessful in their specific aims but definitely gave impetus to further probing the promising Mesozoic Tertiary and Upper Paleozoic beds that lay just tantalizingly north in the Sverdrup Basin.[51] Certainly the Winter Harbour experiment was a appetite-whetter for Jack Gallagher who went on to become a leading and active participant in Arctic exploration.[52] In one sense Gallagher complemented Sproule, taking over practically where the visionary had left off.

Gordon Jones and the Arctic Offshore

Beginning in the 1970s, the oil industry in the North began moving offshore, encouraged by a series of extensive offshore seismic explorations between 1969 and 1973 which indicated that the best Arctic prospects were located offshore.[53] A leading figure in paving the way for this new focus has been local geologist, Dr. Gordon H. Jones. Through his work with J.C Sproule and Associates, Global Marine and Global Marine Arctic Limited, Petro-Canada, and latterly with his own consulting company, Jones has done much to anticipate and further offshore development in the Arctic.

Gordon Jones was born in Northampton, England in 1927.[54] He received his B.Sc. (Hons.) in Geology in 1948 from the University of Birmingham, and his Ph.D. from the same institution seven years later. Between 1951 and 1958 he was geological advisor to the government in Uruguay, where he gained extensive experience in many facets of engineering geology.[55] During subsequent service with Hunting Technical and Exploration Services Ltd., Jones spent time in Argentina in geological engineering work before coming to Calgary via Toronto in early 1959. Here he began his involvement in Arctic geology, and in the next year joined J.C. Sproule and Associates as chief photogeologist.

Jones soon became an integral component in the Sproule organization. He headed the surface geological department, and became increasingly involved in the logistics of northern exploration and environmental studies. Jones was also in charge of Sproule's exploration program in the Arctic Islands, and as such he advised clients in the selection of acreages as well as directing frontier exploration programs. Mention has already been made of Jones's important role in the formation of Panarctic, and indeed it was during the latter part of these negotiations that Jones's nascent interest in offshore development began to take practical shape.

Jones first approached Sproule with his idea of offshore development, and the possibility of adding promising offshore acreage to the package of Panarctic holdings.[56] His latter suggestion was considered inappropriate in the light of the high-risk challenges already facing the embryonic consortium. Sproule, too, was skeptical saying that offshore development would never materialize in his lifetime.[57] Jones persisted, however, and took his idea to Global Marine,[58] a Sproule client and a respectable marine exploration company. Global Marine had already achieved a first of sorts when it drilled Canada's first offshore well in the Grand Banks in 1966, and at the time was interested in further good-risk experimentation. Global thus responded favorably to Jones's suggestion that it drill an Arctic offshore well with Sproule supplying the necessary geological and technological guidance.

In the first half of 1967, the offshore program began to take shape. In March, concessions were secured from the federal government covering offshore development. Engineering costs and environmental studies were allowed against work commitments.[59] In May, Global Marine, operating through Canadian Trust for reasons of secrecy, selected ten million acres and filed on 2.2 million carefully chosen acres including the Whitefish, East Drake and Roche Point structures.[60] Then in July, the liberal government enthusiastically announced the program. Once it was known that Global Marine was heavily involved, other companies followed suit, and the Arctic offshore land rush was on. Within months, the entire Arctic offshore was held under permit by companies that hoped to share in the visions of wealth conjured up by Prudhoe Bay, and by the beckoning promise of prolific oil under ice and water.

Jones left Sproule in 1968 to become Canadian manager for Global Marine. He remained with the company for eight years, becoming president of Global Marine Arctic in 1974. During these years Jones wrestled with the formidable engineering and logistics problems posed by the Arctic offshore environment. Factors like ice movement and varying water depths, together with the environmental parameters supplied by season and distance called for new drilling systems. In 1971, Jones helped design a prototype for an air-cushion drilling system.[61] Though it awaits conversion to practical use, the air-cushion drilling barge remains, in Jones's eyes, the most feasible response to the problems of drilling in the landfall ice characteristic of the Arctic Islands offshore.

The career of Gordon Jones provides another voice in the dialogue of Arctic frontier development first articulated by Sproule and carried on by Gallagher. Jones followed Sproule into the Arctic. Yet in a way his vision of offshore wealth transcended that of the older and senior Sproule. Like Gallagher, Jones has turned his attention to solving the practical problems associated with finding oil under Arctic waters. But, unlike Gallagher who has concentrated his energies mainly in the boardrooms of corporate decision making, Jones has remained very much on the everchanging horizons of technological innovation. Between 1976 and 1979, Gordon Jones was with Petro-Canada where he continued his active involvement in the management of offshore drilling, exploration, research and environmental programs. Since then he has continued this work through his own company appropriately named Gordon Jones Frontier Advisers. Through his many publications[62] and extensive consulting practice, he is able to use his considerable experience to advise others interested in his dream of Arctic wealth, and as such sums up his qualifications modestly and succinctly, "I've done a lot of work in frontier exploration and drilling."[63] Jones continues to live and operate out of Calgary.

The Nodwells and All-Terrain Vehicles

The successful advance of the oil industry into the Canadian north was accompanied by major developments in the field of overland transportation. Traditionally, oilmen have been no strangers to the problems of moving heavy machinery in off-road conditions. In the Turner Valley area, for example, one of the chief difficulties faced by exploration crews in the early period was that of getting their rigs to the drill site.[64] However, the added dimension occasioned by muskeg and extremely cold temperatures presented the oil industry with a new transportation challenge. Once again, the most successful individual response came from a western Canadian independent operator. One could argue that Calgary's Bruce Nodwell was the most important single individual in the development of all-terrain vehicles capable of moving heavy loads through the hitherto impassable muskeg country of Canada's north. Similarly, Canadian Foremost Ltd.[65] directed by his son, Jack, is today a world-wide leader in the design and manufacture of all-terrain vehicles. The Nodwells and Canadian Foremost are excellent examples of how local initiative met and adapted to the specialized demands of an industry that was probing new frontiers.

Bruce Nodwell was born in Asquith, Saskatchewan in 1916. He had an early exposure to automobiles and engines through his father's Dodge dealership in North Battleford, and remembers a memorable three-day journey from Carmangay to Asquith in a 1917 Dodge. Like many boys of the time, he became a jack-of-all-trades[66] after leaving school, and at one time was the youngest licensed electrician in Saskatchewan. His involvement with the oil industry occurred during the Depression years. He wired service stations for Texaco, and as a small contractor who could "fix anything," he secured many odd jobs with the same company.[67] He worked at the B.A. refinery in Calgary, before joining Texaco full-time, where by 1940 he had achieved a senior position in construction and maintenance. Tired of the corporate life, the everrestless Nodwell left Texaco to enter business for himself. In 1943 he set up a contracting business with his brother, and three years later began making moveable camp units for Imperial Oil.[68] Then in 1952 Imperial asked Nodwell if he would build a tracked vehicle to its specifications. Interested in the sideline venture to his profitable camp business, Nodwell agreed and subsequently built two prototype vehicles.[69] Both were failures.

Typically, Nodwell was convinced he could do better, and in 1952 formed Bruce Nodwell Ltd. with the idea of developing a tracked vehicle that would work well in muskeg country. Success came in 1956, when he built a vehicle for Imperial Oil capable of moving a five-ton seismic rig through muskeg. Later he developed a ten-ton unit for Shell Oil. A Nodwell vehicle performed capably at Winter Harbour in 1961/62, and by the 1960s his name was synonymous with northern oil operations. For instance, the Nodwell 110 was considered the ideal vehicle in deep snow and extremely cold temperatures.

There were several reasons for Nodwell's success. First, the market was too small and specialized to attract the big American firms like Caterpillar and John Deere. Second, Nodwell was strategically located in Calgary, both in terms of his contacts with the oil industry, as well as in possessing an on-the-spot awareness of the problems involved. Thirdly, he was by nature and experience an innovator who could adapt or modify existing technology to meet emergent demands. By developing his own splicing technique, he was able to control track length and width, and thus overcome one of the chief obstacles to building more powerful vehicles. A further innovation was his crowned track system with its double sprocket drive and single set of wheels. Organizationally, Nodwell also offset his lack of capital by subcontracting much of the work mainly to local enterprises. Indeed, some like Standen's Springs and O.K. Tires designed and produced components based on Nodwell's specific needs.[70] Finally, one could indicate Nodwell's impeccable reputation for integrity and honesty which enabled him to enjoy the trust and confidence of clients and suppliers, big and small.

During these early years, Nodwell experienced the difficulties associated with designing and developing a largely untested and specialized product. While it is true that he enjoyed the patronage of several large clients[71] who placed multiple orders often with custom requirements, Nodwell was also heavily dependent on local financial support. This investment capital was both limited and unstable. The $3 million realized through the sale of Nodwell units between 1957 and 1965 should be measured against the reluctant corporate merger Nodwell was obliged to accept for survival's sake.[72] Similarly, when he formed Canadian Foremost[73] with his son Jack in 1965, Nodwell was faced with the familiar problem of finding investors prepared to back his plans for meeting the specialized transportation needs of the northern oil industry. He found them not in the money markets of eastern Canada or the United States, but among personal acquaintances in Alberta.[74]

The impetus behind the steady growth of Canadian Foremost to a position of international prominence in the production of all-terrain vehicles was provided by northern oil plays.[75] Initially the company proposed to specialize in low ground-pressure tracked vehicles to various branches of the oil industry. Some examples were the recorder units and vibro-carriers,[76] with the biggest moneymaker being the formidable Husky 8. This giant can move up to forty-five tons of heavy equipment including drilling rig, camp, logging instruments, mud, cement, well casing, men and supplies from airstrip to the wellsite[77] through terrain that would have defied almost any vehicle twenty years earlier.

Today, Canadian Foremost's seven tracked-vehicle models can be readily equipped with auxiliary equipment, be it cranes or mobile workshops. Similarly, the different conditions posed by the Arctic Islands environment led Canadian Foremost to turn to the manufacture of rubber-wheeled vehicles in the early 1970s.[78] All-wheel drive, articulated steering and specially designed low-pressure tires have enabled Foremost vehicles to move up to seventy tons over rough terrain.

Canadian Foremost's success illustrated the ability of a local enterprise to survive and even prosper in a difficult marketplace. The company's four-pronged strategy is based on the paradoxical realization that its most singular advantage lies in the very exclusiveness of its product. Under president Jack Nodwell,[79] Foremost concentrates on high quality, durable heavy equipment supplemented by a commitment to ongoing research. Secondly, Nodwell's individualistic marketing policy emphasizes custom-built products designed to individual specifications.[80] Examples might include the "Sure-Go" units used for seismic work in the Arctic, or the design of vehicles that fit snugly into the hold of a Hercules aircraft.[81] Thirdly, the company has not allowed itself to become capital-intensive. Over 300 subcontractors, most of them Alberta-based, do most of the actual manufacturing for Foremost units. Finally, Canadian Foremost has not relied exclusively on the demand created by volatile northern oil plays. Instead it has sought international markets. Beginning in 1968 with a $12 million sale of thirty-two tracked vehicles to the Russians,[82] the company has looked beyond Canada for orders. In its best year (1981), over 85 percent of Canadian Foremost's sales of $28 million were outside Canada.[83]

The emergence of Calgary's Canadian Foremost Ltd. as a world leader in the design and manufacture of all-terrain vehicles has vindicated the value of the pioneering work by Bruce and Jack Nodwell. Their success is singular in the light of the failures experienced by at least fifteen would-be competitors. The company's current international focus in a way belies its close involvement with oil exploration in the Canadian north. Nevertheless, the prevalence of Nodwell vehicles at oil camps in muskeg country, or in remote areas of the frozen Arctic provides clear evidence of the Nodwells' role in facilitating the northern advance of the oil industry. In 1983 Jack Nodwell was operating president of Canadian Foremost.[84] His father Bruce, though retired, retains an active interest in the company.

The Southerns and ATCO Ltd.

The northern expansion of Canada's resource development in the post-1945 era precipitated the need for modular dwelling units that were both efficient and durable. The subsequent rise of ATCO Ltd. as a world-wide leader in portable housing proved the ability of local enterprises to respond meaningfully to new challenges. In the efforts of Don and Ron Southern, Calgary has witnessed a corporate success story probably unparalleled since the days of cattle king, Pat Burns.

In 1946, Don Southern, a Calgary fireman seeking some extra cash to put his son Ron through medical school, was struck with the idea of renting luggage trailers. The Southerns subsequently pooled their savings amounting to $4,000 to begin their rental business, Alberta Trailer Hire. Don had $2,000 in war service credits while Ron contributed his savings from his summer job as bus boy and room service waiter at the Banff Springs Hotel.[85] Between 1947 and 1951, the Southerns[86] operated their rental business from their Calgary site. Business was good enough to allow for a branch lot in Edmonton, and to enable Don to quit his job with the Calgary Fire Department to devote his full attention to the company, known by this time as the Alberta Trailer Company.

In 1952, the Southerns made the crucial transformation from rental to manufacturing with the impetus being supplied by the demands engendered by northern oil activity. In late 1951, Shell Oil Company approached the Southerns with a proposal to build a kitchen unit and bunkhouse for the Slave River.[87] With the construction of these two warm, strong and durable units, a whole new industry was born.

The period 1952-59 was one of rapid growth and consolidation for ATCO. Demand for its units escalated primarily from oil-related enterprises, and by 1959 ATCO was producing about 2,000 units annually from its factory in a converted aircraft hangar at Airdrie.[88] Unlike the Nodwells who were able to subcontract most of their work, the Southerns were forced into a total manufacturing system.[89] The uniqueness of their product necessitated the development of indigenous production-line techniques, and the establishment of support industries.

In the 1960s, the emergence of international markets and the securing of large contracts from other business sectors somewhat reduced ATCO's dependence on northern oil plays. Yet it was the Trans-Alaska Pipeline project in the 1970s which showed ATCO's enormous capacity and scope. Over a nine-month period, ATCO provided housing and back-up facilities for 16,000 workers.[90] ATCO's spectacular growth continued following its conversion to a public company in 1967. Annual sales topped $42 million in 1968. Eleven years later revenues exceeded $368 million. Today ATCO is a diversified worldwide company with annual revenues around one billion dollars and a payroll of some 8,000. Ron Southern remains as president and chief executive officer; his father, Don, is chairman of the board of ATCO Ltd.

It is difficult to explain the precise reasons for ATCO's success particularly in the light of the several obstacles which confronted the Southerns in the early years. Neither had had any experience in building or housing design. Moreover, money was scarce. The illiberal lending policies of local banking institutions led the Southerns into desperate measures to keep their enterprise afloat. One private creditor charged 20 percent interest; another guaranteed loans for half the profits.[91] Finally there was the looming threat of competition provided by established corporations like Alcan, U.S. Steel, Lockheed and U.S. Homes.[92]

According to Ron Southern a singular factor explaining his company's early success was its location relative to a steady market in isolated areas.[93] Like Bruce Nodwell, he believes that Calgary's proximity to the remote areas it served gave him a distance advantage and a head start. The latter advantage was reinforced by the fact that ATCO was engaged in a unique industry of its own creation, and therefore set the standard for competence far more than for emulation.[94] Southern maintains that ATCO's clearly enunciated and long-standing policy of efficiency of both product and service enabled it to maintain its initial dominance over potential competition.[95] Southern credits the caliber of key personnel as a vital ingredient in his company's success. He refers to a closely-knit managerial component which invested heavily in time and money to furthering ATCO's growth.[96] He is also loud in his praise for several large oil companies who helped ATCO not only through their patronage, but also in their willingness to share their managerial expertise.[97] Finally, Southern identifies adaptability as being crucial to ATCO's success. Whether it was in marketing techniques or control, or in financing, ATCO was continually able to make those "tremendous shifts" necessary for growth.[98]

Ron Southern proudly refers to ATCO Ltd. as the Model T of manufacturing in western Canada with a history that would make an ideal case study for the Harvard Business School.[99] Though it has lost some of its close interdependence with northern oil exploration, ATCO was very much a product of the northern movement of Canada's oil frontier. To founder Ron Southern, it provided "the fundamental reason for the creation of our company."[100]

* * *

The foregoing discussion has emphasized the role of several Calgary-based individuals and enterprises in facilitating the movement of the oil and gas industry into the Canadian north. While Calgary's relationship with oil exploration dated to 1914, the city functioned mainly as an operational base for companies seeking oil in Alberta. Certainly it provided little resident impetus for opening up new areas, or in innovative developments. The northerly movement of the oil industry changed Calgary's role. The city became the focus for new directions in exploration and technology, and as a consequence assumed a more viable position in the forefront of Canada's national oil and natural gas industry.

Footnotes

1. The Leduc discovery was made by Imperial Oil and ended a lengthy but unsuccessful exploration program to discover oil in Alberta. The Leduc discovery well had been preceded by 133 dry holes.

2. Oil was first discovered at Turner Valley in 1914. A major gas well was brought in in 1924, and in 1936 crude oil was discovered by Turner Valley Royalties, a company headed by Robert A. Brown, Sr. father of Robert Brown who in the 1950s and 1960s propelled Home Oil into the forefront of Canadian petroleum activity. Turner Valley hit its peak as a producing field during World War II, but by the time of the Leduc discovery was already a declining field.

3. These included Redwater (1948), Wizard Lake (1951), Acheson, Bonnie Glen and Westerose (1952), Pembina (1953) and Swan Hills (1957).

4. For an excellent discussion on Dr. Link and Norman Wells see *Dusters and Gushers: The Canadian Oil and Gas Industry*, edited by James D. Hilborn (Toronto: Pitt Publishing Company, 1968), pp.227-41.

5. K.J. Rea, *The Political Economy of Northern Development*, Science Council of Canada Background Study No.36, April 1976, p.52.

6. *Oil in Canada*, February 6, 1956.

7. *Oil in Canada*, November 4, 1957.

8. *Oil in Canada*, June 20, 1955.

9. *Ibid.*

10. *Ibid.*

11. *Ibid.* The details for this and the three preceding footnotes were contained in a speech given by William Booth, Commonwealth Drilling Company Ltd. and A.S. Murray, Imperial Oil, to the spring meeting of the American Petroleum Institute, April 7, 1955.

12. Gordon H. Jones, "Economic Development Oil and Gas" paper presented at Symposium, "A Century of Canada's Arctic Islands 1880-1980," Yellowknife: 1980, p.222.

13. In 1959, E.J. Baltrusaitis, Exploration Manager for Dome Petroleum estimated a recoverable 100 billion barrels as "not being overly optimistic." Reported in *Oilweek*, June 19, 1961.

14. The peninsula is situated on Melville Island where Sproule encountered the oil-saturated sands which stimulated his interest in the Arctic. *Calgary Herald*, June 24, 1971.

15. *Ibid.*

16. For biographical information on Sproule see *Herald*, May 22, 1970.

17. *Oil in Canada*, February 6, 1956.

18. *Oilweek*, May 14, 1960.

19. *Ibid.*

20. *Oil in Canada*, January 20, 1958.

21. This and other excerpts from favorable geological reports were contained in a promotional bulletin issued by Trans-Western Oils Limited in May, 1961.

22. Jones, *op.cit.*, p.222.

23. According to Jones who was employed by Sproule at the time, the Conservative Canadian government was quite surprised at the application and had formulated no strategy for dispensing permits in the Arctic Islands. Its favorable response was probably associated with John Diefenbaker's "Roads to Resources" electoral slogan.

24. For description of these regulations see *Petroleum Press Services*, May 1960, pp.187-8.

25. *Ibid.*

26. *Oilweek*, July 5, 1965.

27. Jones, *op.cit.*, p.223.

28. Interview with Dr. Gordon H. Jones, former Sproule associate and leading figure in the formation of Panarctic, January 17, 1983. (Hereafter cited as Jones Interview).

29. R.G.S. Currie, "Successful Exploration in the High Arctic." Paper presented to the Fifth International Congress, "Arctic Oil and Gas: Problems and Possibilities," LeHavre: May 1973.

30. *Ibid.*

31. Jones Interview, *op.cit.*

32. For good account of formation of Panarctic see Currie, *op.cit.*, and Charles R. Hetherington, "A Story of Arctic Exploration," text of an article reprinted from the *U.B.C. Business Review*, 1971.

33. Jones Interview, *op.cit.*

34. *Oilweek.*

35. *Ibid.*

36. Interview with Carl O. Nickle, December 10, 1976. (Hereafter cited as Nickle Interview).

37. Currie, *op.cit.*, pp.10-12.

38. Panarctic Oils drilled the first two wells in 1969, one of which discovered the Drake Point Gasfield.

39. The companies included Bankeno Mines Ltd., California Standard Co., Canadian Southern Petroleum Ltd., Clark Oil and Refining Corp., the Dome Group, the Dominion Explorers Group which included Canpet Exploration Ltd., Mill City Petroleums Ltd., and Sarcee Petroleums Ltd., Round Valley Oil Co. Ltd., The Tidewater Group which included Skelly Oil Co. and Tidewater Oil Co. Other companies included Union Oil Company of Canada Ltd., and the Western Minerals Group.

40. Not strictly accurate. Gallagher agreed to manage some American money. Dome Exploration (Western) Ltd. was formed as a private company in 1950, but went public a year later. At this point Gallagher became full-time president. Canadian majority ownership of Dome did not occur until much later.

41. Peter Foster, *The Blue-Eyed Sheiks: The Canadian Oil Establishment* (Toronto: Collins Publishers, 1979), p.172.

42. *The Oil and Gas Journal*, July 3, 1961.

43. Dome Petroleum Files. Letter from Walter Dinsdale, Minister for Northern Affairs and National Resources, August 23, 1961.

44. The actual choice of Winter Harbour as a wellsite was based on both geological and practical considerations. It was believed that the area around Winter Harbour contained the crest of an apparent elongated anticlinal closure. The primary objective was the Allen Bay reef of Silurian/Ordovician age. Moreover, Winter Harbour itself was known to be ice-free in most years for a period of time long enough to carry out the project.

45. A British Admiralty expedition under the command of William Parry wintered at Melville Harbour in 1819/20. Parry's diaries reported oil showings while further information given in these diaries was used to choose the anchorage location in 1961, for the "Thora Dan" supply ship.

46. Bawden went on to drill the world's most northerly well at Spitsbergen in 1965. He later became M.P. for Calgary South in the House of Commons.

47. For an excellent account of the Winter Harbour project see "The Story Behind the World's most Northerly Drilling Project 1961-62." Special Report by the Staff of Dome Petroleum Ltd., *World Petroleum*, March 1963, pp.44-53.

48. These were: Canpet Exploration Ltd., Triad Oil, Mill City Petroleums Ltd., Sarcee Petroleums Ltd., Share Oils Ltd., United Canso Oil and Gas Ltd.

49. For information of these wells see *Calgary Albertan*, Feb.1, March 6, 1962. *Petroleum Press Services*, February, 1964. Operators had to give up their plans for a second well at Resolute, 409 miles from the first. Similarly a third drilling location on Banks Island failed to materialize because of lack of backing.

50. For examples see *Calgary Albertan*, March 1, 1962; *Financial Post*, November 18, 1961; *Oilweek*, December 11, 1961.

51. Indeed, Panarctic's first major gas discoveries in the 1970s proved to be in the Sverdrup Basin.

52. Reference here of course is made to the much publicized activities in the Beaufort Sea which began in 1976.

53. The ultimate goal was expected to be prolific Paleozoic oil to supplement the large existing discoveries of Mesozoic gas.

54. For biographical information on Jones see "Petroleum Profile," *Petroleum Engineer*, February, 1976.

55. For example damsites, water supply problems and route locations.

56. Jones, *op.cit.*, p.224.

57. Jones Interview.

58. *Ibid.*

59. *Ibid.*

60. Jones, *op.cit.*, p.224.

61. For details here see Dr. Gordon H. Jones, "Arctic Operations Expand with New Technology," *Petroleum Engineer*, February 1977, pp.18-21. Also "Arctic Poses Extreme Technical Challenges," *Petroleum Engineer*, January 1975, pp.22-6.

62. For list up to 1978 see *Who's Who in Oil and Gas*, 1977-78. To the end of 1978, Jones had four publications on the Arctic as well as several private consulting reports and multi-author publications.

63. Quoted in *Alberta Business*, July 13, 1979.

64. Some excellent accounts of the difficulties in transporting oil equipment in Turner Valley in the 1920s were narrated by Bill Renard in an interview with the author, January 1983. Renard used to drive the horse drawn wagons hauling heavy equipment to wellsites in Turner Valley.

65. Canadian Foremost was singled out by Richard Baine in his study of Calgary as an example of a local enterprise that achieved success on an international scale. See Richard Baine, *Calgary An Urban Study* (Toronto: Clarke Irwin and Company, 1973), p.61.

66. Nodwell admits to having scores of jobs including hauling grains at 10¢ an hour, setting up bowling pins and driving a car for the C.P.R. It was in this latter job that Nodwell first encountered the difficulties of driving through muskeg.

67. He relates one risky experience when he fixed a gasoline tank at a service station in Claresholm with a hammer and chisel, all for $5.00.

68. Nodwell was able to build two units a day and by the early 1950s had built up a strong business.

69. The main difficulty with these machines lay in the inadequacy of their power trains. They were unable to travel more than a short distance without becoming inoperative.

70. Interview with Mr. Bruce Nodwell, December 24, 1983. (Hereafter cited as Bruce Nodwell Interview).

71. For example Texaco, Imperial and Shell. Nodwell also beat out Bombardier in securing a big contract with Chevron in the late 1950s.

72. The merger in question was with Robinson Supply Co. The new company was Robin Nodwell which subsequently amalgamated with another operation, Flextrack to form Flextrack Nodwell. This meant that Nodwell through Canadian Foremost was, for a time, actually competing against his own name. In 1976, however, Flextrack Nodwell was bought out by Canadian Foremost. At the time of purchase Flextrack Nodwell had become Canadian Flextrack Ltd. Bruce Nodwell Interview.

73. Canadian Foremost was actually formed in 1964 as a land-breaking company, in which Nodwell units were adapted to break stump land. The decision to abandon the land-breaking business and go into manufacturing vehicles was made in 1965. Bruce Nodwell Interview.

74. These include Percy Smith, Elmer McDougall, Lawrence Harrington, Bruce McLean, John McMillan and a Peace River caterpillar contractor named Vern Easterbrook. Bruce Nodwell Interview.

75. Jack Nodwell estimated that the earlier Nodwell companies and Canadian Foremost have placed about 1500 vehicles in Canada since its inception. The northern market absorbs about thirty vehicles per year. Interview with Jack Nodwell, January 17, 1983. (Hereafter cited as Jack Nodwell Interview).

76. Foremost's buyer catalogue gives details of the various types of vehicles available.

77. *Oilweek*, March 16, 1970.

78. Jack Nodwell Interview. Today Foremost's product line contains nine-wheeled vehicle models.

79. Jack Nodwell is a graduate in mechanical engineering from the University of Alberta and, according to father Bruce, has been largely responsible for placing Canadian Foremost in its present position.

80. Nodwell units last a long time, usually ten years. Customers tend to rebuild them rather than place new orders.

81. "Sure Go" units were basically cabs mounted on tracks and equipped with self-powered recorders for seismic work and were capable of holding five men and supplies for five days. *Oilweek*, May 25, 1970. See also J.M. Robins, "Heavy Air Freighting in the Arctic," *Arctic and Middle North Transport*, edited by B.F. Slater. *Proceedings of a Symposium held by the Arctic Institute of North America*, 1969, p.157.

82. *Oilweek*, March 3, 1969. In 1970 an $11 million deal for seventy large-tracked vehicles was concluded.

83. Jack Nodwell Interview.

84. Canadian Foremost is Canadian-owned and controlled. Though there are about 900 shareholders, some 53 percent of the company is controlled by three major shareholders, all of whom are actually involved in the company itself.

85. Interview with Mr. Ron Southern, President ATCO Ltd., March 23, 1983. (Hereafter cited as Southern Interview).

86. Apparently, Mrs. Southern, Don's wife, was also actively involved with the company at this time.

87. Southern Interview.

88. Airdrie is a town just north of Calgary. In 1965 ATCO located on a 72-acre site in south-west Calgary.

89. Ron Southern states that there were neither sub-shops or wholesalers that could supply the necessary components.

90. Back-up facilities included a fully equipped hospital and recreational facilities.

91. Southern Interview.

92. *Ibid.*

93. *Ibid.*

94. *Ibid.*

95. *Ibid.*

96. *Ibid.*

97. *Ibid.*

98. *Ibid.*

99. *Ibid.*

100. *Ibid.*

URBAN DEVELOPMENT TRENDS IN THE PRAIRIE PROVINCES

Peter J. Smith

The purpose of this essay is to present a broad overview of urban development in the prairie provinces since World War II. Effectively, that means the thirty-five-year period between 1946 and 1981, since the prime source for a survey of this kind has to be the Census of Canada, and the 1981 Census is the most recent that is available.

There are two further observations that should be made, by way of introduction. First, urban development is one of the most obvious manifestations of the great economic and social transformation that has swept the West in recent decades, and to which other contributions in this volume are directly addressed. In the limited space here, however, it will not be possible to do more than offer glancing references to the causes of the phenomena to be described. Second, there are critical differences among the three prairie provinces which make it difficult to generalize about them as though they form a common region. I have tried to draw out the most important of these differences, but I also found I could not avoid giving more attention to Alberta than to the other provinces. This reflects the greater scale of urban development in Alberta, and the greater complexity of its forms and impacts.

The natural starting point for a descriptive survey, since it establishes the most basic fact of all, is the amount of urban growth there has been since 1946. There are many ways in which this might be measured, but by any standard the scale of growth has been impressive. For simplicity's sake, only population trends will be described here and then only in terms of the most basic statistics.

In round figures, the urban population of the three provinces increased from one million in 1946 to three million in 1981. Since the total population increase over the same period was just short of two million it can be said that the entire postwar growth of the prairie provinces has been urban growth. The lion's share, however—about 75 percent—has gone to Alberta, where the urban population actually quintupled. This is illustrated in Figure 1 which shows how Alberta has maintained a consistently higher rate of growth than the other provinces, with the result that it has increased its share of the prairie urban population from about one-third in 1946 to well over one-half in 1981. Manitoba's growth curve, by contrast, has flattened in a remarkably regular fashion, showing that the rate of urban population increase has been falling steadily, census period by census period. Saskatchewan, which still has the smallest urban population, has been more erratic in its growth, but it, too, had shown a definite levelling off before the economic upturn of the late 1970s.

An inevitable accompaniment of this generally strong growth trend, and in its way an altogether more revealing one, since it is more symptomatic of the cultural transformation of the past forty years, has been a marked rural-urban shift in population distribution. Very simply, a rural-agricultural society has evolved into an urban-industrial one. The implications are profound, not just for the material circumstances of people's lives—where they live and what sorts of jobs they do—but because it signalled a complete reshaping of the way of life of prairie people. It was also a process that began remarkably abruptly, particularly in Manitoba and Alberta, and it made its major impact in its earliest stages (Figure 2). In Alberta, for example, two-thirds of the population was classed as rural in 1931, and the proportion remained unchanged throughout the next decade. By 1946, however, the urban share had jumped to 44 percent and it reached 50 percent early in the 1950s. Today it stands above 75 percent, which puts Alberta almost exactly at the national average. Manitoba's urbanization curve, like its growth curve, has been more regular than Alberta's but both have flattened in the last decade, indicating that the rural-urban distribution of population is now more or less stable. Among the three provinces only Saskatchewan is still showing an upward trend, and that is a consequence of its later start. As late as 1951 only 30 percent of Saskatchewan's population was technically classed as urban, and it had not quite reached 60 percent thirty years later. Within Canada, only Prince Edward Island is less urbanized.

FIGURE 1
Urban population increase in the three prairie provinces, 1946-1981.

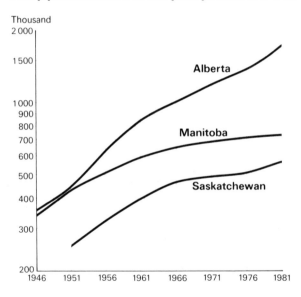

At the same time the official statistics have to be interpreted with some caution. It is never easy to capture people's attitudes and behavior in mechanical formulae, and urbanization is no exception. It is such a pervasive phenomenon that the traditional distinction between rural and urban has lost much of its meaning. Cities are no longer tightly contained; urban workers regularly commute over distances of eighty km. or more; and many rural municipalities have found themselves having to cope with the demands of large new populations of exurbanites, who are urban in everything except their place of residence. In other words, because of the way in which the urban population is counted, it is possible that an important new component of the urbanization process is being overlooked. For example, the boundaries of the Edmonton and Calgary census metropolitan areas exclude tens of thousands of people who function as part of the metropolitan unit, but unless they live in an incorporated urban municipality with a population greater than 1000 these people will not be classed as urban.

FIGURE 2

Urban population as a percentage of provincial population, 1946-1981.

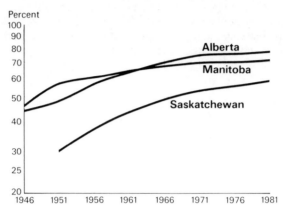

The larger point, however, is that the apparent trend toward equilibrium in rural-urban distribution cannot be taken to mean that the erosion of the traditional rural population has been checked. Rather, it reflects a changing split between the farm and nonfarm segments of the rural population. In brief, while the former has declined consistently in all three provinces, the latter had increased in sufficient numbers to allow the *total* rural population to maintain an approximate balance with the urban population, at least over the last decade in Manitoba and Alberta. In all, across the three provinces, the farm population has fallen from 950,000 in 1951 to less than half-a-million today; that is, it has been roughly halved during a period of great population increase. The implication is obvious: the farm population, which to most people probably still constitutes the true rural population, now accounts for a small part of the total prairie population--less than 10 percent in Manitoba and Alberta and about 20 percent in Saskatchewan.

A third basic trend, which may not be so well-known as either of the two I have just described, is the great increase since 1946 in the number of places that are obviously urban. This can be illustrated most readily by grouping towns and cities into size classes, as has been done in Table 1. The population limits are completely arbitrary but they serve to demonstrate the trend that I will refer to as the enrichment of the urban system. In the 1930s, at the climax of the rural phase of development, the prairie urban system was simple in the extreme. Urban places were few and small, and almost the only reason for their existence was to provide services to the agricultural economy and to farm families. They were rural service centers, or "central places," the stereotypical prairie small towns which, I suspect, dominate in most outside images of prairie life, even today. In Alberta's case, as late as 1946, there were only eight towns with more than 2500 people, and there was a very large gap between Edmonton and Calgary, with 100,000 each, and Lethbridge with 17,000. The pattern was not exactly the same in the other provinces: in Manitoba, with only one dominant city rather than two, the second city (Brandon) was even more overshadowed; and in Saskatchewan, where Regina and Saskatoon were only about half as large as Edmonton and Calgary, there was a more even distribution of places in the different size classes. Yet the general point holds nonetheless. The agricultural economy of the day generated a comparatively modest demand for urban services, with the result that the prairie urban system was weakly developed.

TABLE 1

NUMBERS OF URBAN PLACES BY SIZE CLASSES IN

THE PRAIRIE PROVINCES, 1946-1981

Minimum population	1946	1956	1966	1976	1981
(a) ALBERTA					
100,000	2	2	2	2	2
25,000	0	1	3	4	6
10,000	2	3	1	5	6
5,000	0	4	5	8	16
2,500	4	15	29	32	35
1,000	30	39	39	47	49
	38	64	79	98	114
(b) SASKATCHEWAN					
100,000	0	0	2	2	2
25,000	2	3	2	2	2
10,000	2	2	3	3	4
5,000	4	4	3	4	4
2,500	2	6	12	11	15
1,000	22	28	36	39	43
	32	43	58	61	70
(c) MANITOBA					
100,000	1	1	1	1	1
25,000	0	0	1	1	1
10,000	1	3	2	2	3
5,000	2	2	3	5	4
2,500	2	5	6	6	6
1,000	13	16	15	14	19
	19	27	28	29	34

Notes: 1 Lloydminster is included in Alberta.

2 Flin Flon is included in Manitoba.

3 Winnipeg includes all the communities with which it was amalgamated in 1970.

It is clear from Table 1 that this situation has changed dramatically, particularly in Alberta. The growth impulse has affected every level in the urban hierarchy. Most of the places that were in the smallest size classes in 1946 have moved steadily upward, and their positions have been taken by still smaller places moving up from below, or by newly-created towns. Again, in more restrained fashion, that pattern has prevailed in Manitoba and Saskatchewan as well.

A further dimension of urban system expansion, which is not brought out by Table 1, is that the system is now far more complex than it was forty or fifty years ago. More and larger towns and cities mean also a greater variety of functions being performed, more diverse reasons for growth, and more intricate spatial groupings and arrangements. I will touch briefly on all of these, but I will concentrate on the last, since it is the most obviously geographical. I must also warn that a number of different development processes have been working upon the urban system, and they often overlap and obscure one another. That noted, however, it is possible to identify several major trends, around which I will organize the rest of my remarks.

Perhaps the most obvious trend, certainly as far as Alberta and Saskatchewan are concerned, is the growth that has been generated by the resource-based industries—forestry, mining, recreation and tourism and, above all, oil and natural gas, the effects of which have been especially widespread, in keeping with the extensive distribution of the resources themselves. This has had two consequences of immediate moment.

The first is that much of the resource-based growth has accrued to the existing rural service centers. In Alberta, for example, all the largest central places—Medicine Hat, Red Deer, Grande Prairie, Lloydminster, Camrose—have benefited in some degree from new roles as servicing, processing and manufacturing centers for the oil and gas industry. Many smaller places have also profited, if more sporadically, from the development of nearby oil and gas fields or from the construction of gas processing plants. These effects have been felt ever since the initial Leduc discoveries in the winter of 1946/47, but their greatest impact came in the census decade between 1971 and 1981, when the energy crisis was at its peak. The latest census returns reveal that a strong growth trend was experienced in all levels of the urban hierarchy. Where the great majority of small places were static or declining during the 1960s, most recorded a high rate of increase in the 1970s. Indeed, the impact was even greater than is suggested by Table 2, since 75 percent of the towns and villages in the growing category experienced population increases greater than 25 percent. The expansion of the resource industries was not the only factor in this sudden turnaround, but it must have been a major contributor.

The second consequence has been the increased prominence in the urban systems of all three provinces of single-enterprise resource towns, some of which have become large places in their own right. This is not exactly a new phenomenon—Flin Flon was Manitoba's third largest city in 1951. Nor are the resource towns necessarily assured of a permanent existence, as recent events in Uranium City have demonstrated. But in the current phase of economic development, resource towns have made a substantial contribution to the enrichment of the urban system, particularly in Alberta. Of the thirty urban places with populations greater than

5000 in 1981, seven either began as resource towns or exist primarily from resource exploitation today. In the next size class (2500-5000) ten of the thirty-five places can be classified in the same way.

When the pattern of resource town development in Alberta is looked at more closely, three main features can be noted. First, the earliest resource towns in the modern period, all of which were sparked by the opening of oil fields, were concentrated in the settled areas of the province, which has allowed them to diversify their economic bases. Thus, Devon, in the Leduc oil field, is carving out a new role as a dormitory community and industrial satellite of Edmonton; and Drayton Valley, on the Pembina oilfield, has become the major service center for the agricultural area west of Edmonton. Second, as resource exploration and development began to shift into the unpopulated forest zone of western and northern Alberta, a string of struggling towns along the agricultural frontier, where farming was marginal at best, took on new life. They were the obvious gateways and service points for much of the resource frontier. Third, with the deeper and deeper penetration of the forest zone, completely new towns were built; the advancement of the resource frontier has also meant the advancement of the urban frontier. Fort McMurray, of course, has had the most spectacular career, exploding from a tiny river port twenty years ago to a city of more than 30,000 people today. In the other provinces, the only comparable development is the emergence of Thompson as Manitoba's fourth largest city. Flin Flon is actually larger, but its population is split between Saskatchewan and Manitoba. Still, among the northern single-enterprise towns, Flin Flon is second only to Fort McMurray.

For all the attention received by the resource sector these days, it is by no means the only factor in either urban growth or the enrichment of the urban system. Another factor that has long played a critical part in the traditional rural areas of the prairie provinces is the trend to centralization, or the concentration of development at certain favored places within the central place network. Since I am referring here to the rural service role that most prairie cities and towns still perform, it also follows that the growth I am referring to is derived from the needs of the rural population. At first sight, given the steep decline in farm population numbers, that may seem contradictory. The explanation lies in changing attitudes toward urban-based services, which is reflected in the tendency for service functions to be concentrated in fewer, larger and more widely spaced centers.

The key to understanding the selective effects of growth in a central place system is accessibility. With better highways, better cars and cheap gasoline, all of which have been available since 1946, distance has become less and less of a barrier. Farm families today can travel further in less time and more comfort than those of forty and sixty years ago. Instead of being tied to the nearest center, no matter how small or limited in its services, they can look to more distant but larger centers, where they can enjoy the same quality and choice of services that city residents take for granted. The smallest places thus come to be bypassed by the rural consumers, and their trade areas are captured by their larger neighbors. The "more central" places are able to grow at the expense of the "less central" ones and, in the act of growing, they are able to increase their attractiveness, and their growth potential, by offering still greater arrays of services.

TABLE 2

POPULATION CHANGE IN SMALL URBAN PLACES IN ALBERTA BY 10 YEAR INTERVALS, 1951-1981

Type of population change	Incorporated towns and villages with populations less than 1000 at the start of each period			Incorporated towns and villages with populations between 1000 and 2500 at the start of period		
	1951-61	1961-71	1971-81	1951-61	1961-71	1971-81
Increase of 10% or greater	98	53	138	31	27	34
Increase or decrease of less than 10%	40	53	35	6	15	9
Decrease of 10% or greater	14	63	12	2	1	0
Totals	152	169	185	39	43	43

Inevitably, it is the smallest central places that are least able to compete in the centralization process. Something of the outcome for Alberta is suggested in Table 2, in the evident stagnation and decline of the majority of villages and small towns in the 1960s. For a time, indeed, this trend led to fears that the prairie small town was doomed, and it is true that many of the smallest urban places, the unincorporated hamlets and elevator sidings, have disappeared. In one study of the Red Deer trade area, for example, it was found that more than thirty places were lost from the local system between 1941 and 1971.

Ultimately, any tendency to centralization in a central place system must be reflected in the growth of the cities at the top of the hierarchy. For that matter, growth for any reason anywhere in the urban system must impact, eventually, on the largest cities where the most specialized services are concentrated. This introduces yet another trend that has characterized the urban development of the prairie provinces since World War II—the trend to metropolitanization, or the special, accelerated growth effects experienced by the largest urban places. The simplest way of highlighting this is through a single statistic: since 1946 the combined population of the five leading cities has increased by about one-and-a-half million, which represents three-quarters of the total population increase of the three provinces.

In rather different ways all the provinces have participated in the metropolitan trend, but the most dramatic changes, once again, have occurred in Alberta. In round figures, while Winnipeg's population doubled between 1941 and 1981, and Regina's and Saskatoon's trebled, Edmonton and Calgary increased six-fold (Figure 3). In 1941 Winnipeg was by far the dominant prairie city, three times as large as Regina and Saskatoon. In the ensuing forty years, however, both the Alberta cities have overtaken Winnipeg, and their growth rates have been consistently higher than those of the Saskatchewan cities, as well. In terms of an overall prairie urban system, there are now three large cities of almost equal size (about 600,000) and two medium-sized cities. In fact, despite the strong growth they have shown over the past thirty-five years, Regina and Saskatoon are still no larger than Edmonton and Calgary were in 1951.

FIGURE 3
Population increase in census metropolitan area, 1941-1981.

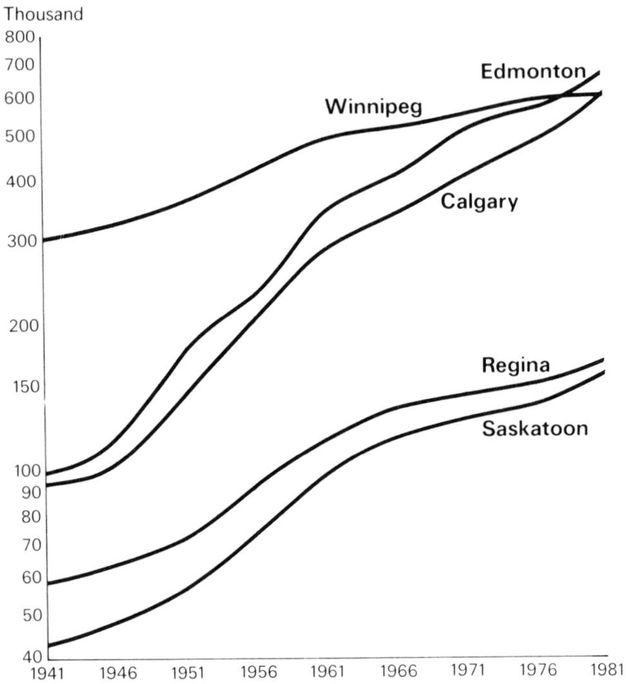

That last point can be related back to Saskatchewan's comparatively low rate of urbanization, and it also suggests that Saskatchewan is likely to show the lowest concentration of provincial population in its largest cities. For all that Regina and Saskatoon have grown at rates well above the provincial average, their share of the total population is still no more than one-third as compared with almost 60 percent in the other two provinces (Figure 4). The growth curve also appears to be leveling off, which suggests that Regina and Saskatoon may never exercise the same dominance over their provincial distribution as the three larger cities do over Alberta and Manitoba. Another way of illustrating this is to calculate the ratio of the largest city's population to that of the largest place at the next level of the provincial hierarchy. In the case of Saskatchewan in 1981 the ratio was 4.2:1 (Regina/Prince Albert); in Alberta, by contrast, it was 12.2:1 (Edmonton/Lethbridge) and in Manitoba, 15.6:1 (Winnipeg/Brandon).

The other particularly interesting feature of Figure 4 is the convergence of the Alberta and Manitoba growth curves and their apparent stabilization. That, of course, does not mean that the metropolitan populations have stopped growing, although Winnipeg's increase over the last census period (1976-1981) was a mere 1 percent. What the flattened curves really indicate is that metropolitan population in Alberta and Manitoba is now increasing in proportion to the rest of the population, so that the trend to an increased concentration in the metropolitan centers has run its course. In other words, some of the urban growth impulse is beginning to shift away from the largest cities, a phenomenon that is known to be

FIGURE 4
Metropolitan population as a percentage of provincial population,
19841-1981.

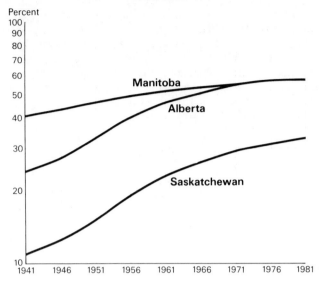

occurring throughout North America. It has also been given the misleading label of counter-urbanization--misleading because the population is not any less urban, either in distribution or in attitudes. Rather, the smaller cities and towns are coming to attract a larger share of whatever growth there is. In the case of Edmonton and Calgary the numerical increase is still extremely large, but their share of the total provincial increase has fallen sharply since the peak period of 1966-1971, when literally all of Alberta's population increase was metropolitan increase (Table 3).

TABLE 3
METROPOLITAN SHARE OF ALBERTA'S POPULATION
INCREASE BY 5 YEARS INTERVALS, 1946-1981

	Metropolitan increase	Percentage of Alberta increase
1946-51	99,020	73%
1951-56	139,273	76%
1956-61	165,177	79%
1961-66	115,214	88%
1966-71	167,137	101%
1971-76	125,134	60%
1976-81	225,655	56%
1946-81	1,036,640	72%

The further consequence of this trend, and another of the factors working to enrich the urban system, is that the group of next-largest cities is now showing much stronger growth. Between 1971 and 1981 the cities of more than 10,000 people increased by 70 percent as compared with a 40 percent increase for the two metropolitan areas. And whereas the metropolitan rate of increase had fallen slightly from the preceding decade, the rate for the secondary cities had taken a large jump (from 25 percent in 1961-1971). Towns lower in the hierarchy experienced the same kind of shift, though not to the same degree. For the towns in the 2500 to 10,000 range, the overall growth rate increased from about 25 percent in 1961-1971 to almost 50 percent in 1971-1981.

FIGURE 5
Structure of the Edmonton metropolitan area.

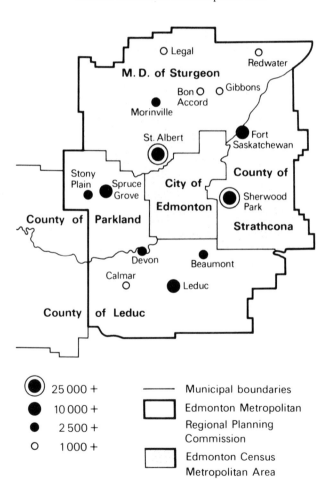

The standard explanation for counter-urbanization is that it is an adaptation to the negative aspects of large city size and highly concentrated development. The difficulty of moving around in increasingly congested cities, for example, may more than offset any locational advantage that comes from being at the hub of a transportation network; the high cost of land may encourage entrepreneurs to look for sites well outside the city, even if they are less accessible; and there are a host of reasons why many people have come to prefer life in smaller cities and towns. Moreover, when described in these terms, the process does not look particularly new or unusual; it began decades ago, in the flight to the suburbs, although Alberta was not affected until the postwar boom years. Since then, however, the trend to suburban and satellite town development has become well established, particularly in the Edmonton area, which is now the most elaborate metropolitan constellation to be found anywhere in the prairie provinces (Figure 5). The trend has developed much later in Calgary, largely because there were fewer towns to act as growth magnets within close proximity of the city. Only in the most recent census returns has the suburbanization of towns like Airdrie and Okotoks become at all pronounced.

What is really new, in relation to the idea of counter urbanization, is the much larger areal scale on which it is operating. There is also, in Alberta, a unique channelling effect into the corridor by which Edmonton and Calgary are linked, creating a new type of development region—new, at least, for the prairie provinces. It is no longer adequate to point to the two metropolitan centers as the most concentrated loci of growth in Alberta. As a group it is the corridor towns between Edmonton and Calgary that have shown the highest rate of population increase since 1971 (87 percent as compared with 34 percent in the previous decade). We must now begin to think in terms of a much larger Edmonton-Calgary region containing many towns and cities, most of them growing rapidly and all linked together in a most complex pattern of interdependence. The emergence of this development region, then, is a final factor in the enrichment of Alberta's urban system. By 1981, thirteen of the thirty largest places in Alberta were clustered there, in the satellite rings around Edmonton and Calgary or in the corridor between them.

The scale and complexity of recent urban development trends in Alberta is a fitting note on which to end. At the beginning of the postwar period it was Manitoba that stood out as the least typical of the three provinces. There were certainly points of difference between Alberta and Saskatchewan, but in their basic patterns they were very alike. Even in Manitoba's case the difference all stemmed from the single cause of Winnipeg's historic preeminence in the economic organization of the western interior. At that time, it still made sense to think of a unified prairie urban system focused on Winnipeg as the regional capital, but that order has passed forever. Despite some general similarities among the three provinces, it is the differences in their urban development experiences over the last thirty-five years that are really more notable. And now it is Alberta that is most different of all.

Acknowledgement

The figures were drafted in the Cartographic Laboratory, Department of Geography, University of Alberta.

PERSPECTIVES ON RURAL WESTERN CANADA IN THE 1950s

B.Y. Card

Introduction

The aim of this paper is to employ a dynamic mix of perspectives to examine the rural West in what amounts to a moment of time, the 1950s. In many ways it is a unique historical, sociological and psychological moment (Erikson, 1975) since it involves persons now living trying to recreate symbolically what has been lived through. This paper introduces processes, points of view, and theoretical perspective in an exploratory, tentative and incomplete way. An attempt is made to combine subjectivity and objectivity heuristically, to make an opening, rather than a last-statement, on the rural West of the 1950s.

The paper has five parts. Parts I and V are concerned with the rural West as an emergent and then as a diminishing symbol or signifying system (Williams, 1981:207-214). Here we continue perspectives already introduced by historians, notably Owram (1980) in his *Promise of Eden*, dealing with the West in the nineteenth century, and Allen (1973), who explored the West and its knowledge as a *Region of the Mind*. Parts I and V underline the view that the rural West, whatever its objective reality, began with words, was developed with words, and was modified and interpreted in the 1950s with words, hence the emphasis on the West as a symbol or signifying system.

The three parts making up the middle of the paper are concerned with the human interactions taking place in the rural West and official and unofficial reports of, and reaction to them. In Part II, the micro-level of decision making is the perspective used to see how some people actually moved into and out of the decade behaviorally. In Part III the macro-level perspective of Statistics Canada and other sources is used to see what these micro-level behaviors added up to for the rural West. Part IV has a still different perspective, which is simply referred to all "social dynamics," in which attention is focused on some of the major responses to change in the rural West during the decade.

In very basic terms, this paper is about three things: (1) what rural West was in talk up to 1950, (2) what the rural West was in interaction and behavior in the 1950s, and (3) what the rural West was in talk during and at the end of the decade. Enough before-and-after the decade will be considered to give the ten years a place in time. Further, disciplinary and geographical boundaries will be freely crossed in order to give a larger contextual view of the rural West in the limited time span under consideration.

The Emerging Symbol System of a Rural West[1]

Where did the term and the notion of "rural" come from in the first place? How did it come to be applied to western Canada? When? What was the symbolic situation around 1950? Partly to illustrate the development and use of a symbol system, and partly to make up for a lack of better knowledge, a story is introduced, based on some fact, and followed with some reputable knowledge from a variety of sources to bring 1950 into focus with its "rural" symbol system.[2]

Once upon a time, many centuries ago and before 1200 B.C., two brothers, Rubus and Dubus, lived in the countryside near the river Tiber. (They are not to be confused with Romulus and Remus of the same locality). Both were agricolae, actually pig farmers who had no name for themselves except "us" or "we farmers." They lived in *rus* (the country) as everyone did. The main topic of conversation was pigs and weather. For the women, it was how the men smelled. One day Dubus, at his wife's request, was bathing in the Tiber. Here he made the discovery of white, crusty salt deposits along the shore line. Entrepreneurial possibilities came immediately to his mind. Very shortly Dubus mined and sold salt to Rubus and the neighbors. Business flourished. He added staff. Soon salt pork was a staple commodity for Rubus, Dubus and neighbors. But Dubus could no longer handle the volume of business living in *rus*. He moved from the pig farm to some adjoining hills.

One day, while Dubus was reflecting on his new life-style as a merchant and employer in the salt business, a Hittite customer from the east came by. Desiring to buy salt at a good price and anxious to make a good impression, the Hittite said: "Dubus, you have a growing uru here." "What do you mean by "uru?" queried Dubus, the cautious merchant. The Hittite, somewhat astonished that his words were not well understood tried to explain. "Uru means where you and your workers live who sell salt. It is different from *rus*, where Rubus and the pig farmers live. You have people around you all the time. You sell. You exchange market news. You have an importance."

When Dubus heard the word "importance" his mind and chest swelled. "I have it!" he fairly shouted. You say I am in uru, but I don't like your word. It's too much like a cow's moo for a person selling salt pork and salt. I need a word with more grunt. I will say I am in urbs, and therefore urban. That sets me apart from Rubus, who lives in rus, and is therefore rural. Urban and rural, what a pair of words, especially since urban is the more important! In fact, urban makes me feel definitely superior."

From these dubious beginnings, the words "rural" and "urban" were passed along by Latin scholars to the people of Western Europe who didn't need them except to pass language courses. They had words of their own such as city and country, la ville et la campagne (Williams, 1976:46-48, 71-72), which they preferred. In the fourteenth and fifteenth centuries, however, "rural" began to be used by writers mainly from the city to talk about the country. It wasn't until the nineteenth century that "urban" came into common usage in England (*Oxford English Dictionary*, 1971; Partridge, 1966: 576-577 and 753).

What about "rural" in Canada? In the West? One of the earliest recorded uses of "rural" was in 1841 in Upper Canada in connection with local government.[3] Meanwhile, Canada became a nation in 1867 and by 1870 had purchased a "West" and began planning a national policy to go with the purchase. The West was surveyed, mortgaged, equipped with railroads and telegraph, a police force, churches, schools, townsites, some merchants and also immigrants with the backing and encouragement of the national government. At first, all this was called "settlement," with little or no concern for the development or creation of a "rural" West. Prior to 1891 the Census of Canada listed persons in towns as "occupiers of land" (*Censuses of Canada*, 1608-1876, V, Table XXII; *Census of Canada* 1880-81, IV, Table E). Though in 1891 the British practice of considering aggregations of fewer than 1500 as "rural," based upon sanitary districts, was adopted and the *Canada Census* "line of demarcation" and used in the 1891 *Canada Census* (*Census of Canada*, 1891, Bulletin No. 5; IV, Table F, p. 401), the term rural was mainly used to talk about population trends outside Canada or in Ontario (*Census of Canada*, 1891, Bulletin No.2:1-6). The West was a source of cheap lands for young Ontario farmers, the overflow of rural Ontario. It wasn't until 1901 that rural and urban tabulations became a featured way comparing Census districts (*Census of Canada*, 1901, I Table IV) There was some lag in the way "rural" was substituted for "occupiers of land." While further research is needed on the usage of the term "rural" in federal circles, the evidence at hand suggests that the term was not used consistently or with any clear meaning, except "occupiers of land" or that remainder of the population not living in incorporated villages, towns or cities, a rather negative definition (*Census of Canada*, 1971, V (Part I), Statement 1:5).

In the West itself, the Territorial government tried with little success to organize "Rural Municipalities" as early as 1883 (Hanson, 1956:24-26) while Manitoba adopted the terms "rural" and "urban" for municipalities in 1886 (Crawford, 1954:42-46). Saskatchewan passed a Rural Municipalities Act in 1908, Alberta a Municipalities Act in 1912, with provision for "rural municipalities." In 1918 Alberta rescinded its legislation on rural municipalities and has not used the term for local government since. In Manitoba and Saskatchewan the term was persistently used through the first half of the present century in local government, where it was "frozen," according to E.J. Hanson (1956:26).

But "rural" in local government hardly signified a "rural" West. South of the border and also in Ontario a North American country-life movement emerged with the Protestant churches prominent in their leadership (Hofstadter, 1955). A more general view of "rural" was expressed by John McDougall in his 1913 Report to the Board of Social Service and Evangelism of the Presbyterian Church of Canada, *Rural Life in Canada: Its Trends and Tasks*. After condemning the evils of the city, the virtues of agriculture and rural living were extolled. A special plea was also made to recruit ministers for the Canadian West. Symbolically the process of creating a rural West had begun, and the salvific role of the rural class asserted.

However, as McDougall needed ministers to help the cause along, there were those who saw the need of secular social scientists for the same purpose. The newly created Manitoba College of Agriculture and Rural Economics in 1917 was offering courses on rural leadership as well as economics, followed soon after by rural sociology in the Home Economics Department. R.W. Murchie, appointed an English instructor in 1917, had contacts with rural sociology at the University of Minnesota. Soon his title changed to "Assistant Professor of Rural Sociology," though he worked out of the Department of Rural Economics (Card, 1973:5). Others proliferated the usage of the term "rural." In the 1930s Saskatchewan's Dean of Education, F.M. Quance was scanning student essays from across Canada to see if there were rural and urban differences in their word usage.[4] The findings were incorporated in the Quance *Canadian Speller*. "Rural sociology" was introduced to Saskatchewan Normal School students in the 1930s and 1940s by instructors Cameron, Lorimer and Mahood (Card, 1973:6). Saskatchewan's native son, W.B. Baker, after postgraduate study of rural sociology in the United States, rose from a member of the Department of Extension to Dean of the College of Agriculture between 1947 and 1950 at the University of Saskatchewan, devoting himself to what was tantamount to a rural-change apostleship (Card, 1973:7). By 1950 leadership in developing a rural-symbol system had clearly fallen to Saskatchewan. Manitoba had its experts on rural life, such as Dean of Education, D.S. Woods. Alberta had its rural symbol users such as Andrew Stewart, a rural economist originally from the Manitoba College of Agriculture and a colleague of Murchie, and a number of extension workers, notably Donald Cameron. Ironically, though Saskatchewan was symbolically and ideologically the Western rural leader, its university preferred to have a Department of Agricultural Economics, The University of Alberta, a Department of Rural Economics. By 1950, the prairie universities and a few government departments and programs appeared to be the main repositories of the rural-symbol system.

But the rural-symbol system's dynamics were not confined to the West. The United States and the Canadian federal government were also involved deeply in creating and modifying "rural" as a meaningful symbol, serving as sources of diffusion to the Canadian West. In 1933, two American sociologists, Brunner and Kolb argued that "society cannot be adequately described or analyzed in terms of the old and arbitrary bifocal divisions" of "rural" and "urban" (cited by Whyte, 1966:8). Louis Wirth, the University of Chicago's widely-read sociologist developed a typology of rural and urban man in 1938 (Wirth, 1938). To help with the large-scale study of the *Canadian Frontiers of Settlement*, rural sociologist Carle C. Zimmerman and his graduate students from Harvard, and Lowry Nelson from Brigham Young University were recruited. The several volumes of this large-scale study began to be published in the 1930s. But even as the term "rural" was thus coming into the Canadian West, it came under increasing criticism in the United States. Wirth in 1951 seriously reconsidered the term and his rural typology (Wirth, 1951). The rural symbol system in the United States by 1950 was showing signs of diminishing.

In Canada, the trend setter for usage of "rural" was the Dominion Bureau of Statistics. In 1951 the definition of "rural" was changed from meaning those not living in incorporated places to those not living in places with population concentrations under 1000 persons, whether incorporated or no. Further, "rural" was divided into "rural farm" and "rural nonfarm." In addition, the Census "farm" was carefully defined to mean a tract of land greater than three acres, regardless of product, with production valued at $250 (*Census of Canada*, 1971, V (Part:1) Statement 2:16). In these changed definitions three influences were at work. One was a larger perspective on rural-urban change from Canadian and internationally-important social scientists. Another was the leadership of the U.S. Census which had already moved in the same definitional direction. Then there was the actual change in rural and urban patterns in Canada to accommodate what was happening in 1951 primarily in Ontario and other provinces, not necessarily the Prairie Provinces. But these changes in "rural" symbolically complicated a rather simple concept. The imagination that could go into "rural" was verbally restrained. One fact was abundantly clear. "Rural" was what was left over, the remainder, after urban populations, incorporated or unincorporated, were considered. Dubus could savor the growing importance of "urban" in Canada and its West at mid-century.

FIGURE 1
Micro-settings for observation of the Rural West in the Cardston area in the 1930s to 1960s.

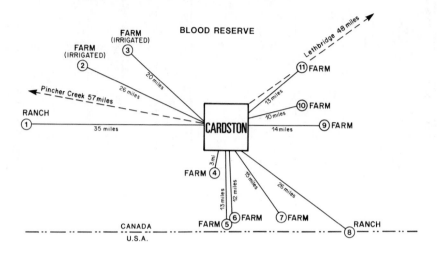

The Rural West from Micro-Perspective

From examining the rural West as a buildup of words and definitions, attention is now directed to particular persons and their micro-situations where hour-by-hour, day-by-day, year-by-year, the deciding, reacting, adapting rural West existed in its most basic way. It is assumed that an adequate picture of the rural West in the 1950s can only be created from aggregating and synthesizing the particular cases, the micro-data so easily overlooked or minimized by the use of "macro" symbols which "rural" and "urban" are. Micro-evidence is needed at this juncture as a way of judging whether symbol systems and macro-evidence of the rural West in the 1950s are "good approximations" to reality or "misleading reification" (Collins, 1981:265-266). Further, the smallest social entities have their own distinctive contribution to make to a broad social science of a larger society such as the Canadian West (R.M. MacIver, cited by Card, 1960:ix). What follows is a small-scale, intimate look at a part of the rural West with the writer as a participant-guide.

The setting chosen is Cardston, in Southwest Alberta, the guide's birthplace. The micro-sample was purposively selected. It consists of the eleven farms or ranches where the guide was employed seasonally in the late twenties and early thirties. The location of the farms and ranches and their distances from Cardston are shown in Figure 1. The data of observation come through "reflective phenomenology" on the part of the guide, supplemented by recent phone interviews and in one instance, a visit to the ranch selected for case study. A table of the eleven micro-settings and observable changes during each decade from the 1930s through the 1960s was constructed as an *aide memoire*, Table 1. The methodology is straightforward, and thoroughly adaptable for other micro-settings. (Zimmerman (1971:28) identified 164 Prairie Province independent trading towns

TABLE 1. ELEVEN RURAL MICRO-SETTINGS IN THE CARDSTON, ALBERTA AREA, 1930's to 1960's[a]

Case	Religion and Ethnicity	Children and Type of School	Previous Occupation and/or Education	Census Status '31 '61 (Deaths)[c]	Family State-P-O-R[b] Farming Mode Mechanization Housing 1930s	Family State-P-O-R[b] Farming Mode Mechanization Housing 1940s	Family State-P-O-R[b] Farming Mode Mechanization Housing 1950s	Family State-P-O-R[b] Farming Mode Mechanization Housing 1960s
1	L.D.S. Irish-Can. German	7 Children 1 Room	Carpenter	F[d] U[d] (late 1930s)[c]	R Family ranch Chickens/livestock horses, Framehouse, phone	R Family ranch — then rented to neighbor	Rented-symbolic survival only for original family	R Moved back from Montreal. Non-Farm
2	L.D.S. Anglo-American	7 Children 2 Rooms Hamlet	Mission	F F	P Family farm Part irrigated Tractor/horses	O Family farm Combine	O Family farm	R Moved to Cardston 2 sons on farm
3	L.D.S. Anglo-Albertan	4 Children Village School	Mission Agric. School	F F (early 1930s)	P Agribusiness Combine/tractors Modern house	P-O Brother farms Agribusiness	O Agribusiness	R Agribusiness
4	R.C. Italian	4 Children Town School	? No data	F U: (1940-killed tractor)	O Family farm Tractor/combine Sons move to Lethbridge	R Farm sold Agribusiness Home modernized	O For sons, in Agribusiness in S.E. Alberta	? Agribusiness out of Lethbridge
5	Protestant Anglo-Ontario	4 Children 1 Room & Village	Civil Engineer	F F (late 1940s)	O Family farm Tractor/horses Moves to Cardston	R Boys farm Combine	Farm management in transition	P Agribusiness Modern House
6	German Anglo-American	3 + Children 4 Room Village	Farm	F F	O Family farm merge to agribusiness	O Agribusiness	R Agribusiness	Decline of Farm Becomes feed-lot operation
7	Protestant German	2 + Children 4 Room Village	? No data	F F	P Family farm Tractor/horses Combine	O Family farm	O Family farm Home modernized	R Retires to Cardston. Farm to son Agribusiness
8	L.D.S. Anglo-American	4 Children Town	Farm University	U (1932-killed/ car)	O-R Agribusiness Closed out with estate.	No Data	No Data	No Data
9	L.D.S. Danish-American	8 Children Hamlet School	Mission Farm Univ.	F F (late 1950s)	O Family farm Horses/tractor/combine Modern house	O-R Agribusiness	R Agribusiness Farm divided on death of owner	Agribusiness
10	Ex-Hutterite German	3 Children 2 Room	Farm	F U	P Family farm	O Moved to Raymond	No Data	No Data
11	Non-denom. Protestant	2 Children Town	Farm	F F	O Family farm Tractor/combine Modern house	O Agribusiness	O Agribusiness	R Sold Farm Moved to Lethbridge

[a]Source: Retrospection plus phone interview.　[b]Family of procreation—P, orientation—O. renunciation—R.　[c]Death of farmer, date and cause in parenthesis.　[d]F-Farm; U-Urban.

or embryo "farm cities" between 1931-66, each of which could be treated as the locus of micro-settings). The strategy followed is briefly to summarize observations from Figure 1 and Table 1, deal with three specific cases for their typological importance, and then to look at local district change as seen by the school superintendent whose entire professional career was, and continues to be, in the area.

As indicated in Table 1, the early thirties marked the end of a stable country-town relationship. Both country and town people lived by three times, diurnal, seasonal and standard. Standard time was operationalized for both by school and train. Concern over seasons, crops and market prices was felt most acutely by country people and those town businesses most closely tied to agriculture. There was a close relationship between country and town in sports, community events such as the local fair, church meetings and especially in the business transactions of elevator and mainstreet stores and offices. Occasionally, business holidays were declared and school absences regularly tolerated to provide farmer manpower needs for seeding and harvesting. For able youth and young men, not working on farms, especially at harvest, was tantamount to community disloyalty. Townspeople did enjoy amenities like a water system and electricity and easy access to stores, schools and churches, but at the same time many lived a semi-country style of life with their large gardens, cows, chickens, ponies, and occasionally pigs and sheep maintained in one's own lot. Outdoor privies were common as backup for faltering water works or a necessity for those places not yet on town water. Country children within walking or horseback-riding distance regularly attended all school grades, while senior students from further away boarded in town from the high school years. In this setting Rubus and Dubus were essentially equals with a recognized division of labor but working in two great common causes, agricultural production and raising and educating families.[5]

It is not possible to report in depth on the sample of eleven country micro-situations of 1931 and all the changes that occurred in them through the 1950s. The major changes to be noted are the deaths of five farmers or ranchers, which necessitated major family adaptations which were still carried over to the 1950s. The mode of farming was also changing. In 1931 there were nine family farms or ranches, where family labor and subsistence production had a dominant place. In the 1950s only two farm families of this type remained. Four were already into or entering an agribusiness mode where scale of operations, mechanization, and emphasis on commercial rather than subsistence production were dominant features. In 1931, one rancher would have been classified as urban; in 1961, this man's descendants, and three other country family units would have been classified as urban also. Mechanization was so well advanced prior to 1950 that no combine harvesters were added for the first time during that decade. Home modernization was started in or before the 1930s in terms of electricity and a water system. The process was still going on in the 1950s. For this particular sample, the 1950s were a transition decade where many changes in country living begun twenty years earlier were still going on, but at the micro-level, it was in the family unit that change was most drastically apparent, as the following three case studies selected from Table 1 reveal. They are reported with permission.

In Case 1, the second daughter of an Irish-Canadian carpenter and rancher and a German-ancestry, practical nurse mother, distinguished herself as a Claresholm Agricultural School student and athlete. In her local district she was renowned as a horsewoman, marksman, and mountaineer, as well as a versatile ranch hand. In a feature article the city daily paper called her "The Girl of the Golden West." Suitors came from two trading centers and beyond. The western-most suitor won out. The couple moved to Montreal in the early 1930s where the husband had a highly productive business career. Two brothers successively tried to make a living off the home ranch, while another emigrated to the United States for work. Two sisters became school teachers and moved on. A third sister also left after the death of the father and mother. Ranching did not produce a living for the boys running the place, so they left for the town and city renting the ranch land but not the house, which was vacant, to a neighbor. The ranch remained in this condition, overgrazed and run-down until the 1960s, when the Montreal couple, who had maintained a financial interest in the property, returned to make it their home for retirement. Case I was the most idyllic, bucolic micro-setting in the Table 1 sample. Families and neighbors cooperated in their near-subsistence agriculture and local social life. In the 1960s it is the only micro-setting which came close to the definition of rural in the *Canadian Junior Dictionary* (1977): "Rural—in, ...belonging to, like that of the country. Rural life is healthy and quiet."

Case 4 starts with an Italian immigrant who arrived in Canada in 1918 and who was killed in a tractor accident in 1940. He had three sons and a daughter. The three boys during the 1930s left home in order to farm land on their own some fifteen miles east of Cardston. They set up headquarters in Lethbridge in a rented house so they would have a place to clean up on weekends. Using trucks to move equipment, they also farmed their mother's land near Cardston. In 1944 they built her a new, modern farm home and looked after her until she too moved to Lethbridge in 1949. The home farm was then sold, and has since been turned mostly back to pasture because it is so hilly, among other reasons. Meanwhile the boys expanded farming operations on large tracts of inexpensive land south-east of Lethbridge, but kept well-appointed homes and a business office in the city. In the 1950s they were among the area's most successful agribusinessmen.

Case 11 east of Cardston was noted during the three decades as a model farm. The farmstead was neat, the equipment up-to-date, and the whole enterprise was operated on the soundest of business principles. The farmer kept a Cardston mailing address, even though there was a hamlet post office closer by. When the newly created large school division was holding its 1942 election, he became a School Board member. After serving with the Board for eight years, where he was noted for sound financial judgment, he left it in 1950 to serve on the Hospital Board when a new hospital was about to be built. In the early 1960s he sold the farm to move to Lethbridge, where his son resided, his daughter having married and gone to British Columbia. The private and public decision making of this farmer contributed to the district's adaptation to change, especially in the fields of health and education.

Another micro-view was obtained from a Cardston citizen who taught in the district and became the school superintendent. It is expressed as a reconstructed interview.

I recall what happened in 1938. The provincial government wanted a big school district. The local people were unanimously opposed. They were being served by over twenty schools of one to four rooms each, where their children attended and where they themselves served as local school boards. The schools were conveniently located for them. However, the Province imposed their new large unit on them and they had to give in. In those years I didn't know what "rural" and "urban" meant, but that is when people began to see themselves as "rural," for that is what they were being called.

I started teaching at the hamlet of Kimball in 1942. The same year a big consolidation took place a few miles east of Jefferson. This took all the Kimball students, so I went west to another hamlet, Mountain View, and from there to other schools. I was at Spring Coulee, east of Cardston, during the construction of the St. Mary's dam in 1945-47. I had construction workers' children in my class. Then I was principal of the Woolford school when it was closed in 1947. In 1948 I came to Cardston to teach. Since Cardston, a town, had been officially "included" in the St. Mary's School Division in 1946, my transfer was easy.

In 1948 we had five Indians from the Blood Reserve as students in the Cardston schools. Their numbers constantly increased in the 1950s. As non-Indian students decreased in numbers from changes taking place on farms and in hamlets, Indian student numbers increased. Thus for many years we have had a very constant School Division student population.

In the 1950s most of the rural and hamlet schools were closed. Their students were bussed to Cardston or to the few village schools that were left. Cardston schools grew till their student bodies equalled half the town population.

It was when I became school superintendent in 1960 that the meaning of "rural" and "urban" really hit me. I was at the annual meeting of the Alberta School Trustees Association. Here there was a real struggle between rural and urban. It was led by Calgary and Edmonton who wanted more say for urban centres. They threatened to split the organization. To prevent this, the school divisions and counties, which up to then each had one vote, agreed to have votes according to their population. In this way the two big cities got what they wanted and the split was avoided.

From these micro-situation reports it is observed that in the Cardston community system there was a country-town harmony and acknowledged interdependence in the 1930s, the end of the horsepower agricultural era. The three case studies show three types of responses to a changing West. For one family, decisions, stored in memory and written contracts, were able to carry their country heritage forward for four decades without the help of senior parents or of occupied land. Another family adapted by moving to the nearest city and from there carried on a large-scale, profitable agribusiness. Lately, one skilled and respected farmer helped a whole community system make adaptation by reorganizing health and education services. From the school superintendent the influence of provincial government and of large cities in insisting upon changes they wanted is observed, and along with this influence, the unplanned effect of polarizing people and organizations into rural and urban. On a personal level, the changes taking place had an emotional cost, reflected in the words of a senior Cardston area resident:

When the school and the church are withdrawn from a community, it is never the same; it dies and only memories remain. (Shaw, 1978:81)

The Macro-Statistical Perspective of the Rural West

While micro-level perceptions of the rural West such as those illustrated, might include nostalgic laments for the family farm and small community, there were at least three types of macro-perceptions that were being generated when the 1950s began and continued thereafter. The first was the image of the empty

West, the nonentity West except for cities. A 1950 portrayal of urban change in the United States and Canada shows the West as vacant except for the stubby rectangles standing for Winnipeg, Calgary and Edmonton. This stood in contrast to the 1946 depiction of rural Western Canada by the Bureau of Statistics which showed a well-settled right-angle triangle of population from the Southeast corner of Manitoba to the slopes of the Rockies, corresponding closely to the ecumene or cropland potential of the West. The northern parts of each province were in fact virtually empty. However, the emptiness view, reinforced by subsequent Statistics Canada depictions of the urban population (*Census of Canada*, 1976:Vol. Map I), by the emphasis on population sparsity and the high cost of space of sociologists such as Kraenzel (1955; 1978), culminated in a view of the Interior West of both Canada and the United States as "The Empty Quarter" (Garreau and Furno, 1980, in Ferkiss, 1980, p. 17). By innuendo and subliminal impression, the rural West of the 1950s was fading on a national and North American scene as the message was repeatedly signalled that cities were what counted.

A second perspective was of a future, flourishing West where intensive agriculture pushed to the northern limits of soil and climate would hold sway alongside an intensive, thriving industrialization based on the West's soil and energy resources, especially coal. This was the vision of the University of Toronto's controversial geographer, Griffith Taylor, whose perspective (Taylor, 1945) was circulated by the Alberta Government soon after it appeared in *Chatelaine* for its own advertising purposes. Taylor's full statement, *Canada: A study of Cool, Continental Environments...* was published two years later (1947). Since Taylor wrote about 2045 A.D., his perspective was probably regarded as more literary, possibly prophetic, than scientific. It was strongly criticized by professional peers (e.g., B. Kaye and D.W. Moodie, 1973:38-40), who claimed that from a macro-statistical view further development of the rural West should not be expected. Through technological change the rural West had peaked and expansion was over. Whatever its scientific demerits, the Taylor view of a new Canadian heartland in the West had ideological potential which the Alberta government recognized, for Alberta would be the new industrial center. How much impact this long-range view of the West as both rural and urban, agricultural and industrial, actually had on persons, agencies and policies during the fifties is a challenge to further study.

The conventional macro-statistical view of the rural West derives primarily from the *Census of Canada*. Census data were used by a variety of social scientists, educators, agriculturists, planners and officials to generate macro-knowledge needed for various purposes (e.g., Hanson, 1959; Card, 1960; Uhlman, 1961; Tyler, 1966). Probably the major statistical portrait was by Whyte (1966), a Manitoba sociologist who later moved to Carleton University. The following resumé of the macro-statistical West follows the Whyte lead.

A statistical view of the rural West from 1941 to 1971 is compressed in Table 2. For the 1950s it is seen that in terms of actual numbers of people the region as a whole had a population increase of 631,041 persons. However, the urban increase was 688,384, while the rural decrease was 57,347. In percentages, this was a 24.8 percent gain regionally, an urban gain of 60 percent, a rural loss of 4 percent. This was the decade when the West's total rural population changed from a majority to a minority, from 55.2 percent to 42.2 percent. However, when provincial and nonfarm rural-urban watershed in the 1940s, when the rural percentage fell from 55.9 in 1941 to 43.4 in 1951. A major trend in the fifties was the decline in the rural farm population from 28.2 to 18.6 percent by 1961, the lowest proportion of the three provinces. Further, by 1961, Manitoba's rural population was evenly divided between nonfarm and farm, unlike Alberta and Saskatchewan where farm populations were the larger.

TABLE 2

PRAIRIE PROVINCE RURAL-URBAN POPULATION, 1931-1971, BY PROVINCE[a]

PROVINCE	1931	1941	1951	1961	1971
MANITOBA					
Total Population	700,139	729,744	776,541	921,686	988,250
Urban	315,969	321,873	439,580	588,807	686,455
Rural	384,170	407,871	336,961	332,879	301,800
Percent Urban	45.1	44.1	56.6	63.8	69.5
" Rural	54.9	55.9	43.4	36.2	30.5
" NonFarm	18.3	21.7	15.2	17.6	17.3
" Farm	36.6	34.2	28.2	18.6	13.2
SASKATCHEWAN					
Total	921,785	895,992	831.728	925,181	926,240
Urban	290,905	295,146	252,470	398,091	490,630
Rural	630,880	600,846	579,258	527,090	435,610
Percent Urban	31.6	32.9	30.4	43.0	53.0
" Rural	68.4	67.1	69.6	57.0	47.0
" NonFarm	7.2	9.7	21.7	24.1	21.8
" Farm	61.2	57.4	47.9	32.9	25.2
ALBERTA					
Total	731,605	796,169	939,501	1,331,944	1,627,875
Urban	278,508	306,586	449,675	843,211	1,196,255
Rural	435,097	489,583	489,826	488,733	431,620
Percent Urban	38.1	38.5	47.9	63.3	73.5
" Rural	61.9	61.5	52.1	36.7	26.5
" NonFarm	10.6	12.3	15.9	15.2	12.0
" Farm	51.3	48.2	36.2	21.5	14.5
PRAIRIE PROVINCES					
Total	2,353,529	2,421,905	2,547,770	3,178,811	3,542,365
Urban	885,382	923,605	1,141,725	1,830,109	2,373,330
Rural	1,468,147	1,498,300	1,406,048	1,348,702	1,169,035
Percent Urban	37.6	38.1	44.8	57.8	67.0
" Rural	62.4	61.9	55.2	42.2	33.0
" NonFarm	11.6	14.5	17.6	18.2	16.1
" Farm	50.8	47.4	37.6	24.0	16.9

[a]Sources: Tyler (1966:317); 1971 *Census of Canada*, Vol. I., Table 10-2; 1971 *Census of Canada*, Vol.V (Part I), Table 2 and Table 5.

Saskatchewan remained a predominantly rural province in the 1950s, 69.6 percent in 1951, 57.0 percent in 1961. The Saskatchewan rural-urban watershed did not take place until the 1960s. Though the province had a growing nonfarm population in the 1950s, the greater growth had taken place in the preceding decade, when the proportion rose from 9.7 to 21.7 percent. In 1961 it was 24.1

percent. During the same twenty years, the fall in farm population was greater proportionately than the gain in nonfarm. In 1941 the farm population was 57.4 percent of the provincial total, in 1951 47.9 per cent, and by 1961 32.9 percent. At the end of the fifties, Saskatchewan still had the largest proportion of farmers of the three prairie provinces, approximately a third, the other two provinces a fifth.

Alberta's rural-urban watershed took place in the fifties when urban percentages soared to 63.3 in 1961 from 47.9 in 1951. The rural proportion fell from 52.1 to 36.7 percent, the largest provincial drop in the prairie region. The nonfarm population held steady at just over 15 percent. The farm population declined from 36.2 to 21.5 percent, paralleling the low percentage of farm population of Manitoba. From these provincial comparisons it is clear that the West was becoming increasingly less rural, but not evenly so. Manitoba and Alberta were leading the trend.

What was happening to other demographic characteristics of the rural West during rural decline? As reported by Whyte (1966:10-27) the rural population had a higher dependency ratio of children and elderly per 100 working-age adults than the urban, 84.6 compared to 61.2 in 1951, and 100 to 82.4 in 1961. While the rural dependency ratio was greater, the gap between rural and urban was narrowing. The sex ratio of males per 100 females was higher for the rural than the urban population, 118.3 compared to 96.1 in 1951, and 116.2 to 99.5 in 1961. Again a slight tendency toward reduced difference is noted. Throughout the decade the rural working-age population was proportionately lower than the urban, the children were more numerous and the over seventy about the same. The overall tendency for the 1950s was the moderate homogenization of the salient rural-urban differences of past decades.

Farm statistics are considered next. The most notable change was increasing farm size (Whyte, 1966:29-31). Between 1951 and 1961 average farm size increased from 498 to 584 acres, a gain of 86 acres per farm. This continued the trend of the 1940s when the decade gain was 93 acres per farm. The proportion of occupied farms decreased 16.1 percent in the 1940s, 15.4 percent in the fifties. In the fifties also, the owner-occupied farms decreased from 61 to 58 percent, the lowest owner-occupancy rate in rural Canada as a whole. Despite these trends, the West had 83 percent of its farms classified as "commercial," over $1200 per year in produce, the highest proportion of commercial farms in Canada. The West also had the lowest proportion of part-time farmers in the nation, 20 percent in 1951, 25 percent in 1961. Despite rural population decline in the 1950s, farming as a business seemed to be improving. Saskatchewan's bushels of wheat per acre and wheat production for the decade had never been as high (Archer, 1980:362-363).

What did these specific tendencies in the rural West reflect? Among other things they reflected improved roads and better transportation, more mechanization, and different farm-management patterns. They also reflected a growing practice of renting or leasing land to obtain a viable economic size of farm. Reflected also was migration of farm families to neighboring towns and of farm youth and young adults to urban areas for school and work (Saskatchewan Royal Commission...Report 7, 1956).

The institutional sector most visibly and publicly affected by declining rural population was education, and specifically the one-room country school. From 1936 to 1950 there had been a moderate decline in the number of one-room schools. In the 1950s the one-room school was phased out on a massive scale. It was reported (Whyte, 1966:70) that between 1950-54 one-room schools had decreased by 20.8 percent, between 1954 and 1957 by 18.4 percent, and between 1957 and 1960 by 38.4 percent. Between 1960 and 1963 the reduction was 21.2 percent. This passage of the one-room school had repercussions for teachers, who were generally underqualified and underpaid in relation to urban counterparts. Despite many strains in the educational system in the 1950s, there was evidence of educational gain for rural students. The proportion of 5-to-9 years olds in school increased by 4.9 percent, the 10-to-14s by 1 percent, the 15-to-19s by 18.3 percent, the 20-24s by 2.2 percent. By 1961 only the 20-24s were below the urban rate of attendance (Whyte, 1966:69-79). The West's response to rural change in the field of education is an invitation for a closer look at the social dynamics, to round out the macro-statistical perspective.

Social Dynamics of the Rural West

A case approach is adopted here to depict macro-level social dynamics in the rural West in the 1950s. The aim is to show by selected examples macro-level responses of contest, conflict, social movements, and institutional reform efforts, which transcended micro-level decision making at the family and local community level.

Case 1. The Problem of Agricultural Societies and the Class "C" Fair
In both Alberta and Saskatchewan the local agriculture societies and their annual fairs, regularly subsidized by provincial funds, were in a state of disorganization. In 1950 the Alberta Department of Agriculture disorganized twenty-two local agricultural societies by ministerial decree, leaving the total of forty-one on the records (Alberta Department of Agriculture, 1951:86-87). In Saskatchewan a special task force held hearings throughout the province for two years in an effort to assess ailing, dormant, disorganized agricultural societies and their Class C fairs. In 1950 they reported that the societies were "caught up in a swirl of changes" affecting all of rural life. Mechanization had displaced livestock, which were essential for local fairs. The declining rural population left fewer local leaders. When mechanized farmers and their families could travel easily 50 to 100 miles from home, their horizons shifted from the local community to a large district. The task force reluctantly concluded that the local agricultural societies and their fairs no longer had an "essential place," though they saw hope in regionalization of agricultural societies and of conferences to share experiences about rural problems and programs. In both provinces a major celebration of rural life, the Class C fair, was either over or rapidly disappearing.

Case 2. The Saskatchewan Royal Commission on Agriculture and Rural Life
In 1952 the Saskatchewan government appointed William B. Baker, rural sociologist and Dean of the School of Agriculture at the University of Saskatchewan to chair a six-member Commission to investigate basic changes and rural social problems in the Province. The Commission reported in 1955, the year of the

Province's golden anniversary. Its fifteen reports covered thoroughly farm economics, the quality of rural life, education, family life, service centers, transportation, finance and other matters. Many of the recommendations were acted upon. One important recommendation virtually extended the Commission process. In 1956 by Order-in-Council, the Saskatchewan Centre for Community Studies was established, with W. B. Baker as director. It was located on the University of Saskatchewan's Saskatoon campus. Its aim was to undertake applied research, leadership training and program development for the benefit of agencies and communities requesting its services.

The two Saskatchewan Cases show response to rural social change in a thoroughly liberal tradition, where research, discussion, education and volunteerism were emphasized. For those with more conservative or radical leanings this approach was threatening or inadequate. In the 1960s the politics of university and province, where differing ideological views prevailed, were a major factor in the phasing out of the Centre for Community Studies (Card, 1973:11).

Case 3. Alberta Town and Rural Planning

In 1953, the Alberta government, motivated by the post-Leduc growth in cities, and encouraged by farseeing civil servants, elected officials and town planners, brought in a revised Town and Rural Planning Act with provision for "interim development" control and urban-rural participation in planning bodies. During the decade, District Planning Commissions in Edmonton, Calgary, Red Deer, Medicine Hat, Grande Prairie, Camrose and Lethbridge were formed to deal with planning matters in the most populous parts of Alberta. The Department of Municipal Affairs provided for or facilitated planning services for the remainder of the Province. This thrust toward urban-rural participation in planning paralleled the growth of similar relationships in the provision of education and health services. At district and regional levels the tendency was to merge and to a degree equalize rural and urban in official decision making. Conflict was not eliminated, but working together became the norm.

Case 4. The Alberta Royal Commission on Edmonton and Calgary's Metropolitan Growth

If the preceding case illustrates dynamics of accommodation and cooperation, this one reflects overt competition and underlying conflict, not so much between rural and urban in any abstract sense, but in the concrete matter of who would control local taxable resources, Edmonton, or the adjoining Municipality where they were located. The Commission's recommendations for the expansion of Calgary by annexation were carried through. They were not in Edmonton. The dormitory community of Campbell town, later named Sherwood Park, remained unannexed, along with Refinery Row, the sought-after tax base, because of an adamantly opposed, country-led Municipality of Strathcona. Here the "rural" power of the M.D., despite its growing urbanization, combined with provincial reluctance to face costs, led to a durable "stand-off." Not only were the 1955 Royal Commission's annexation and compensation recommendations set aside, but also those of another unsuccessful Commission in the 1960s.

Case 5. The Alberta Royal Commission on Education
In 1957, the Alberta government appointed a Royal Commission on Education, headed by Senator Donald Cameron, a noted adult educator. In this decision they were influenced by the growing complexity of educational problems which appeared beyond professional and voluntary organization solutions, and by the example of other provinces who had recently completed or were starting their own royal commissions on education (Stevenson, 1970:396-403). The main thrusts of the Commission's recommendations regarding rural Alberta were equalized opportunities for all with respect to curriculum, facilities, teacher qualifications and support services at the school level, and at the provincial level, development of community colleges and improved agriculture colleges for rural Alberta. Ironically, the Commission generated more debate over the separate, dual system of education concept and the essentialist vs. progressive philosophies of education, than the concept of equality of educational opportunity through public schooling that it championed.

Case 6. The Manitoba Royal Commission on Education
This Commission, headed by Ronald McFarlane, a former Deputy Minister of Education in Manitoba, also was launched in 1957. Compared to the Cameron and Baker Commissions it was modest. Its recommendations also had rural needs in mind—larger administrative units, composite high schools, basic subjects, university-controlled teacher education and government grants to both public and parochial schools. As with the two other Commissions, education was to be a means of bringing rural people, with their surplus of youth, into the mainstream of urban life and opportunity as equals.

Case 7. Rural Consumer Strategies
The last case might be termed a mass response of the rural West to changing circumstances. Studies carried out from the 1940s into the 1960s repeatedly showed rural dwellers, especially in the more isolated and underdeveloped parts of the West, had a level of living considerably below their urban counterparts *(Card et al.,* 1963:229-234). Federal and provincial governments had studies and programs devoted to upgrading rural living. Cities by example and deliberate salesmanship propagandized their way of life. Rural people responded to these overwhelming cultural and economic pressures and their own sense of deprivation by ballot, credit, strategic migration and roving consumership in an effort to improve living standards.

During the decade, the proportion of rural households with running water increased from 10.8 to 36.1 percent, those with bath or shower from 7.2 to 28.1 percent, those with flush toilets from 5.4 to 22.3 percent, and those with a mechanical refrigerator from 16.7 to 74.8 percent (Whyte, 1966: 40-42; Beaman and D'Arcy, 1978). In 1961, rural households had the same proportion of passenger cars as did urban households, 73 percent, but not as may television sets, 54.7 percent compared to the urban 82.7 percent. Through various consumer strategies, aided by government programs, larger high schools, extension workers and the business community, the basic living standards of rural and urban residents were less differentiated in 1961 than in 1951. With this rise in rural living standards, especially in the more prosperous areas, the rural way of life began to be identified with poverty, especially in what remained of the "pioneer fringe," on the marginal agricultural lands, and in the northern areas of the West.

From these cases it is seen that changes in the rural West evoked strong public and private reactions, which included institutional modification and reform. The overall direction taken was not so much the improvement of the rural situation *per se* as it was the merging of rural with the urban. The rural West in the 1950s became more of what it had been from its start, an appendage to and an image of the urban world situated in its country location. It was already beyond a metropolis-hinterland relationship (Davis, 1971), nor was it hardly a symbiotic rural society in close relationship to an urban society (Sanders, 1977:149-152). The rural West was becoming an extension of the metropolis itself, connected by good roads, immersed in metropolitan electronic communication, bound to great shopping centers, linked to cities by highly relevant kin networks, and advocating education for the maximally interchangeable person.

The Rural Symbol System in Question

We turn from the macro-views of the rural West to a further consideration of the symbol system in the 1950s. With all the changes going on at the micro- and macro-levels, how were people on farms or in smaller communities talking about themselves? What was the saliency of the term "rural" for them during the decade? What was the locus of the rural symbol system in their society? These questions could conceivably be answered with some precision if an adequate research effort were made. Here they can be only briefly and tentatively explored.

How did rural people talk about themselves? Eighteen older Albertans who were on farms or in small communities were asked in March 1983, to talk about themselves. Here is a sample of responses, from Red Deer and Edmonton.

1. "We were just a farm district. In the 1950s we talked of being in the country. My children went to a large one-room school. I don't remember it ever being called a rural school. I was never aware of 'rural' and 'urban' until 1963 when I was married a second time." (Wife of a retired farmer).

2. "I never thought of rural, just being in the country. I never heard of urban till the last few years. All I ever went to was a rural school." (Retired farmer).

3. "I always thought of myself as a country person. Urban was a new term, since World War II." (Retired female).

4. "In the 1930s we were 'just on the farm.' In the 1950s we began to think of rural--rural gas, rural electricity, rural telephone lines, and rural cooperatives. The 4-H clubs put 'rural' on the map." (Retired farmer).

5. "I never knew what the word 'rural' meant until I left (my farm home) and came to university." (Former country teacher, female).

6. "The first time I got involved with 'rural', I had to ask what it meant. To me it was always the country. I never knew what rural and urban meant till I became an Ag student at the university after World War II." (Male, small town background, senior government official when interviewed).

The pattern of responses for all persons interviewed was the same. At the level of every-day life "rural" and "urban" were not household terms, for male or females. Their usage in the 1950s applied to services such as electricity , telephones, schools infrequently, and cooperatives. What comes through clearly is that "rural" was used on the receiving end by farmers, whose cues for its usage were provided by others. It was not a term representing a "deep structure" in their thought, nor was it a term for which they could be called the proprietors. Where then was the proprietary locus of the term? For whom was "rural" part of the "language game of power" (Collins, 1982:255-259)?

It was hypothesized that if there were proprietors of the term "rural" in Western society, the provincial departments of agriculture would be one set. With this in mind all Saskatchewan Department of Agriculture *Annual Reports* for the 1950s and samples of *Annual Reports* from Alberta and Manitoba were examined. Mostly the reports were about specific aspects of agriculture, but there were three areas of the work of these Departments where "rural" seemed structurally lodged. One was when the provincial department was involved with federal programs or agencies, such as the Prairie Rural Housing committee, working out of the Prairie Rural Research Centre at Winnipeg in 1951 (Alberta Department of Agriculture, 1951:89). Another was in connection with rural electrification or telephones. However, the dominant proprietors of "rural" were the agriculture extension services, for whom "rural youth clubs," " the rural family," or "the rural community" were key words for agriculture representatives and their supervisors, especially in Saskatchewan.

Another grouping with proprietary interest in "rural" were social scientists, among whom the writer must include himself (Card, 1964). A case in point is Jean Burnet's *Next-Year Country: A Study of Rural Social Organization.* Here "rural" is an indispensable adjective, an aggregative empirical referent for chapters on the rural household, rural village, and the problem of the rural community. There are other usages. They all represent the needs of a professional person communicating with a reading public, but not the language of rural people.

One of the symbolically important trends of the fifties, however, was the growing frequency with which "rural" was omitted or transformed. The Saskatchewan *Royal Commission on Agriculture and Rural Life* culminated its existence in the formation of the Centre for Community Studies, reflecting a shift from "rural" to "urban" anticipated earlier by Zimmerman (1938). A major transformation in the meaning of "rural" was its association with poverty both on the prairies and nationally. "Rural poverty" was linked with regional disparity and called for a different conceptualization. One response was the development of 68 Canadian regions, 288 functional "zones," and 471 subzones based on work pioneered by the federal Department of Defense Production (Camu, Sametz and Weeks, 1965:261-270). Here was a shift from "rural" to "regional" which carried into the 1960s, reflected in the operations of the Department of Regional Economic Expansion and ARDA, which minimized the term "rural." One prairie social scientist openly suggested replacing "rural" and "urban" with "regions" (Page, 1969:38).

The process of diminishing the rural symbol system took on momentum. Montana's Great Plains expert Carl Kraenzel (1955; 1978) talked of "sutland" and "yonland." Dialectician A.K. Davis, former Research Director at the Saskatchewan Centre for Community Studies (1968) favored "metropolis" and "hinterland." Uhlman (1959; 1961), a researcher for the Cameron Commission on Education in Alberta, urged the abandonment of the rural-urban differentiation in education. This was an underlying motif in not only the Cameron, but also the Baker and McFarlane Commission Reports. Sociologist Whyte, hailing from

Manitoba but writing at Carleton University (1966:99), claimed that rural life as ideology was outmoded and at odds with technology's rationalization requirements. He anticipated Saskatchewan critics of the rural municipality as a viable unit of local government, Richards (1977: 142-3) and Archer (1980:20-1). Influencing the diminution of the rural symbol-system in the Canadian West were more critical thrusts by American social scientists which were well-known north of the border, especially Dewey's (1960) article, "The Rural-Urban Continuum: Real but Relatively Unimportant," Copp, 1972 (quoted in Buttel and Newby, 1980:4) was even more emphatic: "There is no *rural* society and no *rural* economy. It is merely our analytic distinction, our rhetorical device."

Conclusion

What has been attempted in this paper is an exploratory, symbolic-interaction examination of the rural West in the 1950s. It has been shown that the West of settlement began without being "rural," and that it was symbolically created as rural over a time span extending into the 1950s. At the micro-level, many of the behaviors and decisions adding up to change were made in decades prior to 1950, and extended into the decades following. When aggregated to macro-level trends it was seen that "rural society" was receding in the three provinces, culminated by Saskatchewan crossing over from predominantly rural to urban in the 1960s. Macro-level responses to rural change were expressed through commissions. These sought to remove educational and other differences between rural and urban populations, which were becoming increasingly indistinguishable in level of living aspirations. As a symbol system, the "rural" West tended to be non-functional for country and small community people, but of direct use to those in a dominant power relationship to those on the land.

Two final questions need consideration. To what extent was the rural West of the 1950s created and maintained symbolically as a fiction (Whyte, 1966:99), as a reification of the dialogue of scholars, politicians and others? Is a better conceptual scheme needed to replace "rural" as a redundancy, and "rural-urban" as a misleading dichotomy?[6] To answer these questions will take more than research. Creative imagination will also be needed for the human development of persons regardless of spatial location. This task requires better theory and concepts (Marx, 1964: 364-365) for the time when "rural" becomes part of our archaeology of knowledge (Foucault in Sheridan: 1980: 91; Wood, 1975).

Acknowledgement

The writer is indebted to the librarians of Red Deer College, The University of Alberta, and Statistics Canada for source material, to persons in the Cardston and Red Deer areas for interview material, to colleagues at Red Deer College for conceptual clarification, and to Naomi Card for editorial assistance. The responsibility for the contents and perspectives used in this article rests solely with the writer.

Footnotes

1. Parts I and V are tentative explorations in the use of symbolic interaction and the sociology of knowledge as perspectives for seeing the rural West. The basic philosophical position implied is that the essence of social science, history and their applications to society building is art, not engineering or science, nor evolution, power struggle, or chance. This approach is not incongruent with Mandel's (1973:208) view of the prairies as a conceptual framework with many possibilities, and with a place always reserved for "ideas not yet present."

2. This original legend was inspired by a short account of "Rome before the Republic," by R.M. Oglivie (1980:245-8). There were pig farmers and salt deposits in the Tiber area. Hittite words were known over the Mediterranean region at that time.

3. The 1841 date needs further verification. It is mentioned in an 1861 report of an 1841 Canadian law (Avis, 1967:648).

4. The undocumented information in this paragraph comes from interviews remembered by the writer in a research traverse of the Prairie Provinces in the spring of 1950.

5. An important biographical work of a Cardston area resident with a remarkable career in the West is N. Eldon Tanner: His Life and Service (Durham:1981). This work is especially good in its depiction of micro-level decision making in the Cardston area up to the 1940s, and in the West on a large scale thereafter.

6. As Friedman (1978) has pointed out, there is a fundamental contradiction between city and country, which he attributed to two basically different approaches to social life, the organizational and the territorial. It is the present writer's view that this dialectical relationship, though persistent, is amenable to modification through the dynamic processes of exchange, maximizing human potential wherever found, synergism, and symbolic interaction in societal creation and adaptation. The creation of the West and its rural change, as has been shown here, tends to support this possibility.

References

Allen, Richard (ed.). A Region of the Mind: Interpreting the Western Canadian Plains. Regina: Canadian Plains Study Centre, University of Saskatchewan, 1973.

Archer, John H. Saskatchewan: A History. Saskatoon: Western Producer Prairie Books, 1980.

Archer, John H. "Some Reflections on the History of Saskatchewan: 1905-1980." In The New Provinces: Alberta and Saskatchewan, edited by Howard Palmer and Donald Smith. Vancouver: Tantalus, 1980, pp. 9-22.

Avis, Walter S. (ed.-in-chief). A Dictionary of Canadianisms on Historical Principles. Toronto: W.J. Gage Limited, 1967.

Beaman, Jay and Carl D'Arcy. "The Changing Saskatchewan Community." In Sociocultural Change Since 1950, edited by T. Lynn Smith and Mah Singh Das. New Delhi: Vikas Publishing House, 1978, pp. 7-35.

Burnet, Jean. Next-Year Country: A Study of Rural Social Organization in Alberta. Toronto: University of Toronto Press, 1951.

Buttel, Frederick H. and Howard Newby (eds.). Rural Sociology of the Advanced Societies: Critical Perspectives. Montclair, N.J.: Allanheld, Osmun and Company, 1980.

Camu, Pierre, E.P. Weeks and Z.W. Sametz. Economic Geography of Canada, with an Introduction to a 68-Region System. Toronto: Macmillan of Canada, 1968.

Card, B.Y. (ed.). Perspectives on Regions and Regionalism. Proceedings of the Tenth Annual Meeting of the Western Association of Sociology and Anthropology. Edmonton: University of Alberta Printing Services, 1969.

Card, B.Y. et al. School Achievement in Rural Alberta. Edmonton: The University of Alberta Bookstore, 1964.

Card, B.Y., G.K. Hirabayashi and C.L. French, *et al. The Métis in Alberta Society, with Special Reference to Social, Economic, and Cultural Factors Associated with Persistently High Tuberculosis Incidence.* A Report on Project A (1960-63), University of Alberta Committee for Social Research, for The Alberta Tuberculosis Association. Edmonton: The University of Alberta Bookstore, 1963.

Card, B.Y. *The Canadian Prairie Provinces from 1870 to 1950: A Sociological Introduction.* Toronto: J.M. Dent and Sons Ltd., 1960.

Collins, Randal. *Sociology Since Midcentury: Essays in Theory Cumulation.* New York: Academic Press, 1981.

Davis, Arthur K. "Canadian Society and History as Hinterland Versus Metropolis." In *Canadian Society: Pluralism, Change, and Conflict,* edited by Richard J. Ossenberg. Scarborough: Prentice-Hall of Canada. 1971, pp. 6-32.

Dewey, Richard. "The Rural Urban Continum: Real but Relatively Unimportant." *American Journal of Sociology* 66 (1960), pp. 60-6.

Durham, G. Homer. *N. Eldon Tanner: His Life and Service.* Salt Lake City: Deseret Book Company, 1981.

Erikson, Erik H. *Life and the Historical Moment.* New York: W.W. Norton and Company, Inc., 1975.

Ferkiss, Victor. "The Future of North America." *The Futurist* (August 1980), pp 17-24.

Friedman, John. "On the Contradictions between City and Country." *Comparative Urban Research* 6:1 (1978), pp. 5-41.

Garreau, Joel and Richard Furno. "A New Map of North America." In the *Washington Post,* reproduced by the *Futurist,* with permission, August 1980, p.17.

Hanson, Eric J. *Dynamic Decade: The Evolution and Effects of the Oil Industry in Alberta.* Toronto: McClelland and Stewart, 1958.

Hanson, Eric J. *Local Government in Alberta.* Toronto: McClelland and Stewart, 1956.

Hofstadter, Richard. *The Age of Reform: From Bryan to F.D.R.* New York: Alfred A. Knopf, and Random House, 1955.

Kaye, B. and D.W. Moodie. "Geographical Perspectives on the Canadian Plains." In *A Region of The Mind: Interpreting the Western Canadian Plains,* edited by Richard Allen. Regina: Canadian Plains Study Centre, 1972, pp. 17-46.

Kraenzel, Carl F. "Sovereignty at Bay for Man and Energy Resources in the Yonland--The price of Corporate Avarice." In *Sociocultural Change Since 1950,* edited by T. Lynn Smith and Man Singh Das. New Delhi: Vikas Publishing House, 1978, pp. 49-68.

Kraenzel, Carl F. *The Great Plains in Transition.* Norman: The University of Oklahoma Press, 1955.

Krotki, Karol J. "Availability and Retrieval of Regional Data in Canada." In *Perspectives on Regions and Regionalism,* edited by B.Y. Card. Edmonton: University of Alberta Printing Services, 1969, pp. 57-76.

Laskin, Richard. "Nonagricultural, Semiagricultural and Agricultural Service Centers." In *Rural Canada in Transition,* edited by Marc-Adelard Tremblay and Walton J. Anderson. Ottawa: Agricultural Research Council of Canada, 1966, pp. 114-77.

Laslett, Peter. *The World We Have Lost.* London: Methuen and Company Limited, 1965.

Lautt, M.L. "Sociology and the Canadian Plains." In *A Region of the Mind,* edited by Richard Allen. Regina: Canadian Plains Study Centre, University of Saskatchewan, 1973, pp. 125-51.

Mandel, Eli. "Images of Prairie Man." In *A Region of the Mind,* edited by Richard Allen. Regina: Canadian Plains Studies Centre, University of Saskatchewan, 1973, pp. 201-9.

Marx, Leo. *The Machine and the Garden: Technology and the Pastoral Ideal in America.* New York: Oxford University Press, 1964.

Mirkovic, Damir. *Dialectial and Sociological Thought.* St. Catherines, Ontario: Diliton Publications, 1980.

Oglivie, R.M. "Rome before the Republic." In *The Encyclopedia of Ancient Civilization*, edited by Arthur Cottrell. New York: Mayflower Books, 1980, pp. 245-8.

Owram, Doug. *Promise of Eden: The Canadian Expansionist Movement and the Idea of the West 1856-1900*. Toronto: University of Toronto Press, 1980.

Palmer, Howard and Donald Smith (eds.). *The New Provinces: Alberta and Saskatchewan, 1905-1980*. Vancouver: Tantalus Research, 1980.

Page, John S.J. "Government Administrative Divisions and Regional Administration." In *Perspectives on Regions and Regionalism*, edited by B.Y. Card. Edmonton: University of Alberta Printing Services, 1969, pp. 33-9.

Partridge, Eric. *Origins: A Short Etymological Dictionary of Modern English*. 4th Edition. London: Routledge and Kegan Paul, 1958, 1966.

Quandt, Jean B. *From the Small Town to the Great Community: The Social Thought of Progressive Intellectuals*. New Brunswick, New Jersey: Rutgers University Press, 1970.

Reiss, Alberta J., Jr. *Louis Wirth on Cities and Social Life*. Chicago: The University of Chicago Press, 1964.

Richards, J. Howard. "The Status of Saskatchewan vis-a-vis the Western Interior." In *The Canadian West*, edited by Henry C. Klassen. Calgary: University of Calgary/Comprint Publishing Company, 1977, pp. 127-46.

Sanders, Irwin T. *Rural Society*. Englewood Cliffs, New Jersey: Prentice-Hall, 1977.

Saskatchewan Royal Commission on Agriculture and Rural Life. *Report No. 6: Rural Education*. Regina: Queen's Printer, 1956.

Saskatchewan Royal Commission on Agriculture and Rural Life. *Report No. 7. Movement of Farm People*. Regina: Queen's Printer, 1956.

Saskatchewan Royal Commission on Agriculture and Rural Life. *Report No. 10. The Home and Family in Rural Saskatchewan*. Regina: Queen's Printer, 1956.

Sheridan, Alan. *Michel Foucault: The Will to Truth*. London: Tavistock Publication, 1980.

Smith, T. Lynn and Man Singh Das (eds.). *Sociocultural Change Since 1950* (In Honor of Carle C. Zimmerman Professor Emeritus, Harvard University). New Delhi: Vikas Publishing House PVT, 1978.

Stevenson, Hugh A. "Developing Public Education in Post-War Canada to 1960." In *Canadian Education: A History*, edited by J. Donald Wilson, Robert M. Stamp and Louis-Philippe Audet. Scarborough: Prentice-Hall of Canada, 1970, pp. 386-415.

Taylor, Griffith. *Canada: A Study of Cool Continental Environments and Their Effect on British and French Settlement*. London: Methuen and Company, 1947.

Taylor, Prof. Griffith. *Canada 100 Years from Now!* (As told to Dallas Bannister). Edmonton: Alberta Department of Trade and Industry, King's Printer, 1945.

Tremblay, Marc-Adelard and Walton J. Anderson. *Rural Canada in Transition: A multidimensional study of the impact of technology and urbanization on traditional society*. Ottawa: Agricultural Economics Research Council of Canada, 1966.

Tyler, Earl J. "The Farmer as a Social Class." In *Rural Canada in Transition*, edited by Marc-Adelard Tremblay and Walton J. Anderson. Ottawa: Agricultural Economics Research Council of Canada, 1966, pp. 228-340.

Donald R. Whyte. "Rural Canada in Transition." In *Rural Canada in Transition*, edited by Marc-Adelard Tremblay and Walton J. Anderson. Ottawa: Agricultural Economics Research Council of Canada, 1966, pp. 1-113.

Uhlman, Harold J. *Rural Alberta: Patterns of Change*. Monographs in Education No. 5. Edmonton: The University Advisory Committee on Educational Research, The University of Alberta, 1961.

Uhlman, Harold Joshua. "A Study of the Impact of Demographic and Economic Changes in Rural Alberta on the Financing of Education." Unpublished Ph.D. Dissertation, Division of Educational Administration, The University of Alberta, 1959.

Williams, Raymond. *Culture*. Glasgow: William Collins and Sons, Fontana edition, 1981.

Williams, Raymond. *Keywords: A Vocabulary of Culture and Social Change.* Glasgow: William Collins and Sons Ltd. Fontana/Croom Helm edition, 1976.

Wilson, J. Donald, Robert M. Stamp and Louis-Philippe Audet. *Canadian Education: A History.* Scarborough: Prentice-Hall of Canada, 1970.

Wirth, Louis. "Rural-Urban Differences." Talk Typescript in 1951, published as an article in *Community Life and Social Policy,* edited by Elizabeth Wirth Marvick and Albert J. Reiss, Jr. Chicago: University of Chicago Press, (1951) 1956, pp. 172-6.

Wirth, Louis. "Urbanism as a Way of Life." *American Journal of Sociology* 44 (July 1938), pp. 1-24.

Wood, Ron (ed.). *The Agrarian Myth in Canada.* Toronto: McClelland and Stewart, 1975.

Zimmerman, Carle C. and Garry M. Moneo. *The Prairie Community System.* Ottawa: Agricultural Economics Research Council of Canada, 1971.

Zimmerman, Carle C. *The Changing Community.* New York: Harper and Brothers, 1938.

MULTICULTURAL REGIONALISM:
TOWARD UNDERSTANDING THE CANADIAN WEST

Leo Driedger

If Canadians tend to see Quebec as a distinctive region, why not think of the Canadian West as a distinctive region also? The American South has often been viewed in a distinctive way as well, where longtime editor of *Social Forces*, Howard W. Odum (1936:8) proposed that "region is a tool for analysis," it is "a gestalt in which all factors are sought out and interpreted in their proper perspective and a framework for social planning." In this short space we obviously cannot pursue such a comprehensive study of the Canadian West, but if we wish to seriously probe western distinctiveness, we need to begin the search for some of the areas of axes of identity and alienation in the process of modernization.

Samuel E. Wallace (1981:431), in his presidential address to the Mid-South Sociological Society, says "the conception of The American south as a distinctive region was well established by 1800" (Hesseltine and Smiley, 1943). Wallace (1981:432) claims that "each section of the country has different needs, interests, ambitions, even different theories and forms of government, and in the South ethnicity and race relations played an important part." He goes on to say "the South is a region, a society, a set of institutions, an attitudinal stance, a people, a symbol, an idea" (Wallace, 1981:438). Wallace laments that sociological theories and models of the last two or three decades have been devoid of any sense of place, and he wonders whether that is why they downplayed regions. Region persists because people have a sense of place;—"to be identified with space means to treat space as part of the self—not simply something to use, abuse, destroy, deface, or pollute" (Wallace, 1981:438). In the deep South the sentiment and symbolism of the land is still important; I suggest in the Canadian West this sense of sanctified and hallowed ground is also emerging. Wallace claims "we lose explanatory power and we also lose history when we abandon the concept of regionalism....Functionalists occupied no space, so they also included neither past nor future in their models. Regionalism however, can develop only over time" (1981:439).

Ralph Matthews (1980:43-61) follows the same argument: "there has been virtually no sustained attempt to develop a 'regional sociology.' He is impressed with the overriding concern of Canadian sociologists with the nature of Canadian unity and identity. John Porter provides no analysis of the regional basis of the Canadian elite in his *Vertical Mosaic*; indeed he declares "it has never struck me that regions provide basic group identities in Canada" (1975:6). Indeed, in this view, modernization tends to obscure a sense of place. Matthews (1980) tries to outline the significance of regional considerations, he tries to prepare the ground for an explanation of regional differences, so as to try to develop a theoretical and analytical framework which is capable of providing insight into the various divisions in Canada. To understand the Canadian West, we propose to do the same.

For sociologists, however, regions are mostly containers in which important social, political and economic interaction and structure may be found. Richard

Simeon (1979:293) says, "We must first recognize that in no sense is region an explanatory variable: by itself it doesn't explain anything; nothing happens because of regionalism. If we find differences of any sort among regions, it remains for us to find out why they exist; regionalism is not an answer." Matthews adds, "We must delve more deeply into their nature and causes" (Matthews, 1980:50). Some studies (Driedger, 1977; Driedger, Vallee, and DeVries, 1981) have focused on language and ethnicity in the various Canadian regions. Ralph Matthews (1980:49, 51) in his call for a Canadian sociology of regionalism talks about "distinctive regional cultures," and suggests that at least socioeconomic, political and cultural (group identity) factors must be considered. Simeon and Elkins (1979) have recently formed a four-fold typology based on efficacy and trust in politics with significant differences in various regions of Canada. They controlled separately for social class, education, party identification, sex, age and size of community, and found that substantial regional differences remained after controls had been introduced (Simeon and Elkins, 1979:43). They conclude that there are "distinctive regional cultures."

There are western differences of consciousness and identity, we suggest. It tends to take a multicultural, multi-political, multi-religious form, because no ethnic group is in the majority, because there are a number of substantial ethnic groups (British, 49 percent; Germans 13 percent; Ukrainians, 7 percent; and French, 6 percent), and unlike other regions in the East, the West has always had a multi-variate socio-ethnic history.

Recently John Conway (1983) has pursued the regional theme in his *The West: The History of a Region in Confederation*, where he tries to make a case for a distinctive Canadian West much as Odum and Wallace did for the American South. He claims that central Canada views the West as a hinterland region to be exploited, and describes the ensuing resentment of Westerners regarding their place in confederation. Conway sees western protest movements as a range of coalitions between the Indians, Métis, and other ethnic groups seeking to find a niche in Canada. It is a regional history which clearly builds a case for a distinctive West.

To understand the Canadian West, we must first discuss the unique diverse western regional context, and then contrast this with the very different perspectives and assumptions of other regions. From the western view we must ask such questions as to why the East sent two armies to suppress Riel; why land claims with native Indians are not being dealt with; why the West produced so many new political parties (Progressive, Social Credit, CCF); why so many Westerners hate Trudeau and the Liberals; why there was so much western opposition to a charter of rights in the constitution. While factors of economic and political modernity are certainly relevant, I propose that traditional factors, of counter-modernity such as ethnicity and religion are also important.

The Perspectives of Dawson, Clark and Porter

The emphasis of three Canadian sociologists will illustrate the importance of a range of perspectives from Dawson's concern with concrete regional communities established in the West, to Porter's preoccupation on the other hand with macro-national trends of power and class, with less concern for regions. Clark tends to be concerned with both macro-historical trends, but usually elaborates upon the trends in distinct regions of Canada as well, placing him between Dawson and Porter.

Carl A. Dawson, a Canadian who studied theology and later took up sociology at the University of Chicago came to McGill in 1922. Soon, he spearheaded ecological research in using the Chicago School approach first in Montreal and later in western Canada. The Chicago School was deeply concerned with correcting social ills where research and social action was often combined, focusing on the region of Chicago. An urban ecological orientation developed where social space became an important factor in community studies. Dawson brought these concerns to McGill, hired the Canadian Everett Hughes (who also studied at Chicago), thereby bringing in large research grants, for the study of social pathology in Montreal. What is relevant here, is that soon Dawson himself and others also proceeded to study western Canada, leading eventually to the *Canadian Frontiers of Settlement* series published during the 1930s.

Dawson's *Group Settlement: Ethnic Communities in Western Canada* (1936), is a good example of his Chicago School approach. He examines the prairies as an ecological area into which a multitude of some thirty ethnic groups entered, establishing their many ethnic communities. He then selects five groups (the Doukhobors, Mennonites, Mormons, German Catholics and French-Canadians), and devotes the entire volume to various topics: their settlement, invasion and succession; means and modes of living; resistance to secularization; community building; establishment of organization; social adjustment and persistence. Dawson's emphasis on ethnicity and religion is similar to many other studies made by sociologists of the Chicago School, who sought to research the patterns of settlement, the forms of community organization, and the extent to which these new immigrants persisted or assimilated. The focus was on a variety of distinctive groups living first in rural segregated bloc settlements, and later converging upon emerging urban areas.

In contrast to Dawson's focus on groups and communities within regions, John Porter at Carleton University focused almost entirely on macroeconomic and political processes. In his classic *The Vertical Mosaic* (1965), his major focus was on an analysis of social class and power in Canada. He saw the structures of class and power concentrated among economic, political, educational, religious and communications elites who were represented most by White Anglo-Saxon Protestants located heavily in urban centers in southern Ontario. This economic and political stronghold in central Canada with its urban industrial concentration has become the power core, and the rest of Canada is seen as hinterland. The Canadian West, farthest away from the core, and most recently settled by Europeans, tends to be viewed as a region which provides opportunities for feeding the Ontario industrial complex with raw materials.

Porter's (1965) overriding concern with stratification, and the need for immigrant groups to forget their ethnic identities in favor of gaining better acceptance in the marketplace, is a more subtle form of anglo-conformity. He leaves the impression that status and power will sweep away all regional and ethnic distinctions. His intense focus on the power of the elite in economics and politics, fails to consider seriously regionalism and multiculturalism. After commenting on his writings on "binationalism which was the founding principle of confederation" he further reviews

> the ethnic structure of Canadian society and its relationship to binationalism which was the founding principle of confederation; the difficulty of imposing on that historic condition a quite different notion of multiculturalism; and some of the dangers and dilemmas of retaining ethnicity as a salient feature of any society. In fact...I come to reject it altogether because in the long run ethnicity only makes sense if we also seek to perpetuate endogamous descent groups. The great value placed on this primordial identity is reminiscent of the German romantic movement with its emphasis on volksgeist (Porter, 1979).

Porter tended to emphasize the overwhelming influence of technology and urbanization as the master trend which sweeps away all forms of ethnic differentiation before it. In Frank Vallee's (1981:641) review of "John Porter's Sociology and Ethnicity as Anachronism," he says "that there is no doubt that Porter would have rejoiced had ethnic differentiation disappeared altogether.... If the choice had to be made between the ideology of the melting pot and the mosaic, he made it clear he would choose the melting pot....What bothered Porter more than anything was that these group or collective rights were ascriptive, that is, determined by the categories into which one was born." In his *Vertical Mosaic* (1965) Porter argued that ethnicity was an impediment to upward social mobility, and he was concerned that all should have the maximum chance to better themselves socio-economically. He clearly opted for the forces of modernity.

Cultural pluralism, more evident in the Canadian West, tends to focus on countervailing forces such as "democracy" and "human justice" which preclude that all people are of equal worth and that all should have the freedom to choose their distinct quality of life. Whereas assimilationists envisioned disappearance of immigrant and racial groups, this theory suggests that there may be greater resistance to assimilate than had formerly been thought. In fact, the trend toward permissive differentiation seems to be set. In Canada we have accepted pluralist religious expressions, which in Europe during the Reformation were hardly tolerated. The same is now true of the political scene, where a diversity of political parties and ideologies exist and are accepted by society.

Multiculturalism in Canada is now also recognized federally, albeit ambiguously, and not without some resistance. In Canada, the large French population (29 percent in 1971) highly concentrated in Quebec, has always made up a very substantial tile in the mosaic, which has not melted, nor has it assimilated into the Anglo-Canadian stream. Pluralists would say that the Native peoples of Canada isolated in Canada's northlands represent more tiles in the mosaic which have not disappeared. Canada's Blacks, Jews, Hutterites, Doukhobors, Italians and many other groups such as the Ukrainians and Germans in bloc settlements in the prairies tend to look more like patches in a highly differentiated quilt, than a homogeneous ethnic blend. Canada's original Natives, dominant charter groups, and a relatively open immigration policy seem to have contributed to a differentiated country more like Belgium or Switzerland than that of either of our most influential neighbors, Britain and the United States. Multiculturalism is especially an important part of the Canadian West.

There is considerable evidence that in the Canadian West the regional, community and group concerns presented by Dawson, as well as the macropolitical and macroeconomic powers in the larger Canadian context, are both relevant for a study of the Canadian West. S.D. Clark who grew up in the Canadian West, and did his major studies and work in the East (McGill, Toronto) in history, sociology and political science, was concerned with both of these major contrasting emphasis (Hiller, 1982). His historical and sociological orientation tends to deal with Chicago School concerns similar to those of Dawson especially in his earlier years, while later he focused increasingly on macro-urbanization trends, while still concerned with questions like urban poverty.

Like Dawson, S.D. Clark (1976) traces many more of the historical, regional, ethnic, religious and urban factors which have shaped different parts of Canada. Clark's approach is more pluralist when he says:

> There is nothing in society that can be fully understood except in relation to how the society developed....In a word, Canadian Society can be understood only if viewed within an historical perspective.

This historical approach opens the way for not one dominant unified end, but a multitude of various strands which together with their many beginnings, processes and ends, make up a heterogeneous patchwork or mosaic, which is quite different than the homogeneous end of anglo-conformity or franco-formity.

Clark's early concern with a study of religion, especially in his *Church and Sect in Canada* (1948), focused on the various regions of Canada such as the Great Awakening and revival in Nova Scotia and the Maritimes, the conflict of church and sect in various parts of Canada, new frontiers like the West and emerging new sects, the rise of the territorial church, emerging urban churches and modern communities. Clark was interested in both specific communities and their histories, as well as the larger global changes over time as illustrated in his *Urbanism and the Changing Canadian Society* (1961), and *The Developing Canadian Society* (1962). This concern for both specific and larger trends continued in his urban studies related to suburbia (1966), multiculturalism (1976) and the urban poor (1978).

The point of this discussion of the perspectives of Dawson, Clark and Porter is that to understand the Canadian West within confederation, we must see it as a distinct region with its unique history, population, communities and aspirations; while at the same time we recognize that the West is only part of a large demographic, ecological, demographic, political and economic whole where power relations do exist and operate. To do this, we shall introduce five axes of relationships between the West and other regions of North America to show that the many demographic, political, economic, ethnic and religious factors play differential roles depending on the region in question. While modernization factors such as political and economic integration may be dominant in some of these axes, counter-modernization factors such as territory, ethnicity and religion may be more important in other axes. Our task is to show that the West is cradled and surrounded by a demographic, ecological, cultural and social milieu very different from that of the other regions of Canada. We hypothesize that this milieu has also created different attitudes, aspirations and perspectives which make it a distinctive multicultural region seeking to deal with modern technological, industrial, urban and bureaucratic change.

The Canadian West in the Continental Regional Network

Thus far we have argued that the Canadian West is a unique region in North America, and we assume that it will also have distinctive aspirations often at variance or in conflict with populations of other regions. In Figure 1 we have isolated at least five other ecological areas, and/or constellations, which greatly affect The Canadian West. The European-Francophone, the Multicultural-Bi and Bi and the New West-British Elite axes illustrate at least some of the potential regions or power blocs with which the Canadian West could come into conflict with when they thwart western goals and aspirations. We propose that in some cases the sources of alienation and conflict are more related to Chicago School questions of community, ethnicity and religion of a counter-modernity variety, while other axes of relationships are more related to economic and political power relationships as Porter suggested. The pattern or mix of factors that each axis represents varies considerably, and we propose that with respect to power, the West is more often on the subordinate end of the power relationship, although not always. We propose that lack of understanding of western aspirations on the part of others, and lack of western power to change things, tends to create alienation.

FIGURE 1

Western regionalism and the impact of five other regional axes.

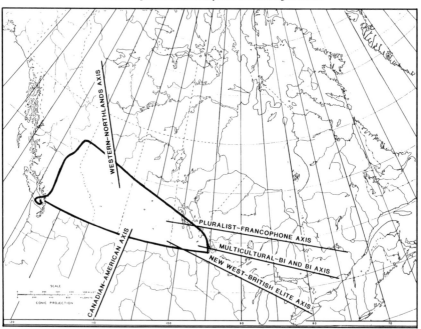

European-Native Axis

The Canadian northlands, represent 80 percent of Canada's territory although the population and political power in the North is small. The majority of the population are native Indians, many of them still in the food-gathering stage. Only 112 years ago, all of the West was still the domain of the Hudson's Bay company where fur-trading was king. The West is closer in time, space and development to the native northlands than any other region in Canada. Indian Reserves dot the West, Native and European-origin children go to school together, many from the North come south into western cities. These natives are multilingual, multicultural, and classified as mongoloid racially.

Westerners, now dominantly of many European origins, are intensely aware of their multicultural neighbors to the north. They tend to view this relationship in somewhat contradictory ways. On the one hand they share multicultural aspirations, because they too support a variety of cultural expressions, they too wish to gain a greater control of their resources and their destiny. On the other hand, Westerners see the northlands as a hinterland of raw materials which can be exploited to benefit the industrial urban needs. Like Northerners they feel Easterners do not understand their multicultural aspirations; and like Easterners, they would like to exploit the north so as to gain greater power in Confederation.

While economics and politics are likely the major factors why land claims have not yet been settled in the Northlands territory of the Dene, I suspect that the fact that they are a powerless minority, of non-European origin, non-caucasian, and perceived as primitive food-gathers is also important. The eleven treaties made with native Indians in western Canada recognize aboriginal rights to their land. However, plans for extraction of oil and minerals go on, despite the protests of natives. Westerners (especially in Alberta), see the northlands as opportunities for economic expansion, but they are often frustrated by Ottawa, where the control of native treaty rights and the Northwest territories is located.

But the northlands also pose a threat. Melling (1967) has shown that many in western cities on the northlands fringe (such as Prince Rupert, Prince Albert and Kenora) which are fairly small, surrounded by large native populations, also perceive these natives as a threat to the white urban populations. Larger cities such as Victoria, Vancouver, Edmonton, Saskatoon, and Winnipeg already have substantial native populations in their ghetto areas. Although economic and political factors are clearly operating, ethnicity seems a more plausible reason why, for example, all four western premiers were against entrenching a bill of rights in the constitution. Data of course need to be collected to test this hypothesis. At the least, economic and political factors cannot be assumed as the only ones which are operating.

It is difficult to know whether the desire to exploit the northland economically, and the close contact of Westerners with natives, is responsible for the negative attitudes of Westerners toward Canadian Indians. Berry et al. (1976:109, 294) found that Canadians in the prairies and British Columbia claimed that Native Indians were better known to them, but less similar to themselves, and their overall evaluation was more negative than that of respondents in Ontario, Quebec and the Atlantic regions. Driedger et al. (1977, 1981) also found in Winnipeg, for example, that university and high school students (two samples), wished to maintain the greatest social distance from Native Indians and the Inuit; only one-fifth were willing to consider marrying them.

We propose that the western-northlands axis provides opportunities for the West to exploit the northland economically, but other jurisdictions such as the United States and Ottawa often set up barriers which make modernization and industrial enterprise in the North more difficult and frustrating. At the same time, traditional ideologies concerned with justice, and forces of ethnic identification ask about the ethics and morality of exploiting the North before land claims have been settled. These countervailing forces slow technological progress and create apparent conflict between traditional values and modernization.

Canadian-American Axis

While the West is dominant in the western-northlands axis the reverse is true for the Canadian-American axis. The industrial giant to the south with its political power, economic capital and communication networks sees the Canadian West as a hinterland of raw resources to be exploited.

In 1869 when Louis Riel tried to get a hearing from the two-year-old Canadian confederation of four tiny provinces in the east, they were too preoccupied with their eastern concerns to pay much attention. Riel was concerned because the Red River settlement of 10,000 inhabitants was developing stronger transportation ties between Fort Garry and St. Paul to the south. "In 1865 on one trip alone, Norbert Welsh travelled with a train of 300 carts; and by 1869 some 2,500 Red River carts lunged and screeched their ungreased way behind the ponderous ox-teams that hauled them along the road to St. Paul" (Stanley, 1963). Riel's negotiations for provincial status in the Canadian confederation, the right to send representatives to Parliament, and a rail link with the East, did not take place until after the first Canadian army was sent to the West. The French-Métis Riel was forced to become an exile in the United States when many now agree that he should have become the first premier of the West (Manitoba). Twice Riel was elected to represent the Manitoba Provencher riding in Ottawa, but was prevented from occupying his seat. Easterners were too preoccupied with their French-English ethnic axis, to deal with western Canadian-American, north-south tendencies which were in the making. The West was greatly neglected.

Three of the western provinces share the great prairie plains with the American states to the south. There is no physical barrier such as the Great Lakes of Ontario, the northeastern forest separating Quebec, and the ocean separating the Atlantic region. The prairies on both sides of the border were considered the wild hinterlands to be settled by their respective easterners. Later, farmers from northern, central and eastern Europe of many cultures broke sod, and settled on both sides of the border, often in bloc communities (Dawson, 1934, 1936, 1940; Anderson, 1977). Similar affinities exist between Canadian and American residents on the Pacific coast. Indeed, many settlements, multi-ethnic compositions, types of occupations are much more similar than their eastern affinities.

Even today these natural tendencies continue. Manitoba water and hydro power flow south to Minnesota; Saskatchewan potash is used by American farmers in the Dakotas, Montana and Kansas; Alberta oil runs engines on both sides of the border; and lumber, coal, water, and fish flow along the Pacific coastal regions. Thus, these populations of the Canadian and American West feel a great deal of kinship, potential for cooperation, and communication north and south. Although economics and politics are intricately bound up in this north-south exchange, American oil companies and mining conglomerates pose an unbalanced labor and capital power relationship which often threatens western industrial independence and self-sufficiency.

It is more difficult to document specific attitudes of western Canadians toward Americans; we are aware only of a few social-distance studies. Card, Hirabayashi and French (1963:361) report that University of Alberta students in 1961 ranking twenty-three ethnic groups, ranked the Canadians first (social distance quotient of 1.19) and Americans second (1.48). These same students ranked Eskimos (2.90), Canadian Indians (3.03) and Métis (3.14) last, which supports our hypothesis of negative attitudes in the previous section. Card, Hirabayashi and French (1963:361) also report results of a second 1962 sample of north-east Edmonton where Americans rank first (1.12 social distance quotient), and Canadian second (1.20) out of twenty-four groups compared. Two Manitoba social distance samples reported by Driedger and Peters (1977:169) and Driedger and Mezoff (1980:8) of University of Manitoba and Manitoba highschool students respectively, show that students are more willing to marry Americans (78 and 75 percent), than any of the other thirty groups considered. More research is needed to compare western Canadian attitudes toward Americans with those of eastern Canadians. Edgar Friedenberg (1978: 135-146), an American writing from Halifax, complains about negative attitudes of Canadians toward Americans in the East. Canadians are clearly underdogs in most of these Canadian-American relationships, and this powerlessness may often result in alienation.

Pluralist-Francophone Axis

French and English fur traders intermarried with the Indians so that by 1871, there were "5,420 French-speaking half-breeds, 4,080 English-speaking half-breeds, and 1,600 white settlers" in the Red River settlement (Stanley, 1963). Had the French-Métis Louis Riel become the first premier of Manitoba, the province might have become bilingual and bicultural. The provincial legislature begun in 1870 was officially bilingual. This, however, changed very quickly, so that the French declined both in numbers and power soon thereafter. By 1971 the 86,500 French-origin Manitobans represented only 8.8 percent of the population in the province. The 46,200 French residents in Winnipeg, heavily concentrated in St. Boniface, the largest French community in the West, represent only 8.6 percent of metropolitan Winnipeg. The St. Boniface French Roman Catholic archdiocese at one time covered all of southern Manitoba, northern Minnesota, and parts of eastern Saskatchewan and western Ontario. Now it is confined to one part of Winnipeg. Elsewhere in the West, the French represent even smaller proportions of the population. They rank fourth, after the British, Germans and Ukrainians. Westerners see the French (6 percent) as one of many other ethnic groups in the region. More are unofficially bilingual (English and their ethnic tongue), than officially bilingual (English and French).

In the Canadian West where the French are one of many groups, there is a reluctance to give the French special status. It does not seem fair that the French (fourth largest and 6 percent) should receive privileges while the Germans and

Ukrainians, for example, do not. Except for the Fort Garry Red River settlement where the British and French first came, many ethnic groups opened up the West together, beginning more than 100 years ago. Thus, Westerners tend to think that the French status that Quebekers are fighting for may apply to Quebec, but not to the West. Many Westerners resent the recent imposition of official French status in the West, because historically it does not apply to them. It may seem logical in the St. Lawrence valley region where the French have built a society for more than 350 years, but western historical, cultural, linguistic and ethnic history is very different.

These negative attitudes are reflected in recent research (Berry, et al. (1976:109, 293); Westerners rank French Canadians less similar to themselves than respondents of the other regions, and in overall evaluations, Westerners again rate French Canadians much lower. According to Berry et al. (1976:293-295) these attitudes seem to be reciprocal; Quebekers judge immigrants in general, and other ethnic groups such as Germans, Italians, Ukrainians, Jews and Chinese less favorably than respondents of other regions. Westerners seem to downplay the status of French Canadians, and Quebekers tend to down play the desirability of new immigrants and multiculturalism.

Thus, Westerners find it difficult to rally to the French cause which seems far away. The pluralist West, influenced by the native northlands axis, and the American axis to the south, views the battle of the status of the French in Canada as one to be solved by the historical Ontario-Quebec power axis, viewed in the West to a large extent as Anglo-French. The new Progressive, Social Credit, and CCF parties which sprang up in the West were several political attempts at getting a hearing. While many of their complaints were economic and political, a case can be made that ethnicity was also important—the ethnically pluralist West versus the monolithic British and French in the East.

Most puzzling of all, is why the four western premiers were recently so adamantly opposed to entrenchment of a bill of rights in the constitution. Many of these belong to the same party as John Diefenbaker, who gave Canada it first declaration of human rights. Was it because of the entrenchment of French bilingual and cultural rights? Were they afraid that both the French and the native Indians in Canada, would gain legal rights which the provinces (especially Westerners), do not wish to grant? This hypothesis needs more research for these are certainly minority and ethnic questions.

Multicultural-Bi and Bi Axis

Table 1 shows that the three prairie provinces, are the only provinces where one of the charter groups are not a majority; the French are a majority in Quebec, and the British a majority in the other six provinces. While the British are somewhat less than 50 percent in the West, the Germans (13 percent), Ukrainians (7 percent), and French (6 percent) make up about one-fourth, and the remaining one-fourth is comprised of members of tens of other ethnic groups. The West is definitely the most multicultural area in the country.

When the Royal Commission on Bilingualism and Biculturalism, submitted its report, it was Jaroslav Rudnyckyj, a Ukrainian from the West, who filed a minority report, calling for more lingual and cultural rights for "other" ethnic groups. Indeed, the strong multicultural pressures from the West, resulted in publication of a fourth volume on *The Cultural Contribution of the Other Ethnic Groups* (1970), which originally had not been envisioned.

TABLE 1

PERCENTAGE COMPOSITION OF THE POPULATION BY EHTNIC ORIGINS FOR PROVINCE OF RESIDENCE, CANADA: 1901 AND 1971

Ethnic	Origin	Total	Nfld.	P.E.I.	N.S.	N.B.	Que.	Ont.	Man.	Sask.	Alta.	B.C.
1901	British	57.0		85.1	78.1	71.1	17.6	79.3	64.4	43.9	47.8	59.6
	French	30.7		13.4	9.8	24.2	80.2	7.3	6.3	2.9	6.2	2.6
	Other	12.3		1.5	12.0	4.1	2.2	13.4	29.4	53.2	46.0	37.9
Total:		100.0		100.0	100.0	100.0	100.0	100.0	100.0	100.0	100.0	100.0
1971	British	44.6	93.8	82.7	77.5	57.6	10.6	59.4	41.9	42.1	46.8	57.9
	French	28.7	3.0	13.7	10.2	37.0	79.0	9.6	8.8	6.1	5.8	4.4
	Other	26.7	3.3	3.6	12.3	5.3	10.4	31.0	49.3	51.8	47.4	37.7
	German	6.1	0.5	0.9	5.2	1.3	0.9	6.2	12.5	19.4	14.2	9.1
	Dutch	2.0	0.1	1.1	1.9	0.8	0.2	2.7	3.6	2.1	3.6	3.2
	Scandinavian	1.8	0.2	0.2	0.5	0.6	0.1	0.8	3.6	6.4	6.0	5.1
	Polish	1.5	0.1	0.1	0.4	0.1	0.4	1.9	4.3	2.9	2.7	1.4
	Russian	0.3	0.0	0.0	0.0	0.0	0.1	0.2	0.4	1.1	0.6	1.1
	Ukrainian	2.7	0.0	0.1	0.3	0.1	0.3	2.1	11.6	0.3	8.3	2.8
	Italian	3.4	0.1	0.1	0.5	0.2	2.8	6.0	1.1	0.3	1.5	2.5
	Jewish	1.4	0.1	0.1	0.3	0.2	1.9	1.8	2.0	0.2	0.4	0.6
	Other Europe	3.9	0.2	0.2	0.8	0.4	2.0	6.1	3.8	4.1	4.1	4.5
	Asiatic	1.3	0.3	0.3	0.6	0.4	0.7	1.5	1.0	0.8	1.6	3.6
	Other & N.S.	2.4	1.7	0.5	1.8	1.2	1.0	1.9	5.6	5.2	4.2	3.9
Total:		100.0	100.0	100.0	100.0	100.0	100.0	100.0	100.0	100.0	100.0	100.0

Source: Dominion Bureau of Statistics, *Census of Canada*, 1921, Vol. 1, Ottawa: The King's Printer, 1924, Table 23. Statistics Canada, 1971 *Census of Canada*, Bulletin 1.3-2, Ottawa: Information Canada, 1973, Table 3.

Official bilingualism and biculturalism did not sell well in the West, so that by the early seventies, Pierre Trudeau called for a multicultural Canada in a bilingual framework. This also seemed to be the recommendation of the Royal Commission on Canadian Unity which came to see that in the West residents were much more unofficially bilingual than officially bilingual (Driedger, Vallee, deVries, 1981), and were multicultural with a strong representation from the British, and only weak representation by the French.

During the past decade, Pierre Trudeau and the Liberal party have pushed for greater representation of French Canadians in high places, and for official bilingualism, for they have to counter French separatism in Quebec. It is difficult to say to what extent the drive for bilingualism by Trudeau and many of his French cabinet members (Chrétien, Pepin, Lalonde), is partly the cause of western alienation. Further research is required to test the hypothesis that Ottawa symbolizes bilingualism, and the English-French central power axis which Westerners increasingly abhor. How else can one explain the great hatred of many for Trudeau? French Canadian politicians such as Jean Chrétien formerly in charge of constitutional change (where French has become entrenched); Lalonde formerly in charge of oil policy in Canada (greatly affecting Alberta and Saskatchewan); and Pepin formerly in charge of transportation which deeply effects western farmers (Crow rates) must be viewed as additional eastern power symbols which fan western alienation. I propose that the ethnic factor is as important as the economic and political factors. To what extent does the multicultural West see itself fighting the two charter groups represented by the French-British axis in Ontario and Quebec, who are perceived as promoting Eastern interests (including bilingualism and biculturalism) and which the West does not share?

Berry et al., (1977:94-99) show that the Anglo-celts and French Canadians view each other more favorably than they view the rest. Both the Anglo-celts and the French Canadians thought English Canadians would be weaker as a result of multiculturalism, yet the other ethnic respondents did not share this pessimistic view (Berry et al., 1976:157). Interestingly the French Canadians thought multiculturalism would also weaken their cause, but the others, including the Anglocelts, did not share this view. On the other hand, other ethnics favored third language broadcasting and teaching more than the charter groups, and the Anglophone other ethnics were least in support of teaching more French. It is data such as this which suggests that western Canadians support multiculturalism more, and agree less with the bilingualism and biculturalism which Ottawa is promoting. These are clearly ethnic factors which have aggravated relations along the multicultural-bicultural western-Ottawa axis.

New West-British Elite Axis

John Porter (1965) has clearly shown that the economic and power elite are heavily Anglo-Celtic, and that they are located strongly in southern Ontario. We do not contest this finding. It will be more difficult to argue the importance of the ethnic factor in the New West-British Elite Axis. At first glance, the battle between Alberta and Ontario, between Lougheed and Davis, is an obvious economic power play. The old urban industrial Ontario does not wish to surrender any of its economic advantages. This certainly is one major factor. Ontario is 82.4 percent urban (1971), has twenty of the forty-five largest cities and nine of the twenty-two major metropolitan centers. Toronto is now the largest center in Canada, representing one-fourth of Canada's total metropolitan population in Canada. Kalbach (1981:23) shows that the share of the GNP is shifting toward the West, but only very slowly. While predictions are that the West's share of the GNP will increase from 34.5 percent in 1981 to 38 percent in 1990, Ontario will decline only from 36.8 to 34.7 percent in 1990. Economic advantages neither shift very easily nor very fast.

The importance of ethnicity in the fight between the New West and Ontario's British elite is more subtle. First of all, as a majority population in the past, and as a large plurality today, British Canadians have not been defined as an ethnic group. British conquests of the French in eastern Canada, speaking the English language, loyalty to the Queen, and the BNA act, are not interpreted as "British" ethnic loyalty; these are defined as "Canadian" issues! Berry et al., (1976:36-38) and Driedger et al. (1982) found that when given a choice of identity (British, hyphenated or Canadian), 81 percent of the British respondents in their sample preferred the "Canadian" category.

I would predict, however, that the British population in the West is in many respects quite different from southern Ontario's Empire Loyalist core which has greatly influenced the whole. Western Canadians of British origin have been moulded earlier by a multi-ethnic milieu in the West. British-Canadians were deeply involved in forming the Progressive, Social Credit and CCF parties in the West to counter-balance eastern economic power then largely in the hands of the British in southern Ontario.

Although Porter (1965) has clearly shown the dominance of the British in the economic, political, educational and religious elite, I propose that southern Ontario is a modernity model for the West to which many aspire. Economically, Ontario is the industrial heartland of Canada, and provincial governments such as Alberta especially seek to counterbalance some of that economic power with oil power. And to some extent, until the recent downturn, Alberta became a visible industrial symbol of economic success with its low taxes, low unemployment, highest urban growth (Calgary and Edmonton), frantic new construction, and general prosperity. However, Ontario is also an economic threat to such western industrialization, and is often seen as a competitor, if not an enemy, despite their respective conservative provincial governments (raising oil prices, abolishing the Crow Rates, etc.). With over one-third of the population of Canada, Ontario also becomes a political threat although, fortunately for the West, its political diversity is not the uniform power bloc as is Quebec's liberal federal representation. Ontario in the New West-British Elite axis, seems to represent the ideal model of modernity, but it also represents an economic and political threat which posits a dialectic fraught with potential frustration and alienation.

Conclusion

We have suggested that the Canadian West is a unique region in confederation which has recently entered the processes of modernization, urbanization, and industrialization, with its accompanying secular and bureaucratic tendencies. The insecurities of change bring with it conflict, frustration, identity crises and alienation. There is considerable vacillation between holding on to some of the best of the traditional past, and exploring the opportunities of industrial modernity as evidenced by the circulation of conservative and socialist governments, the pluralist versus assimilationist ethnic identification, and the resurgence of fundamentalist religions, sects and cults.

The reasons for western alienation are more difficult to find. However, we examined five linkages of the Canadian West with other regions to the north, south and east. The western-northlands axis offers the West opportunities for economic dominance and exploitation, but the political ties of the northlands are with Ottawa so these power opportunities are often frustrated. At the same time the West feels ties of kinship with the native ethnic aspirations of the peoples of the north for greater justice and independence. The American giant to the south provides the Canadian West an opportunity to benefit from American economic needs for petroleum, fresh water, mining and forest products, as well as opportunities for offsetting eastern Canadian political power with American political pressures for economic opportunities. The multicultural-francophone axis, illustrates the potency of Franco-ethnic power which often frustrates western multicultural aspirations politically. The southern Ontario economic elite could act as mentors for the industrialization and modernization of the West, but its industrial power tends to generate more fears and potential for conflict than assurances. In many ways Ottawa is the political giant which western provinces see as their dominant enemy which increasingly infringes on the western regional political domains of the four provinces.

We conclude that the Canadian West has emerged as a regional identity, with social, political and economic distinctives which act as a counter-force or antithesis to the eastern power blocs which create much real and potential conflict. The West is a region, a society, a set of institutions, an attitudinal stance, a people, a symbol, an idea as Wallace suggested for the American South.

We also suggest that the macroeconomic and political power struggles between the West and Ottawa, Ontario, and the Americans are perhaps the major factor in these conflictual power relationships as John Porter suggested. The West has different needs, interests, ambitions, even different theories and forms of government. At the same time, this multicultural region with its many ethnic, religious, and political groups and communities, contains a special social mix which makes it unique in Canada, as the studies of Dawson and Clark would suggest.

The recent emergence of the West as an identifiable region due to interprovincial migration, increased urbanization and industrialization, and a sense of place in the political structures of confederation, has left a gap between what the West feels it deserves, and what the rest of Canada is willing to give. In addition there are internal conflicts as to where modernization will lead, resulting in a dialectic between traditional and modern alternatives. Alienation and frustration are often the result.

References

Anderson, Alan B. ''Ethnic Identity in Saskatchewan Bloc Settlements: A Sociological Appraisal.'' In *The Settlement of the West*, edited by Howard Palmer. Calgary: Comprint/University of Calgary, 1977.

Berry, John W., Rudolf Kalin and Donald W. Taylor. *Multiculturalism and Ethnic Attitudes in Canada*. Ottawa: Supply and Services Canada, 1977.

Card, B.Y., G.K. Hirabayashi and C.L. French. *The Métis in Alberta Society*. Edmonton: University of Alberta Committee for Social Research, 1963.

Clark, S.D. *Church and Sect in Canada*. Toronto: University of Toronto Press, 1948.

Clark, S.D. *Urbanism and the Changing Canadian Society*. Toronto: University of Toronto Press, 1961.

Clark, S.D. *The Developing Canadian Community*. Toronto: University of Toronto Press, 1962.

Clark, S.D. *The Suburban Society*. Toronto: University of Toronto Press, 1966.

Clark, S.D. *Canadian Society in Historical Perspective*. Toronto: McGraw-Hill Ryerson, 1976.

Clark, S.D. *The Canadian Society and the Issue of Multiculturalism*. Saskatoon: University of Saskatchewan Sorokin Publications, 1976.

Clark, S.D. *The New Urban Poor*. Toronto: McGraw-Hill Ryerson, 1978.

Census Canada. *Bulletin 1.3-2*. Ottawa: Information Canada, 1973.

Conway, John E. *The West: The History of a Region in Confederation.* Toronto: James Lorimer Publishers, 1983.

Dawson, C.A. *Settlement of the Peace River Country: A Study of a Pioneer Area.* Toronto: Macmillan of Canada, 1934.

Dawson, C.A. *Group Settlement: Ethnic Communities in Canada.* Toronto: Macmillan of Canada, 1936.

Dawson, C.A. *Pioneering in the Prairie Provinces: The Social Side of the Settlement Process.* Toronto: Macmillan of Canada, 1940.

Driedger, Leo. "Structural, Social and Individual Factors in Language Maintenance in Canada." In *The Individual, Language and Society in Canada,* edited by W.H. Coons, Donald W. Taylor and Marc-Adelard Tremblay. Ottawa: The Canada Council, 1977.

Driedger, Leo. "Maintenance of Urban Ethnic Boundaries: The French in St. Boniface." *Sociological Quarterly* 20 (1979), pp. 89-108.

Driedger, Leo and Richard A. Mezoff. "Ethnic Prejudice and Discrimination in Winnipeg High Schools." *Canadian Journal of Sociology* 6 (1980), pp. 1-17.

Driedger, Leo and Jacob Peters. "Identity and Social Distance: Towards Understanding Simmel's "The Stranger." *Canadian Review of Sociology and Anthropology* 14 (1977), pp. 158-73.

Driedger, Leo, Charlene Thacker and Raymond Currie. "Ethnic Identification: Variations in Regional and National Preferences." *Canadian Ethnic Studies* 14 (1982), pp. 57-68.

Driedger, Leo, Frank Vallee and John deVries. "Towards an Ecology of Language Characteristics in Canada." In *Language and the Politics of Accommodation: Comparative Studies in Education Sociolinguistics,* edited by Robert St. Clair and Moshe Nahir. New York: Human Sciences Press, 1981.

Friedenberg, Edgar A. "Changing Canadian Attitudes Toward American Immigrants." In *The Canadian Ethnic Mosaic,* edited by Leo Driedger. Toronto: McClelland and Stewart, 1978.

Hesseltine, William B. and David L. Smiley. *The South in American History.* New York: Prentice-Hall, 1943.

Hiller, Harry H. *Society and Change: S.D. Clark and the Development of Canadian Society.* Toronto: University of Toronto Press, 1982.

Hughes, Everett C. *et al.* (eds.). *Race and Culture.* Volume 1. *The Collected Papers of Robert Ezra Park.* Glencoe, Illinois: Free Press, 1950.

Kalbach, Warren E. "Continental Shift: Emergence of the New West." Paper presented at the 1981 annual meeting of the Western Association of Sociology and Anthropology, Winnipeg: 1981.

Mackintosh, W.A. *Prairie Settlement: The Geographical Setting.* Toronto: Macmillan of Canada, 1934.

Matthews, Ralph. "The Significance and Explanation of Regional Divisions in Canada: Toward a Canadian Sociology." *Journal of Canadian Studies* 15 (1980), pp. 43-61.

Melling, John. *Right to a Future: The Native Peoples of Canada.* Don Mills, Ontario: Anglican and United Churches of Canada, 1967.

Morton, Arthur S. and Chester Martin. *History of Prairie Settlement and "Dominion Lands" Policy.* Toronto: Macmillan of Canada, 1938.

Newman, William M. *American Pluralism: A Study of Minority Groups and Social Theory.* New York: Harper and Row Publishers, 1973.

Odum, Howard, W. *Southern Regions of the United States.* Chapel Hill: University of North Carolina Press, 1936.

Porter, John. *The Vertical Mosaic.* Toronto: University of Toronto Press, 1965.

Porter, John. "Plenary Address." Annual meeting of the Canadian Sociology and Anthropology Association, Edmonton, 1975.

Porter, John. *The Measure of Canadian Society: Education Equality and Opportunity.* Toronto: Gage Publishing, 1979.

Rioux, Marcel. *Quebec in Question.* Toronto: James Lewis and Samuel, 1971.

Royal Commission on Bilingualism and Biculturalism. *The Cultural Contribution of the Other Ethnic Groups.* Ottawa: Queen's Printer, 1970.

Simeon, Richard. "Regionalism and Canadian Political Institutions." In *The Canadian Political Process*, edited by Richard Schultz *et al.* Toronto: Rinehart & Winston, 1979.

Simeon, Richard and David J. Elkins. "Regional Political Cultures in Canada." In *The Canadian Political Process*, edited by Richard Schultz *et al.* Toronto: Holt, Rinehart & Winston, 1979.

Stanley, G.F.G. *The Birth of Western Canada: A History of the Riel Rebellions.* Toronto: University of Toronto Press, 1960.

Thomas, William I. and Florian Znaniecki. *The Polish Peasant in Europe and America.* Chicago: Unversity of Chicago Press, 1918.

Wallace, Samuel B. "Regional Sociology: The South." *Sociological Spectrum* 1 (1981), pp.-429-42.

Wiebe, Rudy. *Peace Shall Destroy Many.* Toronto: McClelland & Stewart, 1962.

Wiebe, Rudy. *The Temptations of Big Bear.* Toronto: McClelland & Stewart, 1973.

Wiebe, Rudy. *The Scorched Earth People.* Toronto: McClelland & Stewart, 1977.

Wirth, Louis. *The Ghetto.* Chicago: University of Chicago Press, 1928.

Zorbaugh, Harvey. *The Gold Coast and the Slum.* Chicago: University of Chicago Press, 1929.

THE MÉTIS IN WESTERN CANADA SINCE 1945

Murray J. Dobbin

Before elaborating upon the question of the Métis after 1945, two preliminary questions need first be addressed. First, the definition of the term Métis and secondly; the historical background to the question—i.e., the Métis before 1945. The definition of Métis has been increasingly complex since the late 1960s in part because of the constitutional strategies employed by Indians, Métis and Inuit to seek redress of their grievances. The recent establishment of a Métis National Council seems to suggest an effort to clarify the matter, a move which anticipates a legal change in status for those native peoples now referred to as nonstatus Indians.

There are many number of definitions of Métis or half-breed, each serving different purposes and often reflecting different historical periods. The Ewing Commission in Alberta in 1935 gave a nicely circular definition: A half-breed was "anyone having Indian blood in their veins and living the normal life of a half-breed."[1] The Commission was appointed to investigate indigent Métis, hence a pathological definition. We are on safer, more objective grounds if we attempt to define Métis in historical terms. We can do this momentarily but for now this can be stated simply by referring to the social, political and cultural characteristics of those people who called themselves Métis and half-breed in the fur trade era of the Northwest. Technically, this definition serves us today as well. Any descendants of that group—and only those descendants—are Métis. Biological definitions such as those given by Lussier and Sealey (whereby the first Métis arrived "Nine months after the white man set foot in Canada")[2] are ahistorical to a fault and serve no useful purpose. The Association of Métis and Non-Status Indian of Saskatchewan (AMNSIS) use two criteria in planning their upcoming census. To qualify as a Métis one must (besides having Indian blood) firstly identify oneself as a Métis, and secondly be recognized by one's community peers as a Métis. The question of definition will be dealt with repeatedly in this paper but for the moment I shall move on to historical background, for it is here that we will find the roots of the present question.

To put the matter as concisely and simply as possible the Métis people, as a distinct people, developed out of the colonial fur trade, beginning in the mid-1700s and reached their political and social peak in 1869/70 (although their final 'national' struggle took place, of course, in 1885). The Métis (interchangeable with the term half-breed except for a small elite of Scottish half-breed businessmen at Red River) can best be described, during this period, and especially after 1821, as Bourgeault does, as "an oppressed nationality."[3] Strictly speaking, the Métis were not a nation. They had no control over or access to capital and did not exercise political control over the common territory which they shared with others. These two crucial factors were controlled by the Hudson's Bay Company. Indeed, the Hudson's Bay Company, British colonialism incorporated, was, indirectly, the engine of Métis nationalism. Its systematic discrimination against the Métis in terms of access to the profit sharing positions in the hierarchy, was implicit in its recognition of the fact that the Hudson's Bay Company saw the Métis for what they were: the resident nationals[4] of the territory; the first people of (partly) European descent who saw the Northwest as their homeland. It was precisely this discrimination against the Métis, together with the Hudson's Bay Company's monopoly power over the economy after 1821, which fostered the growth of Métis nationalism.

Much could be said about the various dimensions (cultural, social, linguistic, economic) of the Métis nationality, but I will restrict myself to its social structure for it is in this factor that we find explanations of the Métis' situation in the twentieth century. It can be said that the Métis were characterized by an embryonic class structure. There were wage laborers (including the militant voyageurs), subsistence farmers, buffalo hunters, free traders and transportation entrepreneurs, and a small but important class of Métis intellectuals who articulated the grievances of all classes in liberal-nationalist political terms.

This nascent class structure of the Métis, whose unity depended on continued domination by the Hudson's Bay Company, was retarded by the Company's efforts to undermine any economic development which did not suit its interests. When settlement did come, it came with a flood, unleashing the full blown, competitive, capitalist social structure on the Northwest. The Métis national unit rapidly disintegrated. Those with marketable skills and appropriate socialization —mostly the businessmen and intellectuals—integrated into the new economic order. Those without value in a racist market were pushed aside and marginalized. For almost three generations this group of Métis suffered under a system of benign neglect by the state and from structural racism in the social and economic system. There was no political opposition for it was the Métis businessmen, farmers and intellectuals who had always provided the political leadership—and these Métis were now a part of the new order. So it was that each new generation of Métis gave up its most promising individuals to the dominant society—it was everyone's goal to "escape" the Métis world.

The first sustained political movement of the Métis began in Northeastern Alberta in 1928 with a spontaneous agitation by destitute, seminomadic Métis whose squatters rights were being threatened. This movement, formally organized as L'Association des Métis d'Alberta et des Territories du Nord Ouest in 1932 was followed in Saskatchewan by the formation, in the southern half of the province of the Saskatchewan Métis Society. A brief look at these two popular movements reveals some constant themes in twentieth-century Métis history.

The Alberta struggle was fundamentally a struggle for land which the Alberta government wanted to open for homesteading. After an on-again, off-again battle which lasted ten years, the government established ten settlement areas or "colonies" for exclusive use by the Métis.[5] The movement, while started by illiterate hunters, was led by educated middle-class Métis, mostly land owners, whose national or racial consciousness was sparked by the destitution of their cousins.

The Saskatchewan group was quite different. Initiated by educated working-class Métis, it was motivated partly by the depression conditions but in the context of what its leaders felt was a genuine aboriginal land claim against the federal government. In the end, this movement failed in its principal objective, in part because its leaders chose a difficult constitutional strategy (unlike their

Alberta counterparts), but principally because most of them were too closely tied to the Liberal party.[6]

A number of themes can be identified in examining these two prewar movements, themes which shed light on the present day Métis situation. The first is the role of leadership. Parallelling the nineteenth-century Métis national struggle, these two movements saw the mass of the Métis highly dependent upon a leadership socially far removed from them. If that leadership was effective, the Métis benefited, if it was not, they were helpless to change matters. In short, the social distance between the leaders and led was extraordinarily great—particularly in the Alberta case.

A second, and more enduring theme, is that of the almost exclusive focus of the Métis movement on the state. As a marginal group, whose exclusion from the mainstream was the reason for their movement, the Métis inevitably went to the modern state—the ''arbiter'' of the system—to seek redress. No other group, save Indian and Inuit had been so systematically excluded from social and economic development. The state was their only possible resort.

A third theme is demonstrated by the Alberta movement: the policy of the Canadian state, whether federal or provincial has been to centralize dispersed, seminomadic peoples when it opened up new areas of natural resources for economic exploitation. The establishment of the Alberta Métis colonies was never opposed by the province—the real issue was their purpose and who would wield political authority[7] —for in order to open the forest and farm land, the nomads had to be removed from the land.

A final theme is that of uneven development and it relates directly to the last one. For various reasons, different resources in the West were developed at different times. Thus, the Métis of the southern prairies were quickly over-whelmed by the new industrial order; many were relegated to the status of ''road-allowance people''—the only ''marginal'' land left for a ''marginal'' people. The Métis of north-central Alberta, where the movement of the thirties flourished, were spared that fate for almost forty years until the drought effectively redefined marginal land.

In viewing the Métis of pre-1945, we generally get a view of a quasi-colonial situation in the sense that the mass of Métis (exclusive of those who had integrated successfully into the dominant society) were a highly dependent group: dependent both on a fickle leadership which often tired of the struggle, and also on the state for salvation. They had no effective control over their future and were effectively outside the political and economic system. Finally, when the resources they occupied were needed they were subject to centralizing policies which left them *de facto* wards of the state like the treaty Indians before them.

In examining the situation of the Métis in the postwar period one could begin by stating that by 1945/46 there was virtually no sign of the political movements which the Métis created in the 1930s. Both the Saskatchewan and Alberta organizations faded during the war years.[8] For some fifteen years until the early 1960s, nowhere did the Métis establish viable political organizations. In part, this is a reflection of the same factors which made Métis leadership so problematic. One of the principal reasons that the Alberta Métis movement faded during the war was the loss of leadership. With improved economic conditions the landowning, educated Métis no longer identified strongly enough with the Métis cause (which was, after all, mainly the salvation of the most destitute Métis) to remain actively involved. It was essentially a conflict between racial or national identification and class identification. With the economic situation returning to "normal," the Métis leaders and many of their followers no longer saw the need for a movement exclusively in the interest of Métis. The prosperity of the prairies during the fifties, led by farmers, had its effects as well. It should be recalled that it took abject misery and virtual threat to life to prompt the Alberta Métis to organize. Less than this extreme duress apparently meant an end to their movement.[9]

To examine the very broad topic we will, for practical reasons, narrow the view to the province of Saskatchewan. For the themes I wish to examine the example of Saskatchewan is adequate as developments there were paralleled in other provinces.

One question immediately comes to mind in the postwar period when we return to the problem of definition. Just who are we discussing and what criteria should we use to define "Métis?" The goal here is simply to gain some understanding of the present situation facing native people and the historical underpinnings of that situation. I will not try here to answer that broad historical question. But we can, however, deal with two important historical aspects of the question in order to qualify the use the term Métis.

The first historical complexity has already been referred to the history of uneven development of the Métis, as determined by the development priorities of industrial capitalism in the West after 1885. This uneven development had a significant impact on the racial/national consciousness of the Métis, and clearly this consciousness is crucial to this discussion. Nowhere in the prairie West was development so uneven, as between north and south, as it was in Saskatchewan. The northern part of that province—the commercial forest area and north—was virtually undeveloped till the postwar period. For the native population the church and the Hudson's Bay Company had remained the *de facto* government after 1885.[10] The Canadian state had almost no presence. When government did enter the north via the CCF in 1944, virtually no native individuals referred to themselves as "Métis." To be sure, it was on the plains that the Métis made their mark. Nonetheless, the voyageurs were quintessentially Métis and were northerners. While any conclusion is necessarily speculative it seems that northern Métis, faced by the disintegration in the south of their national unit, gradually ceased to identify as Métis. Their special fur trade role over, their unity broken, these Métis and their descendants reverted back to hunting and trapping. They rarely left the north. By 1945, the cultural and social characteristics of the mixed-blood people and the treaty Indians were all but indistinguishable. The conditions for a specifically "Métis" identity had ended by the turn of the century.

Métis consciousness in the south fared better, but for different reasons was scarcely more visible. In the south, Métis consciousness was suppressed. The post-1885 settler onslaught, the defeat of Batoche, the betrayal by their priests, the racial discrimination by all levels of white society—all of those factors demoralized the Métis. So did the almost total failure of their political efforts of the 1930s. Integration was the only practical solution, although one certainly had the option of quietly taking pride in one's Métis heritage. In the north the Métis gradually drifted, according to the demands of their environment, toward the Indian side of their ancestry; in the south, faced with an overwhelming nonnative reality, they suppressed their Métis identity. Vastly different situations led to a similar result—there was no Métis political expression. Such expression as there was, annual gatherings at Batoche and the pilgrimage to the St. Laurent shrine were more a cultural and ethnic, rather than political, expressions.

As mentioned above, there were two complexities regarding Métis identification. The second involved the relationship of the Métis to their close cousins, the nonstatus or ex-treaty Indians. The Indian Affairs Branch throughout the 1930s and 1940s implemented various policy decisions aimed at reducing the number of Indians on their rolls—including the encouragement given to treaty Indians to become enfranchised. These policies had the effect of swelling the ranks of native people for whom the province had responsibility. And provincial govern- ments were more concerned about indigency as a trait than they were about distinctions between Indian and Métis. In Alberta, at least, it was these nonstatus Indians who made up a very large proportion of the most desperate and destitute native people.

It is interesting to note that the two Métis organizations took quite different views of the question of definition when it came to membership. This fact in part reflects the above-mentioned theme of uneven development, and as well, the different strategies employed by the two movements. The Alberta Association made no distinction at all, for any person of Indian ancestry could belong, indicative of its provincial, direct-action strategy. The Saskatchewan Métis Society strictly enforced, or so one of its leaders claimed,[11] a Métis-only rule in its constitution. This membership rule was very likely prompted by necessity, as they were pursuing the federal government on the basis of a strict, legal land claim for the Métis.

The first real change came in the 1960s, and not surprisingly in Alberta and Saskatchewan. In 1961, efforts were begun to revive the old Métis Association of Alberta. In Saskatchewan, Malcolm Norris, a key figure in the Alberta move- ment in the 1930s initiated the Métis Association of Saskatchewan (MAS). These were the predecessors of the organizations we know and see today. Yet when they are analyzed and described, any similarity with today's bureaucratic native organizations will seem incidental. The reasons for this returns us to that all-important factor in the native struggle—the state.

As indicated, Malcolm Norris initiated the MAS in 1964.[12] Yet Norris might easily have made this move four years earlier had not other factors intervened. I suggest this because conditions were changing rapidly in Saskatchewan and on the prairies in general. A number of factors come together simultaneously in Saskatchewan, which had the effort of forcing white society finally to confront the native fact in Canada, and its own racism.

In 1960, both the federal government and the Saskatchewan government passed legislation enfranchising treaty Indians. The provincial government at the same time passed legislation permitting Indians to consume alcohol.[13] This, combined with a powerful trend to urbanization and overcrowding of reserves created the conditions for serious racial conflict. It was not long in coming, and by 1963 Saskatchewan was being characterized as "Canada's Alabama."[14]

State policy in the 1930s had been little more than benign neglect of Indian Métis people. At best, it was a sort of modern day "whiteman's burden," disguising a need to get native people out of sight and out of mind. The political culture of Canada in the sixties would not, could not tolerate that attitude, for in rhetoric, at least, it had to be different. Semantics had moved somewhat toward the concept of self-determination, summed up in the phrase "self-help," and reflected the full-blown development of the welfare state.

But the state faced a crisis. It was confronting a situation it had been content to ignore and now could not cover up. The crisis was to be found in the fact that the state had no information on which to build an informed social policy to deal with the dilemma of Indian and Métis people. Academics, like politicians and the general public, had also ignored the ugly reality of the reserves. The so-called "Indian problem" had been addressed by no one.

The state response, particularly at the federal level was to seek out those individual Indians with whom it would converse; that is, those educated Indians who had successfully bridged the gap between the two social realities. In place of informed policy created in the traditional bureaucracy, there would be a process of almost continuous consultation with integrated Indians. Eventually, these Indians, the educated elite, would join the bureaucracy, for the state was creating the conditions for a native bureaucratic elite. Until then, Indian ancestry was a burden, a barrier to a successful career. But in a few short years it became, for some, a material advantage for the first time.

For the most part this new elite was, in fact, not new at all—only the urban context was new. The elite was drawn from what Edgar Dosman calls the "leading families" of the reserves.[15] These families, he argues, had long cooperated with the Indian Affairs Branch on reserves and had benefited as a result. The were in fact, a neo-colonial elite. The move to the cities of large numbers of Indians was thus followed by a nearly simultaneous utilization of the leading families in the new urban context.

The cities however presented special jurisdictional and political problems. The federal government, which had over decades made efforts to reduce its responsibility for Indians, would eventually attempt by 1970 to ease out of its responsibilities for "off-reserve" Indians. In any case, the urban situation tended to blur the legal lines: all newly urbanized native people—Métis, nonstatus and status Indians —faced a similar dilemma. As a result, the Secretary of State began, tentatively, to take some responsiblity for Métis both on its own and through cooperation with the provinces. This process led to the now infamous "White Paper," relegated so decisively to the dust bin earlier this year.

I have digressed here with a purpose: to touch on the question of leadership. For what the state accomplished in the process of attracting the elite to its ranks was, at the same time, the development of a pool of leadership for future native political organizations. What was a spontaneous process of racial and national consciousness among educated leaders in the 1930s became in the 1960s a process encouraged, if not wholly fostered, by the state.

Not all native leaders fell into this category of ultimately state dependent leadership. While decades of colonial dependence and absence of both political rights and political experience on isolated reserves dictated a cautious approach by treaty Indians, this was not always the case with the Métis. To some extent socially isolated and dependent on the state, the Métis nevertheless had a broader political experience; they were not at this time preoccupied with legal questions and were free of debilitating dealings with the Indian Affairs Branch. In short, many Métis were more independently-minded than their Indian cousins.

This statement, however, requires some qualification. As stated earlier, there were significant differences between the mixed-blood people of Northern Saskatchewan and the Métis of the South. After nearly five generations of domination by Euro-Canadian society, the southern Métis were politically very cautious —to what extent we will see shortly. The northern Métis were just coming into their political consciousness. This was not a "Métis Nationalist" consciousness, but a political awareness which grew out of fifteen years of CCF government in the north which had effectively destroyed the old social and economic order, while denying native people access to new resource industries.[16] The northern mixedbloods (some now referred themselves as Métis after persistent categorizing by assorted anthropologists) were ripe for leadership and action after years of little or no collective action.

Malcolm Norris was to provide that leadership. Norris and his brilliant Métis colleague, Jim Brady, had both moved to Saskatchewan from Alberta after the war. Norris knew virtually every popular leader in the north. A socialist and Marxist, Norris had little use for the endless string of consultation meetings with the Secretary of State. He put high value on politcal independence and was determined to avoid any ties with government, especially the new Liberal government in Regina.

Norris was a political anachronism in the context of ceaseless state activity and the "partnership" with native leaders which it fostered. While other leaders were content to discuss the fate of native people with bureaucrats, Norris promoted a radical democracy and a focus on political education of the MAS membership. The issues were social and economic and the strategy militant: native people would demand access to resources as a basis for self-determination and jobs.[17] Norris had hoped for the broadest organization possible, one embracing all native people. But treaty Indian leaders sensed a real danger in allying themselves with the Métis, fearing this would dilute or undermine their special status. While Norris saw the north as the critical area for organizing the MAS, he also wanted a province-wide organization. This, too, would elude his grasp.

There was little interest shown by southern Métis in any organization in 1964. A meeting of Indian and Métis leaders from around the province, called by the Liberal government in Regina, attracted only one Métis from Saskatoon. The process of assimilation, buttressed by the suppression of Métis consciousness, seemed to have nearly eliminated the political base enjoyed by the Métis Society of the 1930s and 1940s.

There were, however, a small number of Métis in Regina who were interested in a Métis organization. Norris's efforts to enlist them for his northern MAS, and their reluctance to join, set the stage for political intervention by the provincial government—an intervention which set the stage for the future relationship between the state and native organizatons for the next two decades.

When Norris met with southern Métis leaders, their arguments against joining the MAS clearly reflected the uneven social development experienced by the Métis after 1885. The northern Métis said the southerners, were, closer to their Indian side; they wanted different things from government such as control of resources versus vocational training in the south. They were also perceived as too militant, for southern leaders, who were historically tied to the Liberal Party and saw government as a partner, not an adversary. Norris's appeals for unity thus failed to move the cautious and suspicious southerners.[18]

The southern Métis proposed that there should be two Métis organizations, with the CN line through Saskatoon the dividing line. This was agreed upon, and shortly after, the Métis Society of Saskatchewan (MSS) was formed. From the outset, Norris was suspicious that the Liberal government was manipulating certain of the southern leaders. He was correct in this assumption. According to the director of the governments' Indian-Métis branch (IMB), the Liberals considered Norris a serious political threat. Cabinet ministers and MLA's were instructed to seek out and encourage alternative, moderate Métis leaders. Norris was fired from his government job and later forced to resign as director of the Prince Albert Indian-Métis Friendship Center. Officials of the IMB were instructed to deny assistance of any kind to Métis involved with Norris.[19]

Finding effective alternate leaders to counter Norris, who was an extremely articulate and experienced leader proved difficult. Joe Amyotte, the president of the southern MSS had great difficulty organizing southern Métis: there was considerable resistance to the very *idea* of an organization exclusively for Métis. Amyotte complained, "We had to have four or five meetings just to explain the reason for the organization...The people were afraid to fight, afraid they would be laughed at."[20] It took Amyotte and his colleagues eighteen months to organize six locals and hold the first annual convention. Norris and a single colleague accomplished the same in five months.

At this point in the organizational fortunes of the Métis, the provincial government felt it necessary to assist the MSS financially. The slow progress of the organization prompted the government to let it be known that funding was available for organizing. Through a treaty-Indian acquaintance of Amyotte (the Federation of Saskatchewan Indians had been receiving $10,000 from the province annually since 1959) the Métis leader was urged to apply for $10,000, encouraged in the belief that it would be forthcoming. When Amyotte, a leader of the old school, only asked for $500 the future pattern was set. In 1967 he accepted $16,000.[21]

Two consequences of this funding initiative are worth noting—one fully anticipated by the government, the other not. In the first case the government's objective was accomplished. With government funding assured for the future, Amyotte shifted ground and began promoting the amalgamation of the two Métis groups. Norris, who was by this time seriously ill, vehemently opposed taking any government funding, attacking it on the basis that it would destroy Métis political independence and provide an open invitation to opportunists and interfere with Métis political priorities. Norris's northern colleagues did not heed his warnings. The amalgamation took place: Amyotte was declared the new organization's President, its name was the southern group's (MSS) and its headquarters were in Regina. The northern MAS, so feared by the provincial government, was simply absorbed by the more cautious MSS.[22]

The other consequence of government funding, though it did not materialize for several years, was the rapid increase in the number of individuals identifying themselves as Métis. As government funding expanded into service programs, vocational training, housing, etc., Métis ancestry entailed a material benefit for the first time since the issuance of scrip. Pride in heritage, encouraged by the political efforts of the MSS and bolstered by the availability of government assistance in various areas, had the effect of liberating Métis consciousness, and sometimes creating it where it had long since disappeared. From one perspective it could be said that the price paid by the government for its political manipulation was many times greater than it had anticipated, for it legitimated the demand by all Métis for special consideration.

The political benefits were not immediate, either. For five years the anticipated passivity of the MSS was noticeably absent. Joe Amyotte was quickly replaced by Howard Adams (author of *Prison of Grass*) and the MSS gained a reputaton as one of the most aggressive and independent native groups in the country. But by 1973/74 the effect of government funding was showing. There was no more political education (for which there was now no money), confrontations over economic issues disappeared and the MSS began to take on the bureaucratic structure and the political tone which today characterizes nearly all native organizations.

It was also in the mid-seventies that the Métis Society began to consider more seriously the aboriginal rights question, in other words, the constitutional strategy. In my view, this was a logical outcome of the gradual decline of direct-action politics and it was encouraged by the federal government's willingness to provide funds for ''ab rights'' research. While a conclusion can only be tentative without further investigation, it seems to this writer at least that a constitutional strategy was arrived at less through debate about alternatives than by default; default by way of intervention of the state. It is perhaps appropriate to quote Jim Brady, the leading Métis intellectual of this century, on the constitutional question: ''Constitutional 'principles' in the abstract have no significance in our struggle...We must establish the fact, at the outset, that the relation of social forces will determine the constitutional issue at any given historical time....''[23] It was the Alberta Métis of the 1930s for whom Brady was speaking and at that time the social and economic crisis faced by the Métis determined that their strategy would not be constitutional but direct-action, public lobbying. What I am suggesting is that today the state, through manipulation of grants to native organizations, has distorted the ''natural'' political decision-making process and in so doing has drawn the Métis movement into a political strategy which is both less threatening and, secondly, under the ultimate control of the state itself.

In general, the history of the Métis movement since the early seventies has been dominated by state intervention. What political rewards does the state receive for its funding of native organizations? First, as suggested above, the government faces far less militant organizations and because the constitutional process is so lengthy, it effectively delays the day when the state is obliged to deal seriously with the social and economic crisis faced by native people. Secondly, because the Métis organizations have become largely service organizations, they must share with the state the failure of service programs to come to grips with the underlying crisis—a failure guaranteed by the nature of the programs which treat symptoms, not causes. Thirdly, and perhaps most importantly, the highly visible presence of articulate native leaders pacifies progressive nonnative public opinion. In this context, it should be pointed out that the native people, a small minority in the country, draw their political power from their capacity to confront the dominant society with its own intrinsic standards of civilization. All classes of white society are eager to believe that something is being done to improve conditions for native people. The existence of well-established native organizations helps establish the largely mythical notion, that the problems of native people are being met.

These are the political advantages accruing to the state as a result of its intervention. The other side of the coin is the political price native organizations pay for accepting this intervention. First, the constitutional strategy divides native people. The Métis, until now allied in one movement with their nonstatus Indian cousins, are now one group among three: Métis, status Indians and nonstatus Indians. Secondly, pursuing the constitutional strategy eliminates the need for native organizations to engage in political education of their membership and in the mobilization of numbers—i.e., it neutralizes the only political weapon an economically weak minority has—organization. Lastly, because the strategy implies a degree of separateness, it tends to draw attention away from and make more difficult, the building of alliances and support with sympathetic nonnative individuals and groups.

We have looked briefly at the question of the Métis after 1945 and it would seem appropriate to look even more briefly at where that question leads with respect to the future. From the Métis perspective there is already a growing consciousness about the implications of ten years of state intervention. Social and economic questions are once again beginning to dominate the debate and we shall very likely witness a period of internal dissension among ordinary Métis regarding their political future. With respect to the Canadian state and its ability to genuinely come to grips with the native question I again quote Jim Brady: "...no capitalist government would ever agree to the complete abolition of the Métis question...Thus it will not be a question of rehabilitation...but of restricting certain undesirable sides of (the question) and limiting certain excesses... objectively, no reconstruction of the Métis will come about."[24] It is not within the political spectrum of liberal-democratic, capitalist society to address the fundamental causes of the native crisis. The state will, therefore, continue to treat the symptoms; to try to eliminate the politically embarrassing "excesses."

Footnotes

1. Oral Testimony at the Ewing Commission Hearings, as quoted in Murray Dobbin, *The One-and-a-Half Men* (Vancouver: New Star Books, 1981), p.95.

2. D.B. Sealey and A.S. Lussier, *The Métis: Canada's Forgotten People* (Winnipeg: Manitoba Métis Federation Press, 1975), p.1.

3. Ron Bourgeault, various unpublished papers, including "The Role of Class in Nineteenth Century Métis History," presented at the Learned Societies Conference, Saskatoon: 1979.

4. *Ibid.*

5. Dobbin, *The One-and-a-Half Men*, pp.54-138.

6. Murray Dobbin, "Métis Struggles of the Twentieth Century," four part series in *New Breed Magazine*, September-December, 1978.

7. *The One-and-a-Half Men*, Chapter 8.

8. *Ibid*, Chapter, and "Métis Struggles...," part 4.

9. *Ibid*, p.135.

10. Vernon C. Serl in "A Northern Dilemma; Reference Papers," Vol.1, edited by Arthur Davis, as quoted in Dobbin, *One-and-a-Half Men*, p.167.

11. Joesph Ross, Métis organizer, in interview with the author, 1977, tape in Sask. Archives.

12. *The One-and-a-Half Men*, pp.218-19.

13. *Ibid*, pp.202-3.

14. Ibid.

15. Edgar Dosman, *Indians: The Urban Dilemma* (Toronto: McClelland and Stewart, 1972), pp.47-68.

16. *The One-and-a-Half Men*, pp.184-5.

17. *Ibid*, pp.230-2.

18. *Ibid*, p.221.

19. *Ibid*, p.231.

20. *Ibid*, p.241.

21. *Ibid*, p.239.

22. *Ibid*, p.241.

23. *Ibid*, p.90.

24. *Ibid*, p.135.

DEVELOPMENTS IN HEALTH CARE IN THE POSTWAR ERA

J.A. Boan

Introduction

The interjection of universal, comprehensive hospital and medical care insurance overshadows all other postwar health-care developments, including the "medicare crisis" that has recently received a lot of media attention; so a large part of what follows will be devoted to examining this particular facet. Developments have been on a broad front, however, involving an expansion in the number and scope of voluntary associations, sweeping changes in public health services, and a rapid acceleration in scholarly analysis of the phenomenon. In what follows, the medicare problem will be examined in some detail, highlighting the apparent causes of the high and rising costs, summarizing suggested solutions, and concluding with a proposal that may help. But first, some concurrent developments will be considered.

Concurrent Developments in Health Care

Voluntary associations dealing with health care were well established by the end of World War II, and had proven to be an important adjunct to traditional health care.[1] The Red Cross Society (1896) and the Victorian Order of Nurses (1897) are but two examples of the half dozen or so agencies whose work began early on, but which continued in expanded form in the post-World War II era. The Canadian Paraplegic Association began in 1945 as a direct result of the need to care for war casualties. Yet other societies to follow included the Canadian Arthritis and Rheumatism Society in 1947, the Multiple Sclerosis Society of Canada in 1948, the Muscular Dystrophy Association of Canada and the Canadian Heart Foundation in 1950, the Canadian Diabetes Association in 1953, and the Cystic Fibrosis Foundation in 1960. By 1962, there were twenty-four national voluntary health organizations, eighteen of which had developed since 1945 (Govan, 1965).

These agencies provided services that included promotion of health, the prevention of illness or disability, and the discovery, treatment or rehabilitation of persons suffering from disease or disability. They were funded for the most part through charitable donations and fees charged for services, and have been well supported until recent times by the public.

By 1961, thirteen of the largest organizations had revenues totalling approximately $26 million (Govan, 1965, p.95). To illustrate something of the growth that has taken place, by 1982 the Canadian Cancer Society alone had expenditures of $46.0 million, nearly double the revenue of the thirteen organizations in 1961 (*Annual Report*, 1982). About 18 percent of these expenditures will have been dispensed through the provincial branches in the four western provinces. It may not be possible to derive an exact figure for the current total voluntary association expenditures for health care, but by extrapolating on the basis of the increases in certain key agencies' expenditures, it appears that a figure of $300 million would be conservative.

In the health departments of the western provinces, increases in services of a similar magnitude can be discerned. Advances were made in all the provinces in western Canada in the provision of services complementary to those delivered by the hospital-medical system. These services, in many cases, were intended to be preventive rather than reactive. Examples include immunization, maternal and child hygiene, public-health nursing, psychiatric services, care of the aged and infirm (in partnership with the private sector), air ambulance service, alcohol treatment services; in Saskatchewan, a dental plan to cover pre-school and school children, the SAIL program (Saskatchewan Aids to Independent Living Program) "...designed to assist handicapped persons to live as independently as possible in their own homes through provision of the mobility, environmental and respiratory equipment..." (Saskatchewan, 1980), and physical fitness programs.[2] Services similar to those provided under SAIL began concurrently in British Columbia and Alberta, and Manitoba in the late 1970s (Mennie, 1982a).

Probably the outstanding changes in the postwar era have been those concerning the care of the elderly and mental patients. Although statistical data are sparse, Mennie (1982) estimates that between 1962 and 1972 beds for the elderly requiring only residential and boarding care increased from twenty-three to forty-two beds per 1000 elderly population. Similarly, facilities for the elderly requiring some medical care (type three beds), increased between 1962 and 1972, from thirteen to twenty per 1000 elderly. The western provinces have moved toward a uniform system of charges for nursing home-care broadly equivalent to the income of a single person receiving old-age security and the guaranteed income supplement. The significant change in mental health care consists of the emptying of the mental hospitals, and the provision of vastly expanded psychiatric care in the larger centers. It is widely agreed that this has been an improvement therapeutically, but whether it has been cheaper is still being debated (Mennie, 1982a).

Scientific research can only be touched upon. Everyone knows that developments on all fronts have been staggering. Many people who died of Hodgkins Disease in the 1960s would still be alive today, if what is known now had been known then. Examples can be multiplied. The rapid changes can be epitomized in the current statistics, widely accepted in medical circles, that the half-life of a medical education in 1983 is now only four years!

The output of scientific literature in the field of health economics during the past few years has accelerated rapidly, where earlier there was very little interest. Prior to the end of World War II, it seems there were only four items of this kind in existence. They appeared one at a time in 1914, 1920, 1927 and 1939. This pace continued after the war for a while with another item appearing in 1946, one in 1950 and one in 1952. After that things picked up a bit, but by 1961, when the The Royal Commission on Health Services was appointed, there were only some thirty items in existence in the English Language—none by Canadians (Culyer, 1977). The Royal Commission generated the first health economics literature in Canada, some of which appeared as chapters in the Report, and some as monographs (Canada, 1964, 1965). From then on, a good deal began to be done in this field; in 1974, the last year for which data has been compiled, ninety-nine books and articles appeared, and today it is doubtful if anyone can keep abreast of what is turned out.

Access to all of this published data has deepened our understanding of the economics of health care, but has not resulted in any definitive solutions. It has largely served to explode myths and to provide insight as to where to turn next.

Medicare

Reasons for High and Rising Costs

Economists tend to examine matters from a demand and supply point of view because prices, and therefore costs of health care, seem to reflect developments in these two basic factors.

Four federal acts largely explain the increases in supply of service; these acts came into effect by the decade: 1948, 1958 and 1968, and the fourth in 1966. The first one, the National Health Grants Act, 1948, a brain-child of Paul Martin (Taylor, 1978, p.163), inspired an increase in hospital and related facilities such that by 31 March 1970, when the program ended, Canada had 7.0 beds per 1000 population, compared to 5.5 per 1000 in the United States (LeClair, 1975, p.14). The next Act made possible the use of these splendid facilities. This was the Hospital Insurance and Diagnostic Services Act, which came into effect on 1 July, 1958 (although it was passed on 12 April 1957).

The financial arrangements for hospital care encouraged the allocation of more resources to the health field. The formula made it possible for low-cost provinces to have well over half of their total hospital costs paid for by the federal government. Thus, in 1972/73, Saskatchewan received 53.3 percent of its hospital costs from Ottawa. This formula acted as a brake on high-cost provinces, but they were already putting a good deal of money into hospital care. The third of these Acts is the Medical Care Act, which came into effect on 1 July 1968. Its formula went further still in encouraging low-costs provinces to spend more. In 1972/73, Saskatchewan received 61.9 percent of its medical care costs from Ottawa, but this went down over time to only 59.6 percent in 1975/76.

The fourth Act of significance was the Health Resources Fund Act, 1965, which came into effect in 1966. It provided "...for assistance in the planning, acquisition, construction, renovation and equipping of health training facilities" (LeClair, p.24). As a result, the number of medical schools increased from twelve to sixteen, and some existing schools were enlarged. The graduating classes increased from 881 in 1966 to 1,292 in 1972, and to 1,761 in 1978.

Immigration of physicians jumped during the period 1961-69 in response, one can infer, to the excellent opportunities that a wealthy country, equipped with health insurance, afforded. During the investigations of the Hall Commission, immigration was merely a factor to consider; numbers in the 200-300 range seemed generous estimates for the future, based on what was at the time, recent experience. In fact, by 1969 immigration of physicians had reached a peak of 1,347, after which it began to taper off, and in 1978 it had dropped to 263 for the year.

The number of active civilian physicians increased from 29,658 in 1969 to 43,192 in 1979. Population per active civilian physician, which was 1004 at the time of the Hall Commission, fell to 636 per physician by 1981, excluding interns and residents (Mennie, 1982b). Additional evidence of the increase in supply is found in the increase in the percentage of the labor force in Health Sciences. In 1961, it was 2.1 percent, by 1971, it was 3.8 percent, and by 1981, 4.2 percent (*Census of Canada*).

These figures are indicative of a significant increase in the supply of hospital and medical services. Supposedly, if the government overshot on this, hospital wards would be idle, doctors would be underutilized, and prices of health services would tend to fall. History shows, however, that there was no idle capacity of either capital or manpower in the postwar period. Demand was able to keep up to supply and, if the ensuing upward pressure on prices can be relied on as an indicator, demand surpassed supply.

The evidence on price trends is not complete. There has been an increase in prices, but, in respect of dental care, as of 1975, it was just a bit more than enough to offset inflation; there is some evidence that physicians' fees lagged behind the rate of inflation in the mid-1970s but caught up by the end of the decade (Hall, 1980, p.33). The price index of nonprescribed drugs has gone up much faster than the rate of inflation, but prescribed drug prices as of 1975 had kept ahead of inflation by only a small margin (Soderstrom, 1978, pp. 236-238). But hospital costs per patient day rose between 1972 and 1979 at a rate of about 14 percent (in Saskatchewan, about 15 percent), about double the annual average increase in the Consumer Price Index (S.H.S.P. 1972 and 1981, and *Bank of Canada Review*, 1982). More work needs to be done on the contribution of rising prices to the rise in expenditures on health care, but for the moment one can conclude that if prices rose, there must have been an increase in demand that exceeded the increase in supply of service, so let's look at that aspect.

This is too large a field to be treated fully here, but its dimensions can be probed. Basically, demand will be a function of population size, health status, and taste.[3] Health status, in turn will be a function of many things: genetics, life-style, environment and so on. Regardless, however, of health status, the proclivity to seek care, which may be called "taste," is an important factor, and is probably fed by the media as well as by health promotion activities in schools and government departments of health. But here we run into a substantial difference between health care and other consumer commodities because, in the case of health care, most of the demand is physician-induced. The individual of his own volition sets the process in motion, but from then on, it is largely up to the doctor. He is the one who says, "Go to the hospital, have these tests or that treatment, take this medicine, and come back in days or weeks to see me again."

An interesting theory to explain the alleged increase in tendency to use health care is found in the concept of moral hazard. The term moral hazard comes from the insurance industry, and means essentially that an insured person will not be as prudent as an uninsured person. Applied to health care it means that the patient will seek more care than he would if he were paying directly for it. Fuchs (1974) uses the restaurant analogy. If a group goes in to eat on the understanding that the bill will be split evenly among them, they will probably order a more expensive meal than if there were individual checks.

The concept has been broadened to include physician and hospital behavior. Fisher (1980), a Philadelphia internist addressed this problem in a book with the subtitle "Distortions Imposed on The Medical System By Its Financing," and by the latter he meant insurance. He said "the moral hazard expressed itself in a mindless extension of the idea that nothing is too good for our patients..." (p.178).

A well-received theory of medical behavior is that the doctor wants to do everything in his power to help the patient. This is the way they are trained, to leave no stone unturned. The more sophisticated technology becomes, the more stones they can turn. And the insurance scheme is paying, so why not? Why not indeed, if by leaving one test undone, the doctor may find himself in court on a malpractice charge? Whether, like Fisher, you call this moral hazard is a question of taste.[4] By whatever name, however, to the extent that it describes actual behavior, it is a powerful explanation for increased demand. When considered in connection with the technological explosion in medicine, it takes on additional meaning.

In almost every area of medicine, especially in diagnosis, technological developments have been rapid, e.g., Nuclear Magnetic Resonance, which is superior to the C.A.T. Scanner, will be sought after shortly by major teaching hospitals in Canada, if experience in the United States is any guide (Time, January 31, 1983). It will have to be accompanied by personnel trained in its use, running up both capital and operating costs. Other areas where developments have caused costs to rise include open-heart surgery, dialysis and kidney transplant, chemotherapy, etc. The fact is, people are being restored to health, at least for a few more years, in many cases that would have been fatal just a few years ago.

Technology is cost-reducing, too; the fact is, there is insufficient knowledge about its overall effects at this stage on costs. The add-on type of technological change probably raises costs, but the substitute kind has the opposite effect, e.g., injecting a drug into the "slipped disc" of a patient suffering back-pain cuts the costs to a fraction of surgical procedure that has been used in the past. The point is that just as more physicians means higher health costs,[5] an expansion in the treatments they can perform for people tends to raise costs still further.

In economic terms, what seems to have happened is this: a rapid increase in hospital capacity occurred as a precursor to national health insurance. Utilization rose because the number of physicians and the things they could do for people increased, and since physicians could improve their own productivity by substituting cost-free (to them) hospital resources for their own costly (to them) time, hospitals tended to be used to capacity.

Regardless of the precise cause-effect relationship, we do know that costs rose form a little less than $1 billion in 1955 (about $50 per capita) to slightly over $15 billion in 1977, the year that the federal government announced a new formula for financing health care that would encourage constraints on the rapid growth in costs. To the extent that these constraints were effective we can be thankful, for, in fact, by 1981 the total bill for health care exceeded $25 billion (about $1,000 per capita),[6] and one wonders what it would have been without the constraints![7] (See Tables 1 and 2).

Absolute dollar costs do not, however, portray real costs accurately. Generally inflation raises costs of nearly everything. Population growth increases health costs, but it also generates the human resources to provide those services. A more reliable statistic than current dollar costs, *or* the costs of care paid through government, is the share of the gross national product devoted to health care. Whatever share of GNP that personal health services takes up, the money could have purchased other items—consumer goods of various kinds, for instance. The sacrifice *of the latter* so that health care could be purchased instead is the real cost of those health services.

Interestingly, the share of the GNP has been fairly constant, hovering around 7.5 percent, since 1971 (Mennie, 1982b). In the United States, by contrast, the figure for 1982 is 8.9 percent (*Time*, August 9, 1982, p.53). It is estimated that Canada's share in 1981 will be below 8 percent, but owing to the economic downturn, when production fell but health costs went right on, the share in 1982 may be above 8 percent (Rehmer, 1983).

TABLE 1

HEALTH CARE EXPENDITURES

THE WEST AND CANADA, 1970-1981

(in millions of dollars)

Year	B.C.	Alta.	Sask.	Man.	Canada
1970	$ 609.3	$ 447.8	$ 235.4	$ 291.1	$ 6,151.9
71	689.6	531.4	260.7	321.4	7,007.3
72	753.0	576.4	273.4	348.8	7,665.2
73	854.4	648.2	297.1	393.9	8,580.3
74	1,061.1	752.4	354.9	439.7	10,083.5
75	1,338.7	957.3	447.7	531.1	12,154.3
76	1,526.4	1,109.7	523.9	618.2	13,882.9
77	1,711.0	1,289.3	579.5	680.2	15,171.3
78	1,946.4	1,443.8	643.2	746.9	17,086.6
79	2,175.8	1,691.9	711.5	829.5	18,983.7
80	2,669.3	2,175.9	822.6	957.5	22,027.0
81[a]	3,129.6	2,582.2	988.3	1,134.0	25,614.3

(a Provisional

Source: Policy Planning and Information Branch,
     Health and Welfare Canada. March 23, 1983

Two other bits of information are relevant. First, the *Parliamentary Task Force on Federal-Provincial Fiscal Arrangements* (1981) found that allowing for inflation, the *per capita* cost of health care in Canada had gone up by less then 20 percent in the 10-year period, 1971-1980 (p.112), when costs in current dollars had increased from $7.1 billion to $20.9 billion, or by almost 200 percent. Second, a careful reading of the Report of the *Royal Commission on Health Services* (Canada, 1964, pp.800 ff) shows that although future costs were a bit underestimated, history has unfolded much as was predicted.

TABLE 2

PERCENTAGE INCREASES IN HEALTH CARE EXPENDITURES
THE WEST AND CANADA, 1970-1981

Year	B.C.	Alta.	Sask.	Man.	Canada
1970	--	--	--	--	--
71	13.2	11.2	10.7	10.4	13.9
72	9.2	8.5	4.9	8.5	9.4
73	13.5	12.5	8.7	12.9	11.9
74	12.4	16.1	19.4	11.6	17.5
75	26.2	27.2	26.1	20.8	20.5
76	14.0	15.9	17.0	16.4	14.2
77	12.1	16.2	10.6	10.0	9.3
78	13.8	12.0	11.0	9.8	12.6
79	11.8	17.2	10.6	11.1	11.1
80	22.7	28.6	15.6	15.4	16.0
81 (a	17.2	18.7	20.1	11.8	16.3
Annual Average 1970	16.0	16.6	13.9	13.2	13.8

(a Provisional

Source: Table 1.

If the burden of health care has been kept at about 7.5 percent in Canada, while it has gone to nearly 9 percent of GNP in the United States, there must be a reason. The explanation lies, of course, in the controls over cost increases made possible by putting the responsibility for paying the bill into the hands of a public agency. These controls have taken the form of cutting hospital budgeted increases, forcing hospitals to economize. Public agencies cannot very well tell a hospital where to economize, but by keeping the payments down, these public bodies can force the hospital to decide which procedures have priority and which services can be cut.

The other approach is to put a lid on physician fee increases. Applying this rigorously has resulted in extra billing, and coupled with cost controls in the hospital sector has given rise to a morale problem, expressed in various forms, including a statement by the President of the Canadian Medical Association to the effect that insufficient money is provided to ensure the availability and quality of health care (Regina *Leader-Post*, March 24, 1982). Evidently more resources could be poured into this field, but at 7.5 percent of the GNP, it already exceeds the combined share taken up by agriculture, forestry and fisheries[8] and, judging from the public debate over costs, there is little enthusiasm for making more resources available. In fact, a great deal of the debate centers on ways and means to curtail demand.

Suggested Solutions

The debate over health care reveals two approaches to curtailing demand. One, greater use of the market system as an allocator of resources; and two, various nonmarket approaches. Those favoring less regulation and more opportunity for market forces to guide the behavior of consumers of health care have proposed a number of strategies: these involve the patient in the payment, whether it be through co-insurance, a deterrent such as Alberta is experimenting with, an income-tax approach, or extra-billing by physicians. With co-insurance, the patient would pay the first x dollars and the insurance company everything over that amount, or the insurance company would pay up to a certain amount and the patient all the rest, or, alternatively, the patient would pay a certain, usually small, percentage of any bill, the insurance company the remainder. The deterrent charge is designed to discipline the patient to discourage frivolous use of health services. The income-tax approach is designed to encourage the patient to be frugal: what it would do is allow the person to deduct a certain amount from income tax on a sliding scale depending on how much had been incurred that year in health costs. In essence this approach would tax heavy users higher than light users of health services.

Those favoring control through nonmarket mechanisms would lean heavily on devices to increase productivity, so that resources currently used to produce health services would be encouraged to raise their aggregate output. This school of thought would also encourage preventive measures so that people would not need so much health service per capita, and self-care, so they would not call so often on the health system. And finally, they would encourage selective de-insurance.

The case against the market approach has been made by Barer, Evans and Stoddart (1979). They evaluated each of the many proposals in terms of two health insurance objectives and two health-care delivery-system objectives. The health insurance objectives consist of risk reduction and wealth transfer. The former needs no elaboration; the wealth transfer attribute, however, may be less clear. What it says is that wealth will be transferred from those with a low probability of use to those with a high probability. The first objective attributed to a good health delivery system is that it should improve the health status of the population through its effect on levels and patterns of use of health services. The second objective is that it should work in the direction of improving efficiency.

Except for the minuscule case of the Saskatchewan drug plan, which appears to have some virtue in terms of encouraging technical efficiency in the delivery of prescriptions, all of the schemes considered failed one or more of those tests. Above all, they would not reduce costs: they might spread them so that it looked like they were lower because the government's bill would be reduced, but the balance would be picked up by patients on a personal basis, and if anything, such schemes would result in more resources being poured into the health sector.

It is no wonder the market approach fails, since there is no market in any meaningful sense in health care as we know it (Culyer, 1982). In order for a market to work toward greater efficiency, the consumer must be able to appraise the merchandise. This not always easy, but in the case of most other goods and services, through the application of standards of weight, measure and purity, and other less formal means, an appraisal can be made. Not so with health care. In this case, the consumer has to rely on the advice of his agent, the physician. In addition, there are the instances where the person is in no condition to make an informed judgment, because of physical or mental problems. And finally there are public health aspects—externalities—that would not come within the purview of the patient. Even without health insurance, there is no significant meaningful market for health care, but with health insurance, any semblance of a market disappears. The market solution does not appear to be very promising.

Among the items included under the nonmarket approach, one proposal that has received considerable attention is that of changes in life-style. It has become known through the work of a number of people (Cochrane, Illich, *et al.*)[9] that better housing, sanitation and nutrition are responsible for the lion's share of the increase in life expectancy that we have experienced—not medical intervention. In fact, except for recent times when the "wonder drugs" came into existence, the contribution by medical intervention to life-expectancy has been almost negligible. Meanwhile, through the work done on smoking and health and related matters, it has become obvious that there are diseases of choice. As Dr. Lorne Vinge (1982), Okanagan Mission, British Columbia said, "If you cross off your list of diseases all those that are diseases of choice, you'd have a small number left."

The movement to curb costs through a more healthful life-style, called "The Blame the Victim" paradigm by Victor Sidel, provides another approach to the treatment of high and rising health costs. According to the evidence available there has been a significant reduction in male mortality in the United States from ischemic heart disease, and it is associated "...with reductions in intake of saturated fat and cholesterol, increased consumption of poly-unsaturated fats and a reduced incidence of smoking" (*Task Force*, Ontario, 1982, p.41). Similarly, a large proportion of cancer deaths seem to be related to environment and life-style. According to the same Ontario *Task Force*, "...of the deaths caused by cancer, 35% come from cancer caused by diet, 30% from cancer caused by smoking...," and so on. Improvement in reducing mortality caused by cancer clearly lies in the area of life-style. A reduction in cancer incidence would materially affect the demand for health care. Another area of significance is accidents, particularly car accidents associated with alcohol, where improvement in life-style would reduce demand. The same is true with self-care. Evidence abounds that properly understood and practiced self-care could take an appreciable load off the health care system (Kronenfeld, 1979).

Although the life-style argument has potential, the problem is how to sell it. It is probably unethical to force people into a life-style they do not want (Wikler, 1978), and persuasion itself is expensive. Thus, the life-style approach is not a "quick-fix."

Selective de-insurance (Barer, Evans and Stoddart, 1970, pp. 99-104) basically means the refusal to reimburse patients or providers for services considered to be inefficacious. That this is a field of great potential there seems little doubt. In this respect, a Toronto physician David Horrobin undertook in 1977 to answer the charges of Illich (1976) that the health system itself is the organism causing people's health problems, and though he took Illich to task throughout most of his book, he also supported him in a number of instances. On the subject of procedures without medical value he had this to say:

> We do not know whether most of the things which we do to patients are better for the welfare of that patient than if we had done nothing at all. And on the whole we most of us prefer to remain warmly ignorant rather than coldly knowledgeable about the situation. It is I think obvious to anyone who looks at medical practice with anything like a critical eye that many of the things which are done to patients either have no influence on the outcome of the illness or may increase discomfort and hasten death. Much money would be saved and many patients would be better off if less medicine were practised. But which bits of medicine should be discarded? The only way to find out is by an effectively designed controlled trial in which the consequences of no treatment

are compared to those of treatment. If more such well designed studies were performed, I have little doubt that many currently used treatments would be dropped and many proposed treatments, after careful trial in a limited number of centers, would never be widely introduced. (Horrobin, 1977, p. 122).

Evidently this is a long-term solution. Yet there are steps that could be taken now by an interested medical association. Some procedures, still being practised, are known to be harmful or to do no good whatever, except possibly for the placebo effect (Fineberg and Hiatt, 1979).

Approaches of this kind bring into relief the role of "need" in health care as opposed to the notion of demand (Culyer, 1976, 1978; *Task Force*, 1982). As Evans (1981) points out, "...there is obviously some meaning to the notion that a person after a car accident needs care in quite a different sense than somebody exercising the preference for a chocolate bar" (p.19). The problem is, in health care, there is a wide spectrum from care in a life-threatening case to care that is going to make someone feel a little better. To the extent that the GOMER Syndrome ("Get Out of My Emergency Room," *Time*, April 11, 1983) is a problem, a place for de-insurance surely exists. The problem, of course, is to establish an imposing list of procedures that could be de-insured. Who would do it and how would it be received by physicians?

In any event, in order to have the desired effect, assuming such a list of procedures could be agreed upon, patients would have to be informed, first of all as to why they will have to pay for such procedures themselves, or else, they might simply go ahead and have the procedures done and the cost would merely be shifted from the health insurance scheme to the patient, with no necessary decrease in overall costs. Secondly, the professional involved would have to cooperate. If, because of differences in clinical opinion, providers kept recommending the de-insured procedure there would not be a noticeable decrease in demand.

Another nonmarket approach with a lot of promise is to make use of new delivery systems, with built-in incentives to induce economies. It is well known that services could be increased dramatically if physicians and dentists would devolve duties on less highly trained personnel trained on the job to do certain tasks (Reinhardt, 1975). Some insurance companies have been using registered nurses to do their medicals for them at a fraction of the cost. There is no doubt that a great many services could be delivered every bit as well by nurse-practitioners and dental assistants, but under our present system there is no incentive to go to the trouble to train such personnel, and as it now stands, such persons have no incentive to take the training. The nurse-practitioner (Lomas and Stoddart, 1982 and Denton, *et al.*, 1982) has been trained in Canada, but there is no tendency to make full use of them. Beyond the nurse-practitioner, there are opportunities elsewhere. It seems to be widely accepted that nurses between midnight and morning are able to perform all sorts of tasks and that they become unable to do once 8 a.m. rolls around—the "reverse Cinderella syndrome" (Hall, 1980, p.72). What is needed in order to get on with the great potential that exists of increased productivity is a thorough overhaul of professional licensing.

A delivery system to parallel those already existing would help. It could be patterned on the Hastings (1972) idea, a system of care for short-term stay—no more than a day—staffed by nurses, psychologists, social workers, and dental assistants, with a modest complement of physicians and dentists as resource people. Such a center would take the pressure off the emergency room at the hospital, and also to some extent off the doctor in his office.

The picture that emerges is something like this: first, health is considered to be a human right, in Canada, as a consequence of signing the United Nations Universal Declaration of Human Rights in 1948; second, health services for the most part are underwritten by health insurance, which in turn sterilizes the market approach to the distribution of health care; technology is marching along at a very rapid pace, which in other areas (electronics, computer, even automobiles) has led to a drop in real costs, but this has not been true in medicine, possibly because of constraints on the market designed to keep profits high, or safeguard incomes in some way. What is missing? Chapter three of Fuchs (1974) names him--"The Physician: The Captain of the Team." That's who is missing. (In dentistry, read Dentist).

A Proposal That May Help

The physician is the person who defines what health and sickness are. The system can't work well without his cooperation. Medicare, like the National Health Service in Britain (Garner, 1979), was put into place over the strong objection of the medical association. Doctors have worked within the insurance scheme on both sides of the Atlantic with less than overwhelming enthusiasm. Surely, however, this is shortsighted. Judging from the way history is unfolding, one of three possible scenarios will prevail. The first is one where, beginning with extra-billing and the possible development of private hospitals for those who can and will pay, a two-tier system will develop: free, hopefully quite good care for the poor, and costly but excellent care for the rich. The second is one where the two-tier development is scotched at birth and substituted in its place by a much more closely government-regulated scheme, reminiscent of the field hospital during wartime, tightly organized on a hierarchical basis. The third, and vastly to be preferred in terms of a harmonious outcome with high quality health care, involves the physicians burying the medicare hatchet, and resolving to make medicare work. Without leadership from the professions none of the suggested solutions referred to above has much chance.

The time for medical statesmanship is now. Otherwise, hardening of the regulations may descend on us, in the name of economy, and Canadians will find themselves commiserating with one another in words my mother is fond of quoting: "Of all sad words of tongue or pen, the saddest are these, it might have been."

Footnotes

1. I am indebted to one of my students, Brian Johnson, for compiling the data on which the following remarks on voluntary associations are based.

2. The definitive history of health care development western Canada has still to be written, but an account of this development in Saskatchewan has been published. (See Smishek, W.E., "Health Care in Saskatchewan," *Socialized Health Services*, 1976, pp. 69-74.)

3. Normally, income and prices of the goods and of substitutes would play a prominent role as arguments in the demand function, but once first dollar health insurance is in place, these variables play almost no part in the determination of demand: dental care, which in the West, however, is rapidly becoming insured, drug use and the purchase of out-of-province health care are exceptions. If income appears to be statistically significant in an analysis of demand for health care, it surely must be acting as a surrogate for better education, knowledge about the availability of health services, and related matters. The only reasons for putting arguments like price and income into the equation is because they are traditionally determinants of demand, but if, through insurance, everyone is equally rich, and price is zero, what determining do they do?

4. Arrow (1974, p.35) defines moral hazard as the difficulty of distinguishing between genuine risks and failures to optimize.

5. A common cost indicator used to be that each physician added to the total of physicians increases costs by $250,000, but lately a figure of $500,000 has been used.

6. Health care in this context consists of services of hospitals, physicians and dentists, as well as services of the professionals such as chiropractors, osteopaths and naturopaths, optometrists, podiatrists, physiotherapists, private-duty nurses and Victorian Order of Nurses; also, eyeglasses and appliances, drugs, and nursing-home care. It includes expenditures on health service prepayment and administration, government public health activities, research and construction. The expenditures of a very large number of voluntary health societies are also included. (Canada, 1975).

7. In the U.S.A., by 1982, health costs had reached $1,225 per capita. (*Time*, August 9, 1982, p.53).

8. Dr. Ludwig Auer, Economic Council of Canada, in a personnel communiqué.

9. Cochrane (1972); Illich (1975); Knowles (1977); Kronefeld (1979); McKeown (1976); Horrobin (1977); and Fuchs (1976).

References

Arrow, K.J. *The Limits of Organization*. New York: W.W. Norton and Company, 1974.

Bank of Canada Review, January 1982.

Barer, M.L., R.G. Evans, and G.L. Stoddart. *Controlling Health Care Costs by Direct Charges to Patients: Snare or Delusion?* Toronto: Ontario Economic Council, Occasional Paper 10, 1979.

Canada. *Royal Commission on Health Services*. Two Volumes. Ottawa: Queen's Printer, 1964 and 1965.

Canada. Dept. of Health & Welfare. *National Health Expenditures in Canada 1960-1973*. Ottawa: 1979, pp. 25, 31.

Cochrane, A.L. *Effectiveness and Efficiency*. London: The Nuffield Provincial Hospitals Trust, 1972.

Culyer, A.J. *Need and the National Health Service*. London: Martin Robertson, 1976.

Culyer, A.J., J. Wiseman, and A. Walker, *An Annotated Bibliography of Health Economics*. London: Martin Robertson, 1977.

Culyer, A.J. *Measuring Health: Lessons for Ontario*. Toronto: Ontario Economic Council, 1978.

Culyer, A.J. "Health Care and the Market." *Journal of Health Economics* 1 (1982), pp. 299-303.

Denton, F.T., *et al. Potential Savings from the Adoption of Nurse Practitioner Technology in the Canadian Health Care System*. QSEP Research Report No. 45. Hamilton: McMaster University, July 1982.

Economic Council of Canada. *Patterns of Growth*. Ottawa: Queen's Printer for Canada, 1970.

Evans, R.G. "Beyond the Medical Market Place: Expenditure, Utilization and Pricing of Insured Health Services in Canada." In *National Health Insurance: Can We Learn From Canada?*, edited by S. Andreopoulos. New York: John Wiley and Sons, 1975, pp. 129-79.

Evans, R.G. "Changing Dynamics in Health Care." Paper delivered at the Saskatchewan Health Care Conference, Regina, 1981. (Mimeo).

Fineberg, Harvey V. and Howard H. Hiatt. "Evaluation of Medical Practices." *New England Journal of Medicine* 301(20), Nov. 15, pp. 1086-91.

Fisher, George Ross. *The Hospital That Ate Chicago.* Philadelphia: The Saunders Press, 1980.

Fuchs, Victor R. *Who Shall Live?* New York: Basic Books, 1974.

Garner, Lesley. *The NHS: Your Money or Your Life.* Markham, Ontario: Penguin Books Canada, 1979.

Govan, E.S.L. *Voluntary Health Organizations in Canada.* Ottawa: Queen's Printer, 1965.

Hall, E.M. *Canada's National-Provincial Health Program for the 1980's.* Ottawa: Health & Welfare, 1980.

Hastings, John F.F. *The Community Health Centre in Canada.* Ottawa: Queen's Printer for Canada, 1972.

Health and Welfare Canada. *Canadian Health Manpower Inventory, 1980.* 1981.

Horrobin, David F. *Medical Hubris: A Reply to Ivan Illich.* Westmount, Quebec: Eden Press, 1977.

Illich, I. *Limits to Medicine: Medical Nemesis--The Expropriation of Health.* London: Marion Boyars Publishers, 1976.

Knowles, J.H., ed. *Doing Better and Feeling Worse.* New York: W.W. Norton and Company, 1977.

Kronenfeld, J.J. "Self Care as A Panacea for the Ills of the Health Care System: An Assessment." *Social Science and Medicine* 13A (1979), pp. 263-7.

Lalonde, M. *A New Perspective on the Health of Canadians.* Ottawa: Health and Welfare Canada, 1974.

Le Clair, Maurice. "The Canadian Health Care System." In *National Health Insurance: Can We Learn From Canada?*, edited by S. Andrepoulos. New York: John Wiley and Sons, 1975, pp. 11-93.

Little, Stephen, Executive Director. Canadian Paraplegic Association, Saskatchewan Division, 1983. (Personal Letter).

Lomas, Jonathan and G.L. Stoddart. *Estimates of the Potential Impact of Nurse Practitioners on Future Requirements for General Practitioners.* Hamilton: McMaster University Department of Clinical Epidemiology and Biostatistics, 1982.

McKeown, T. *The Role of Medicine, Dream, Mirage, or Nemesis?* London: The Nuffield Provincial Hospitals Trust, 1976.

Mennie, W.A. "Health Insurance and Long-Term Care in Canada." Prepared for presentation at the 110th Annual Meeting of the American Public Health Association. Montreal, November 14-18, 1982. 1982a. (Manuscript).

Mennie, W.A. "Health Care Cost Containment Policies in Canada." Prepared for Expert Group Meeting on Economic Efficiency in Health Care Delivery, sponsored by The International Social Security Association. Turku, Finland, September, 1982. 1982b. (Manuscript).

Rehmer, L. Personal communication, March 23, 1983.

Reinhardt, Uwe E. *Physician Productivity and the Demand for Health Manpower.* Cambridge, Mass.: Ballinger Publishing, 1975.

Report of the Parliamentary Task Force on Federal-Provincial Fiscal Arrangements. *Fiscal Federalism in Canada.* Ottawa: Minister of Supply and Services, 1981.

Saskatchewan. Department of Health. *Annual Report for the Year Ending March 31, 1980.* 1980.

Saskatchewan Hospital Services Plan. *Annual Reports.* Regina: Queen's Printer, 1973 and 1981.

Soderstrom, Lee. *The Canadian Health System.* London: Croom Helm, 1978.

Task Force. *Report of the Task Force on Medical Manpower.* Toronto: Council of Ontario Universities, 1982.

Taylor, M.G. *Health Insurance and Canadian Public Policy*. Montreal: McGill-Queen's University Press, 1978.

Venge, Lorne. Panel Discussion. Health and Healing Conference, Luther College, Regina, February 6, 1982. 1982.

Williams, Allan. Paper presented to the Graduate Health Economics class, University of York, on the work of the Royal Commission on Health, November 10, 1977. 1977.

Wikler, Daniel I. "Persuasion and Coercion for Health: Ethical Issues in Government Efforts to Change Life-Styles." *Milbank Memorial Fund Quarterly* 56(3), 1978.

THE PRAIRIE THEATRE AND THE PLAYWRIGHT

Diane Bessai

Interest in the development of a dramatic literature on the prairie has been relatively late when we compare it to the strong achievements in fiction over more than sixty years as represented by the work of such novelists as Grove, Ross, W.O. Mitchell, Laurence and Wiebe. It is axiomatic, of course, that a successful drama cannot develop without the presence of theatres that encourage the writing of new plays and audiences that want to see them. In practical terms, we have to view drama as a collaborative art, a three-way collaboration between playwright, performers and audience. Because theatre has had to come first on the prairie, as elsewhere in Canada, I shall approach my subject, "The Prairie Theatre and the Playwright," by briefly surveying the growth of theatres as it relates to the initiating of a prairie drama.

The foundation of professional theatre over the past twenty or so years can be divided into two historical waves, first the creation of the major regional theatres and then the smaller alternative groups. This is a very rough division and the historical pattern is not always identical from place to place; but what I find most telling about this general pattern, as we will see it, is that the failure, in large measure, of the first wave to fulfill a specifically regional mandate (including a specifically Canadian one) has led to the necessity of proliferating more theatres, often as a form of underground protest. That the second wave theatres are the source of much of the new prairie play-making is a revealing comment on the persistence of a colonial mentality in other quarters; this seems to me the failure to accept that a regional culture need be neither provincial nor parochial, that regionalism, in fact, is the most characteristic mode of native Canadian artistic expression.

The first wave began in a very promising manner with the foundation of the Manitoba Theatre Center in 1958; in fact, for some years following, this organization was held up as the model of regional theatre development for Canada as a whole. One of the most striking features of the young M.T.C. was its strong commitment to a regional ideal of theatre, which is to say that something more was involved than the mere physical location—the M.T.C. did not spring whole from somebody's head or start its life in a vacuum. It began as an amalgamation of the Winnipeg Little Theatre, a dedicated amateur group of ten-years standing, with a fledging professional company called Theatre 77 which had been started a year before by W.L.T. graduate Tom Hendry and John Hirsch. These two were inspired by the idea of professional theatre, the one, Hendry, because he hoped for a theatre to write for, the other because he wanted to direct professionally in his own home town. The pooling of their energies with W.L.T. gave a strong impetus to wide community support, perhaps because Winnipeg had always been a good theatre town, dating back to the days of the touring circuits and continuing through the era of the amateur movement that was spearheaded by the Dominion Drama Festival in the 1930s. In return, the Centre undertook community outreach of various kinds: through a theatre school, a children's theatre, regional touring and a studio theatre. The mainstage itself would offer a full slate of eight plays a season and new work would also have its place in the scheme.

By the end of the first five years, with Hirsch as its artistic director, the M.T.C. had put in motion almost everything the founding groups had planned. This included a few new works written for the children's theatre and the occasional new mainstage show, two by Toronto radio writer Len Peterson and one by Bernard Slade. Since a modern Canadian drama hardly existed at the time, this was not a bad record. In a 1974 retrospective, Hirsch spoke warmly, if nostalgically, about these early days, recalling the excitement that comes from a theatre that grows out of a community; he also spoke of the way the M.T.C. responded to its community by creating "an organic connection between the audiences and what went on stage." Hirsch was referring particularly to the careful programing in his day of plays calculated to appeal to Winnipeggers specifically, Brecht's *Mother Courage*, for example, and his own adaptation of the Jewish folk-play *The Dybyk*. Nevertheless, it was not until 1967 that M.T.C. actually commissioned a mainstage work by a native Winnipegger, a play actually set in Winnipeg. This was Ann Henry's *Lulu Street*, a piece about the General Strike based on the author's memories and stories of her youth. With this production M.T.C. enjoyed a gratifying popular response, drawing people who had never gone to the theatre before because the play was about events they remembered.

These were the zenith years for M.T.C. and I dwell on them in some detail because unfortunately they were too soon gone. Once M.T.C., initially out of necessity, caught building fever, this and related worries about budget deficits encountered in the move to the new Market Street building, gradually eroded the initial activity. The school was closed in 1972, touring petered out and the programing switched to "commercially expedient extravanganzas." While financial stability was eventually restored and subscriptions increased, the long era of professional complacence had set in from which M.T.C. only began to bestir itself a little in the 1980s. The possibilities of local playwriting were never carried very far; at best the second stage, named the Warehouse after its relocation in 1969, scheduled some of the new Canadian plays that were being developed elsewhere.

Thus, as the monolith flourished in its artistically unadventurous way, the would-be Winnipeg playwrights languished in a professional vacuum virtually unmatched in any other prairie city. Recently a group of them formed the Manitoba Association of Playwrights, and with the financial assistance of the Manitoba Arts Council some of their work is now being run through workshop programs. As a consequence two plays by Alfred Silver have been mounted in the past two seasons at the Warehouse, *Thimblerig*, in 1982 and the *Climate of the Times*, in 1983. Silver is actually a product of the Manitoba Theatre Workshop, a virtually underground theatre organization of several years standing that came to the surface in 1981 as a late starter in the second wave of alternate professional theatre movement. Its new name is Prairie Theatre Exchange and in the 1983 season they mounted another workshop play, *St. Peter's Asylum* by Winnipeg writer William Horrocks, also a founding member of The Manitoba Association of Playwrights.

The other elaborately appointed would-be regional monolith on the prairie is Edmonton Citadel Theatre, founded by Joseph Shoctor in 1966. However, there are important differences between the Edmonton theatre scene and that of Winnipeg which relate both directly and indirectly to new play development. For example, unlike the M.T.C., the Citadel *began* unequivocally with what theatre parlance calls mainstream ambitions rather than regional or community intentions. Nor did it evolve from local theatre organizations as did M.T.C., and later, Theatre Calgary. In the postwar years Edmonton was being served, first by Studio Theatre, established in 1949, as an organization that branched out from the University of Alberta Extension Department (as in another direction did the Banff School of Fine Arts). In 1958, an additional amateur group was formed, Walterdale Theatre Associates, taking its name from its first permanent home in the old schoolhouse on the Walterdale flats. From Studio Theatre came a combination of modern, traditional and new plays—most remarkable, in the 1960s, the epic-absurdist plays of Canadian poet, Wilfred Watson; from Walterdale, a nice balance of contemporary and light modern fare, sometimes of near professional quality.

However, the Citadel went about establishing its competence as if it were the only theatre that had ever happened in town, appointing artistic directors and also the majority of its actors from the United States and Britain. Programing was also established repertory, essentially unexciting, although spiced with Broadway and West End hits from time to time. Shoctor's ambitions for his theatre became more apparent in the mid-1970s when he hired John Neville as artistic director in order to pave an international artistic road to his expanding operation which was about to take up residence in a new glass and brass theatre. More sensational were the two and some seasons following Neville's departure in 1978 with British director Peter Coe placed in charge of the Citadel: Coe brought big stars and big ambitions through the production of shows supposedly destined for New York and Broadway—in other words, instant internationalism was the order of the day. Thus outreach to the local community was unabashedly in the direction of the shared delusions of grandeur Edmonton is sometimes prone to. The second stage, the Rice Theatre, like the Warehouse at M.T.C., carried the occasional burden of producing a sampling of well-established Canadian plays, rather than risking untried new ones.

Perhaps because the Citadel has never pretended to be anything else but what it is, a mainstage house that happens to be situated on the prairie, other kinds of theatres quickly proliferated in Edmonton in a way that has never happened in Winnipeg until very recently. On the second wave of prairie theatre development, Theatre 3, Northern Light, Theatre Network, Catalyst Theatre and Workshop West were all spawned in the 1970s, each in some degree of healthy reaction to the Citadel. And although it is never easy for a budding playwright to break successfully into professional theatre, it has not been for lack of encouragement from these quarters. Workshop programs, play-development, collective creations, premieres of new plays, the production of other Canadian works have all taken place at those newer theatres.

However, there is still one historically first-wave theatre that has succeeded by itself in fulfilling a specifically regional mandate similar to the original M.T.C. plan. This is the Globe Theatre of Regina, like the Citadel, founded in 1966, by Ken Kramer and the late Sue Kramer. The beginnings in Regina were very modest. The Kramers came there after studying participatory young people's theatre with Bryan Way in England. Their first four years were spent in establishing a school circuit in Regina and southern Saskatchewan towns. By 1970, however, they were ready also to establish an adult stage in Regina itself. After several locations in that city over the years, three seasons ago, the Globe was granted permanent space in the Old City Hall that was renovated for its use. The theatre has earned its credentials as a dedicated regional voice and shows every sign of sustaining that commitment without lapsing into parochialism or indulging in flighty aspirations.

This is a moderately left-wing theatre politically, its programs showing an emphasis on drama from the mainstream that proves social and political issues— Shaw, Ibsen, Brecht, for example. But it also has led prairie theatres on several specific regional counts: by regularly touring its adult shows to other centers of its area; by commissioning new plays from a variety of Canadian writers both inside and outside its region; by appointing its own writer-in-residence, playwright Rex Deverell, on a continuing basis. This last is a fruitful relationship both for writer and theatre; together they work out the new ideas for a given season. Deverell's writing for the Globe's school tours has also given him a nation-wide reputation for young people's plays. His writing for the mainstage has included such works as *Boiler Room Suite, Drift, Righteousness;* he has also participated in collective theatre with the Globe company, the collaboration with actors in the research and improvisation of local documentary material. The documentary has become a tradition at the Globe, dating from 1971 when Toronto playwright Carol Bolt and the company developed *Next Year Country,* a revue-like history of Saskatchewan with episodic depictions of Depression life, the Estevan miners' strike, the Regina Riots, etc. With Deverell they produced *Number 1 Hard,* a critical look at the grain industry; he has also written his own version of the documentary-style play: *Black Powder,* a full treatment of the Estevan strike for the fiftieth anniversary of that event, and *Medicare!,* the latter, which he calls his one-man collective, the compilation of the documents and events of the 1962 doctors' strike, is a highly skillful achievement in the shaping of historical records into drama with a minimum of fictionalization. One of the vivid features of the *Medicare!* production was the presence in the audience of some of the actual participants in this history-making controversy; it also happened that the Globe was temporarily performing in the Trianon Ballroom that year, which is to say, on the actual location of important confrontations between doctors and government all those years before.

In a very specific instance these coincidences with *Medicare!* point to the immediacy of relationship between performance and audience that the Globe's kind of grassroots theatre cultivates; theirs is a theatre partially designed for the recovery and re-creation of its audience's own life, backgrounds and traditions; thus its work illustrates how theatre arts can give popular currency to specific local and regional identities in a direct way. The premiere performance of *Black Powder* in Estevan itself is yet another vivid example.

The Globe serves as the suitable bridge to the discussion of the second or alternative wave of prairie theatre because it has consistently managed to heed a number of the concerns motivating later theatre development in other prairie cities. Indeed its alertness to new playwriting throughout the 1970s reflects the increasing pressures for a native Canadian theatre and drama that were starting to infiltrate the whole country in an almost underground way. While the source of this energy was chiefly Toronto, the Globe is one prairie theatre that responded to the challenge early by commissioning work from a variety of playwrights: Len Peterson, Carol Bolt, Rod Langley and Ken Mitchell; and some of these plays also went out from the Globe for production elsewhere, for example Langley's *Bethune* was joint commission with Montreal's Centaur Theatre; Carol Bolt and Theatre Passe Muraille transformed *Next Year Country* into *Buffalo Jump.*

A more radical if narrower step was taken in 1972 by Alberta Theatre Projects in Calgary, this the first theatre on the prairie to establish itself as a totally Canadian alternative theatre. Founders Douglas Riske and Lucille Wagner proposed to commission local plays on historical subjects and to produce these and other Canadian plays only. Meanwhile Theatre Calgary was mostly trying to look after the mainstream. It had been established in 1968, indirectly evolving from Calgary's strong amateur movement in the 1950s and 1960s under the leadership of Betty Mitchell, famous in the days of Workshop 14, while Mac 14, a semi-professional group, was Theatre Calgary's actual founding organization. The smaller group, A.T.P., with the aid of a L.I.P. grant, began operating in the old Canmore Opera House at Heritage Park with the aim of reaching audiences who had never been to the theatre before through their local plays. The opener was called the *History Show*, written by Paddy Campbell in both a children's and an adult version. Later this became the script *Under the Arch*. The plan of the founders flourished for a time. Bonnie Le May wrote a comic mystery based on the days of the silk train's passage through Calgary, entitled *Roundhouse*; Sandra Jones and Jan Truss wrote young people's plays; Paddy Campbell collaborated with William Skolnik in a very successful musical comedy, about the semi-legendary Bob Edwards, called *Hoarse Muse*. However, by the end of the 1975/76 season, the need for financial retrenchment and the difficulty in continuing the flow of good plays resulted in a modification of Alberta Theatre Projects' programing policy. While Canadian plays would be the nucleus, they could no longer be the sole content. The next season John Murrell, in his second year as A.T.P.'s writer-in-residence, contributed two plays, *A Great Noise, A Great Light*, set in the Calgary of the Aberhart rise to power and *Waiting for the Parade*, a piece about the experience of several Calgary women waiting out World War II at home. The latter turned into a hit; it was remounted in several Canadian theatres, was chosen by the National Arts Centre for a cross-Canada touring production and later was performed at the Lyric Hammersmith in London, England. Following Murrell, Sharon Pollock also served as playwright-in-residence at A.T.P., working with children's theatre. In 1981, the theatre premiered her adult play *Generations*, an exploration of contemporary pressures on farm family relationships set in southern Alberta.

Sad to say, the impact of Alberta Theatre Projects on developing prairie drama has begun to dwindle since that time. The limitations of space appear to be confining its artistic development as well. However, it is still interested in contemporary Alberta plays, as indicated by its recent collaboration with Edmonton's Northern Light Theatre in the formation of the Alberta Playwriting Centre for the workshopping of new plays.

Theatre Calgary, on the other hand, with its more spacious facilities at the QR Centre, has in recent seasons shown a concentrated interest in mounting plays by local writers for which it can offer more elaborate productions than Alberta

Theatre Projects. This is particularly so if the writers are W.O. Mitchell or Sharon Pollock. Theatre Calgary's history has been mixed, which is to say it was never so rigid as the Citadel about risking itself on a new playwright now and then--even though, like the Citadel, it has in its time been concerned with star attractions and flashy productions; in Theatre Calgary's case this reflects the pressures of audience-building for the eventual arts center space that Calgary has long been expecting. Yet even in 1973, the then artistic director Harold Baldridge ventured what turned out to be Sharon Pollock's first important work, *Walsh*, a play about the ignoble Sitting Bull in Canada episode, a work that went to the Stratford Third Stage the next summer. This has been popular as a teaching text since its publication in 1974 and, in revised form, was offered during the 1983 season at the National Arts Centre in Ottawa. Baldridge also provided W.O. Mitchell with the opportunity for the stage version of his television play, *Back to Beulah*, in 1975, a work that has been much performed in Canadian theatres since, and which initiated further production of Mitchell plays at Theatre Calgary.

The case of W.O. Mitchell as a playwright offers an important comment on the role of the professional theatre as a new artistic vehicle for a writer with an established reputation in other literary forms. Thanks to the pioneering work of Theatre Calgary even the Citadel now puts pre-tested Mitchell on its mainstage. But more important than that, Mitchell is a natural writer for the theatre, particularly with his rich gift for comic character. He himself noted that if conditions for the playwright had been as good in his younger days as they seem to him now, he might have started his writing career with the theatre. The present artistic director, Rick McNair, seems to have come to the interesting conclusion that his theatre can attract audiences with Canadian plays almost as well as any other. Thus he has produced four of Mitchell's plays up to date, and also commissioned a new play form Sharon Pollock in the 1983 season entitled *Whiskey Six*, a vivid evocation of prohibition days in the Crowsnest Pass town of Blairmore.

Themes from regional history have probably done most to stimulate the writing of modern prairie drama, for reasons, I think, that have to do with the urgency to give stories a popular currency before they are forgotten or homogenized out of existence. Local history, as we have seen with the Globe and Alberta Theatre Projects, is also a direct way of putting a theatre in touch with its audience. One of the best advocates of "the community family portrait" past and present in Canada has been Paul Thompson of Toronto's Theatre Passe Muraille; his influence on prairie theatre in this regard is important to record. His theatre works in a collective presentational style that tries to extract the myths of history and community rather than precisely documenting the facts. This is the essential difference between Passe Muraille Plays and the documentary work of the Globe; the former are really improvisations on historical themes.

The best example of the Passe Muraille approach in the West comes from 25th Street Theatre in Saskatoon. Initially this was a cooperative theatre, founded in 1972 by a group of University of Saskatchewan graduates, most prominently Andras Tahn, who performed new plays, often their own plays, whenever they could find the money and the space. Their populist identity emerged with their phenomenally successful show, *Paper Wheat*, a collectively written play about the founding of the Saskatchewan Wheat Pool. Their interest in collective creations was initiated during the visit of Passe Muraille in 1975 when the Toronto theatre came to develop material for its own *The West Show*. For several years this company had been successfully play-making in Ontario by the unique method of moving into particular communities to live while they improvised material for plays from the people and the stories they encountered: *The Farm Show*, created from a summer's experience living in the rural community of Clinton, is one of the best examples. 25th Street Theatre learned through their first collective, directed by Thompson with the unlikely title, *If You're So Good Why are You in Saskatoon?*, and by their application of Thompson's method, beginning with a vaguely formulated idea to do a "Co-op Show."

As Don Kerr describes the process in *Paper Wheat: the Book*, during the winter of 1977 the company went visiting in several Saskatchewan towns to collect their material, calling in at local cafes for leads on people who might reminisce about coops. Gradually they decided to combine the stories they retrieved about pioneer life with the history they were learning about the Wheat Pool. The result was a tremendously popular response on the circuit of small towns they returned to, this leading to further development and improvement of the play and further tours in and beyond Saskatchewan over the next two years. The company discovered that theatre's capacity to make its audience relive the heroic endeavors of a not-so-distant past had great local appeal, an appeal that readily transferred to other part of the country as well. Part of this success was the style of presentation itself: minimal props and sets; engaging multiple characterization, song, mime, and seriousness tempered with comic irony; in Kerr's words: "a little like a Christmas concert or an amateur hour."[1] It is not surprising that Andy Tahn said in 1980, "The kind of theatre I dream of is like hockey—part of the community."[2]

Another theatre that began to work in this way in the late 1970s was Edmonton's Theatre Network. Under the direction of Mark Manson, the company began by moving into the small town of Elnora, near Red Deer, to explore the character of a declining community (*Two Miles Off*, 1976). Next they went to Fort McMurray to explore the life of a burgeoning one since the coming of Syncrude. Theatre Network also went north to do a collective on the contemporary life of Inuvik (*Kicker*, 1978), and more recently developed *Rigs* (1981), a play about the work and people of the Alberta oil patch. Thompson originally started the collective method because there were no Canadian plays that spoke in the genuine local voice of a given community—more likely, in American movie language. In the West his "texture work," as he called it, transferred well for the same reason. Collectives and documentaries are not crafted plays in the conventional sense: they are theatre pieces, not dramatic literature. But they are important notations that identify the areas that a native playwright can further explore, not only to give the life and traditions of the region a popular currency, but as a concrete basis for the expression of individual vision. Thus collective creators and the documentary dramatists have had an important function as map-makers for a developing prairie dramatic tradition. Ken Mitchell, for example, has drawn on two historical figures for plays, *The Shipbuilder*, the story of the eccentric Tom Sukanen (to whom Passe Muraille devoted a sequence in *The West Show*) and *Davin: The Politician*, a play about one of Regina's founders.

I began my account of the prairie theatre and the playwright by talking about the regional ideals first posited by the Manitoba Theatre Centre in the early stages of its development. Such concerns, I believe, are the most important *raison d'être* of a developing native theatre, while the continuing reliance on importation, in other words a continuing neo-colonialism, eventually proves a sterile enterprise. The theatre and the drama, like the other arts, have to put down roots in their natural habitat if they are to thrive.

I would like to conclude my not entirely unbiased survey by referring to some remarks made recently by John Gray, author of *Billy Bishop Goes to War*. At the Canadian Theatre Today Conference in Saskatoon in October, 1981, Gray was very outspoken in attacking what he called the "regionals," meaning in particular the theatre I have described as the monoliths, of which the prairies has two outstanding examples as we have seen. They are "white elephants," he said and "should be blown up;" they are the consequence of the Canada Council's "branch plant mentality" that merely duplicates big centers in the form of little centers, all preoccupied with blandly representative seasons, a little of everything, including the occasional slot for a new play. He also remarked that Canadian plays generally do badly on large main stages, thus discouraging their continuing production, because they have been developed for the small alternate spaces— usually renovated factories, warehouses, churches or meeting halls. More recently, Gray, in his inimitably explosive way, said something further that I think the facts of this presentation also identify as a decidedly Canadian (and prairie) theatre anomaly. Here Gray makes two related points that I will quote:

> In Canada you can get away with a lot because a play is true, because it relates to the audience. And well you should.

This refers to both the strengths and weaknesses of much alternate theatre. Second, he says:

> Because Canadian theatre exists on the dregs, a Canadian play never gets to move into a Regional theatre where it might have to answer to ... questions of structure and form, where it might have to measure up as a work of art.... If they'd make room for us in the Regionals we could probably become more structured, more formalistic, cleaner.[3]

In other words, the effect of the split between the two kinds of theatre is beginning to show, perhaps more severely in some centers than others, but in a way that casts some doubt on the future of Canadian drama. In my own view, the weakness lies in the failure of Gray's "Regionals" to be properly regional.

Footnotes

1. *Paper Wheat: the Book* (Saskatoon: Western Producer Prairie Books, 1982), p. 23.

2. *NeWest Review*, Jan., 1980, p. 7.

3. *The Work: Conversations with English-Canadian Playwrights*, edited by Robert Wallace and Cynthia Zimmermann (Toronto: The Coach House Press, 1982), p. 55.

WINNIPEG WEST: THE POSTWAR DEVELOPMENT OF ART IN WESTERN CANADA

Christopher Varley

Winnipeg West is the first exhibition to attempt to account for the spread and development of art in Western Canada after World War II. A cut-off date of 1970 brings it very close to the present. At one time I considered calling it *A Tale of Six Cities*, for the art of the period was an urban phenomenon, and was heavily dependent upon personal exchanges and travel between the widely separated cities of British Columbia, Alberta, Saskatchewan and Manitoba. Like the London and Paris of Charles Dickens's tale, Vancouver, Edmonton, Calgary, Regina, Saskatoon and Winnipeg each had its own character and "scene," for western Canada was never a homogeneous cultural block.

Although this is not a study of modernist art *per se*, all of the art discussed falls within modernism's various traditions. We may therefore learn something about the ways in which western Canadian artists perceived the world and coped with their isolation. And we will certainly learn something about the nature of modernism *in* isolation.

The *raison d'être* for this undertaking, however, is to draw attention to the many aspects of postwar western Canadian art. Although most of the artists' names are familiar by now, we still do not have a discriminating understanding of the contributions of many of them, and continue to think of them in mutual isolation. I therefore hope that this study leads to further interest in these artists, and to a deeper understanding of their achievements and importance to one another.

École Du Pacifique

Vancouver, 1945-60

Our tale begins in Vancouver,[1] which enjoyed undisputed hegemony over the other western Canadian cities for nearly the entire period of this survey. Its status was reflected in Canadian exhibitions travelling abroad, the pages of *Canadian Art*, and by the other five cities themselves. When H.G. Glyde resigned as Head of the Department of Art at the Provincial Institute of Technology and Art in Calgary in 1946, he invited J.W.G. ("Jock") Macdonald of Vancouver to take his place. Likewise, Joe Plaskett of Vancouver replaced Lionel LeMoine FitzGerald as Acting Principal of the Winnipeg School of Art in 1947/48.[2] And when Kenneth Lochhead reorganized the Emma Lake workshops in Saskatchewan in 1955, he did not turn to eastern Canada or to the United States for workshop leaders, but to Vancouver. Jack Shadbolt led the session that first summer, and Plaskett followed in 1956. B.C. Binning and Shadbolt also served on the juries for the prestigious *Winnipeg Show* in 1956 and 1957 respectively. Furthermore, many prairie artists were attracted to Vancouver.

But what, besides the scenery and climate, made Vancouver so attractive? Existing cultural and educational institutions were certainly a factor, for through the work of The Vancouver Art Gallery and Vancouver School of Art, something akin to traditions and tolerance of the visual arts had been established. Two major figures, Emily Carr and F.H. Varley, had already left their marks on the province, and Lawren Harris added new life to the city when he moved there in 1940. Having adopted abstraction in the mid-thirties, he encouraged Jock Macdonald and B.C. Binning with their forays into this new form of expression. And in his role as Chairman of the Exhibition Committee of The Vancouver Art Gallery, and later as a member of the Gallery's Council, he promoted an adventurous exhibition program and close ties with the Vancouver School of Art in the mid-forties.

One of the most intriguing results of this collaboration was the Gallery's *Art in Living* exhibition of September 1944, "Organized by a group of young artists under the direction of Mr. Fred Amess Principal of the art school...designed to show the people of Vancouver what might be achieved in the future by careful planning of our city and of the homes it will contain."[3] Binning, who taught drawing and architecture at the art school, arranged the architectural component of this exhibition. Starting with his own home in West Vancouver, built about 1940, he introduced modernist architecture derived from Frank Lloyd Wright to the Coast. The "post and beam," flat-topped style that later won wide acceptance in Vancouver owes a lot to him.

But in the mid-forties Binning was also known as a pen-and-ink virtuoso. His whimsical depictions of the coves and beaches of West Vancouver spoke of the pleasure of life on the Coast. They had much in common with Dufy's and Matisse's genteel visions of the French Riviera, and revealed a delightful sense of the ridiculous. Donald Jarvis was so impressed with the wit and facility of these works that he decided to become an artist after seeing one of Binning's classroom demonstrations. His own pen-and-ink drawings of the late forties owed something to Binning's vision.

The other major figure at the Vancouver School of Art was Jack Shadbolt. A controversial teacher who raised the pitch of art-school polemics, he countered Binning's amused detachment with art that was outspoken, engaged and steeped in the anxiety of the age. Although he moved quickly toward abstraction after the war, some of his most remarkable paintings were the city street scenes that he recorded in watercolor from about 1942 to 1946. These affirmations of his attachment to Vancouver were as frank as they were affectionate, and often included superb passages of atmospheric washes.

Most of Vancouver's painters looked to Britain or to the American West Coast for artistic leadership after the war. The Vancouver Art Gallery, under the direction of Jerrold Morris in the early fifties, undoubtedly reinforced the interest in British art with its well-chosen purchases of paintings by Graham Sutherland, Ben Nicholson, Ivon Hitchens and others.

Although Lawren Harris did not respond to these new works himself, he also helped to clear the way for abstraction through his own enthusiastic commitment to it. A devout Theosophist, he held the utopian view that a universal reality of harmonious order existed beyond the chaotic world of temporal appearances. He developed a symbolic abstract language of his own through which he tried to bridge the gap between the universal and the particular, and while he seems to have been possessed by dull, geometric formulas during the forties, he burst into the next decade and the age of retirement with more energy and fireworks than any other Vancouver artist. Propelled by buoyant feelings of spiritual exaltation, he painted some beautifully crafted and highly individual—some might say eccentric—canvases that alluded to the mountains, waves and vistas of the Coast.

Binning and Shadbolt were much younger than Harris, and clearly influenced by the new British art. Binning, who befriended Henry Moore while studying in England just before the war, looked as hard at Ben Nicholson as at Paul Klee and Joan Miró when he started painting abstractions in 1948. He borrowed Nicholson's device of roughing up the surfaces of his paintings on masonite, and adopted the British painter's playful method of superimposing planes and destabilizing spatial relationships. Although the results tended to be repetitive and lightweight, the gaiety of these paintings suggest once again that Binning had found a bit of the Mediterranean on the West Coast.

By comparison, Shadbolt's vision was sombre and perhaps more apt. He saw the sodden reality of Vancouver, with its opaque gray light, months of drizzle, and tangled profusion of growth. But, like many artists of the time, he seemed to trade art for "ambition" when he turned to abstraction in the late forties. Fine as his "metamorphic" abstractions often were, they lacked the tender insights of his Vancouver street scenes. Many were indebted to Graham Sutherland, whose paintings were filled with mechanical symbols for violence and metamorphosis in nature. Shadbolt, then Jarvis, adopted the English painter's spirals and spikes. As in Sutherland's paintings, the results all too often looked melodramatic, as if the postwar art world was still hung-over from too much violence, too much despair and too much Picasso [Fig. 1].

FIGURE 1

TITLE: Ritual Forms in Black, White and Brown 1950

In 1958 Shadbolt won the Canadian Section Award at the Carnegie International Exhibition in Pittsburgh. This brought him attention abroad, and earned him acclaim in Canada. By this time he favored oil paints over watercolor, and his paintings of the period were generally influenced by the late-cubist abstractions of Hans Hofmann and Nicholas de Stael. The acidly brilliance of his palette certainly owed something to Hofmann, although he never acquired the older American artist's vitality of touch.

The influx of students to the Vancouver School of Art after the war was so great and so sudden that some had to be given teaching positions, and others stayed on after graduation. Donald Jarvis and Gordon Smith were among these; Bruno Bobak, who received his early training from Carl Schaefer in Toronto, joined the staff in 1947.

Jarvis was one of several Vancouverites who studied with Hans Hofmann in New York in the late forties. Upon returning home, he turned to the rain forest and city streets for subjects. Initially indebted to Shadbolt, he tried to integrate cubist figures into naturalistic settings. While his paintings of the early fifties were exceedingly gloomy—colored by the sentimentality of youth—by the late forties he had grown into a finely discriminating and highly responsive painter. His abstractions of the period combined atmospheric color and figurative elements in a lyrical and evocative dance. Smith also benefited from Shadbolt's advice and example, and helped to establish Vancouver's reputation nationally when he won first prize at the *1st Canadian Biennial*, organized by The National Gallery in 1955. But he constantly changed styles, and seems to have been lionized as much for his gentility and life-style as for his achievements. Whether alluding to Rufino Tamayo, or to the "lyrical abstraction" of Ivon Hitchens, he always painted with discrimination and refinement. Much the same can be said of Joe Plaskett, a latter-day Edouard Vuillard, whose pastel landscapes and darkened interiors reflected a chic "French" sensibility. Although he spent most of his time in Paris, he maintained close ties with artists and collectors in Vancouver, who seem to have regarded him with a certain amount of envy and awe.

This fascination with style and social acceptance was both a blessing and a curse. It brought the artists to public attention, and helped to sell their work. Vancouver had commercial galleries specializing in contemporary art long before most of the other cities of the West. But all the talk of a Vancouver "scene" also created confusion and led to self-consciousness and entrenchment. Bruno Bobak felt so bitter about the results that he eventually decided to move:

> I grew to hate the attitude that you measured the quality of an artist by the possessions he owned. There was always a scramble to see who could outdo somebody else: the chic wife, the beautiful house...eventually it was a question of whether you had a twelve foot sailboat or a fourteen foot sailboat. If you had two sailboats you were twice the artist of someone who had just one. It was a kind of raw, monied life. Nobody ever really talked about art. You just talked about the good life.[4]

Not unexpectedly, this anger was reflected in Bobak's own art of the late fifties. After paying the customary homage to British artists like Paul Nash and John Piper, and looking closely at the American West Coast painter Morris Graves, he turned to prewar European expressionism, especially to the panoramic cityscapes of Oscar Kokoschka. The biting charcoal drawings that followed were filled with sweeps and scrawls. Busy and melodramatic, yet also dense and full, they greatly enhanced his reputation as a graphic artist [Fig. 2].

FIGURE 2

"Stone Face" by Bruno Bobak   Courtesy of The Edmonton Art Gallery

Vancouver was not as cosmopolitan or as "in the know" as R.H. Hubbard, Allan Jarvis, and other visitors from the East seemed to think. In hindsight, we can see that they should have given Montreal more attention. And it should be clear that in settling for such a comfortable position on the rear deck of the official postwar avant-garde, Vancouver's artists were liable to grow complacent.

They would have been better off with less recognition and more criticism. Still, traditions the later artists would build upon or reject were established. As we continue this tale, we shall see what an advantage this was.

One final word though, for the isolation and spongy intellectual climate of provincial art centers are not always a disadvantage. Highly independent or visionary artists, who create their own histories or might be crushed in a more competitive environment, may actually thrive there.

FIGURE 3

"Howe Sound, B.C., 1955" by E.J. Hughes   Courtesy of The Edmonton Art Gallery

The most important of British Columbia's "independents" was E.J. Hughes, who was trained in Vancouver, and lived on Vancouver Island. His "picture postcard" landscapes of the forties and fifties were among the most guilelessly original and pictorially accomplished paintings made on the Coast. They displayed real insights into both the province's Mediterranean charms and its darker, primeval undertones. And he somehow managed to hold them together, although most were painted in saturated, strongly contrasting colors. It seems ironic that Hughes, who cared so little for recognition or success, is now the most sought after West Coast painter of the period that concerns us here [Fig. 3].

What's Wrong with Winnipeg?

Winnipeg, 1945-70

Of all the cities in the West, Winnipeg would appear to have the most historical advantages.[5] It was the "gateway" to the region, and the site of its first permanent settlement. Somewhat more sophisticated than other western communities, it opened a public art gallery eleven years before Edmonton, and nearly twenty years before Vancouver. One of the artists represented in the inaugural exhibition of December 1912 was Lionel LeMoine FitzGerald, Winnipeg-born, and since 1930 recognized as a major figure in Canadian art.

But Winnipeg has produced few such artists, and it has always projected a cloudy image to the rest of the country. Even the nationally acclaimed *Winnipeg Show*, organized annually by the Winnipeg Art Gallery between 1955 and 1961, and biennially between 1962 and 1970, failed to establish the city on the visual arts map. For, while the gallery devoted time and attention to this national survey, it was perceived as remaining aloof from the local art community. LeMoine FitzGerald and Ivan Eyre were practically the only artists to receive its ongoing support and patronage.

The Winnipeg School of Art, which became affiliated with the University of Manitoba in 1950, offered the semblance of a context, and employed some influential teachers, but its relationship to the rest of the art community was never as strong as it might have been. Even during the two decades when FitzGerald was principal, it never held a clear position of leadership. Yet FitzGerald was unquestionably the most widely recognized artist working in the city at the end of the war. He was curious and perceptive, albeit cautious and tasteful, and his still-lifes of the period were among his finest achievements. Many of these drawings, watercolor, and oil paintings employed the simple yet dynamic formula of setting vertical forms against diagonal planes. Like Cézanne's paintings, most were asymmetrically balanced, and as if in homage, FitzGerald placed apples in many of them [Fig. 4].

FitzGerald also practised abstraction between 1950 and his death in 1956. He was encouraged to take it up by Lawren Harris, whom he periodically visited in Vancouver during the forties. The only clear influences that his abstractions revealed, however, were of Lyonel Feininger and Russian-German constructivism. The proximity of the Chicago Bauhaus may have been a factor in determining this, as we will see that artists in Saskatoon later looked to the same sources for models. But FitzGerald produced too little too late to contribute anything to abstraction's acceptance or development in Canada, and while the best of his abstracts transmitted some of his feelings for spirituality and "pure" form, most were wistful, naive, and marred by spatial incongruities.

FIGURE 4

"Still Life with Flower Pot" by L.L. Fitzgerald
Courtesy of The Edmonton Art Gallery

In 1950, a year after FitzGerald's retirement, William Ashby McCloy was hired by the University of Iowa as the first director of the reorganized University of Manitoba School of Art. This was but the first postwar link between Manitoba, then Saskatoon, and the American Mid-West. In fact, McCloy brought two other University of Iowa graduates, John Kacere and Richard Bowman, with him to Winnipeg; and Richard Williams, a third, was hired to replace him when he returned to the United States in 1954. Winnipeg does not seem to have looked to eastern Canada at all for guidance. Nor did it look to its own artists and administrators, which may be another reason why it did not establish strong, ongoing traditions. Outsiders did not tend to stay long, and were not always accepted by, or interested in the art community.

Nor did their art "stick." While Douglas Morton still remembers the excitement raised by an exhibition of McCloy's, Kacere's, and Bowman's paintings in 1952 at Coste House in Calgary,[6] it may now be impossible to find anything by Kacere or Bowman in Winnipeg, and the Winnipeg Art Gallery only owns one painting by McCloy—a weak pastiche of Picasso.

Nevertheless, Winnipeg received considerable regional attention during the forties and fifties. Simply having an art school and a gallery were enough at the time, for they provided opportunities for advanced study, exhibitions and employment. George Swinton, who served as the first curator of the Saskatoon Art Center from 1947 to 1949, took a teaching post at the art school in 1954. Ivan Eyre left Saskatoon the year before to continue his studies at the school. Eyre recalls that Swinton and Robert Nelson, whom McCloy brought to Winnipeg from the Chicago Art Institute School, were the two most influential teachers at the school in the mid- to late fifties.[7] Swinton counteracted Nelson's Picassoesque surrealism with a personal form of romantic naturalism. He showed a propensity for hot colors, and however poor some of the results, his biblical paintings and landscapes were always *tours de force*. He seems to have exerted an influence at the school similar to Jack Shadbolt in Vancouver, and is either remembered as broad-minded and energetic, or opinionated and condescending.

The art school produced its fair share of talented students, and appears to have been ahead of the rest of the community in terms of amibition, but many of its finest graduates left Winnipeg, and of those who stayed, few developed. Kelly Clark, for example, was looked up to as a student, and the Winnipeg Art Gallery bought two of his paintings from Winnipeg Shows, but he apparently stopped painting in the early sixties in favor of a career in music.

Other Winnipeg artists have quickly come and gone from the National scene over the years, including Jack Markell, a devotee of what Clement Greenberg called the "Boston school of Jewish expressionism,"[8] and Esther Warkov, who studied at the art school in the late fifties, and received considerable praise and attention while her paintings were handled by the Marlborough-Godard Gallery in Toronto and Montreal. But she dropped out of sight when this commercial gallery stopped representing her. This was unfortunate, for her enigmatic, sometimes witty, dream-image paintings were highly individualistic. Curiously, Warkov is almost the only artist in this survey who was directly influenced by art that she saw from eastern Canada. She greatly admired Jack Chambers of London, Ontario, and her early paintings often included floating objects and pale, close valued colors that were similar to his.

Ivan Eyre, who emerged on the national scene in the mid-sixties, is unquestionably the most widely admired Winnipeg painter since FitzGerald. He has received ongoing support and recognition from the Winnipeg Art Gallery, and is respected by his fellow Winnipeg artists for his independence and commitment. He began his studies with Ernest Lindner and Eli Bornstein in Saskatoon, then enrolled at the University of Manitoba School of Art in 1953. His paintings of the fifties were influenced by Pierre Bonnard and Eduoard Buillard, whose "camouflaged"[9] figures interested him and by Max Beckmann, whose paintings he saw in Chicago. In 1958 he entered the graduate program at the University of North Dakota, encouraged by Robert Nelson, who left Winnipeg to head its art department. The following year he briefly lived in Dover, Massachusetts, then returned to Winnipeg to teach at the art school.

In 1961 he decided to purge himself of external influences, and began making large numbers of drawings to determine what was essentially his. The paintings that followed still owed something to Bechmann's allegorical images and biting line, but Eyre littered his crawling, twisted, haunted figures across the vast space of the plains. These symbols of alienation, suffering and paralysis bespoke of folly and ignorance. The large acrylics that followed in the late sixties were more immediately attractive, but hardly less unsettling or mysterious.

Like FitzGerald, Eyre never counted on the interest or support of the Winnipeg community. But this indifference is a rare luxury anywhere in the West, and can only be afforded by those who have found secure employment or have achieved success elsewhere. For artists who are not so fortunate, Winnipeg is still a good city to leave.

Seeds on Rocky Ground

Calgary and Edmonton, 1945-70

> The three Prairie Provinces have proved themselves even less sympathetic to the original artist than the rest of the country. Talent appears here as elsewhere; but an unsympathetic environment acts as an emetic force on those who do not conform to its philistinism, or do not care to put up with its indifference.[10]

Thus began Maxwell Bates's attack in a 1948 issue of *Highlights*, published by the Alberta Society of Artists to help inform and hold the small Alberta art community together. Nowhere was the philistinism that Bates referred to more oppressively felt than in that province. Calgary and Edmonton were still in the cultural wilderness in 1945.[11] Compared to even Vancouver and Winnipeg, their histories were short, and their isolation more complete. No major painters had lived in the province, and few institutions existed for artists to gather around.

And yet some seeds had been planted. The Edmonton Museum of Art (now The Edmonton Art Gallery) was incorporated in 1924, and under the guidance of Maude Bowman, had collected with some flair. In the early thirties in Calgary, A.C. Leighton had run the art department of the Provincial Institute of Technology and Art, and organized the Banff School of Fine Arts. In 1936, H.G. Glyde, another expatriate Englishman, became head of the Department of Art at the "Tech," and of the art department in Banff. A devoted art educator, he deplored the backwardness of Alberta and wanted to bring other artists, writers—even theatre troupes and small orchestras—out from Britain to build the foundations for a stronger culture. But Alberta was poor, and this sort of British domination of the school system was starting to meet resistance.

When Glyde moved to Edmonton in 1946 to organize the art department at the University of Alberta, he asked Jock Macdonald, a Scotsman living in Vancouver, to replace him at the Tech. But Macdonald stayed only a year, and when he left for Toronto, he recommended Saskatchewan-born Illingworth Kerr to take his place.

Kerr oversaw the rapid expansion and the "Canadianization" of the art department after the war. Like the Vancouver School of Art, the Tech grew so quickly in the immediate postwar years that students stayed to teach, and some real momentum was generated. Following Macdonald's example, Kerr and Marion Nicoll, a former student of Leighton's who taught design, took up "automatic" painting. Although Kerr's experiments with this surrealist-derived technique always ended up looking like animals, Nicoll's robust watercolor doodles earned her a reputation as Alberta's first committed abstract artist. Many were stronger than Macdonald's own automatics, which all too often were embroidered with fussy embellishments. Nicoll now receives most recognition, however, for the large, flat patterned canvases that she began painting after studying with Will Barnet at the Emma Lake workshop of 1957, then in his class in New York. She made distant reference to Indian hieroglyphs and cityscapes in these paintings through which she sought to express her feelings for universal, classical order— a far cry from her seemingly random automatics [Fig. 5].

FIGURE 5

Nov. '48 "Untitled" by Marion Nicoll
Courtesy of Glenbow Museum

Kerr, who studied with J.E.H. MacDonald, and other members of the Group of Seven at the Ontario College of Art in the twenties, was primarily an animal and landscape painter who occasionally experimented with abstraction. He admired

Franz Marc, and like him, tried to visualize the relationship that animals felt with their environment. He is much better known for his boldly designed landscapes, however, which emphasize the carpet-like patterns of the rolling Alberta farmland and massive angularity of the Rocky Mountains. His large, broadly laid-in watercolors of the fifties were especially vivid, and displayed his gifts for color to the full.

In lieu of a municipal art gallery, the Calgary Allied Arts Center also played an important role after the war, and helped to bring the various factions of the cultural community together. Douglas Morton, who was curator of the Center from 1951 to 1953, recalls that Bob Kerr wired it for sound, and held musicals every Sunday night. And sandwiched between these other functions was an exhibition program that included both locally organized and touring shows, such as those provided by the Western Canadian Art Circuit, and other art organizations.[12]

Calgary's art community tended to divide between "mountainpainters," like Roland Gissing, and what the young-blood called "real painters," the most admired of whom was Maxwell Bates. He was something of a moral force in the city, for his honesty and dedication apparently impressed nearly everyone. Roy Kiyooka, who met him while studying at the Tech, later described him as an important model in his own life,[13] and Morton thought that he was the best painter in Alberta.[14]

Bates was tough and uncompromising, yet fundamentally generous. A cynical streak constantly reappeared in his expressionistic art. Like the *Nene Sacklichkeit* realists of Weimar Germany whom he admired so much, he often took aim at the vanity, hypocrisy and stupidity of his fellow man. This criticism was especially barbed in his studies of human relationships. In his depictions of games, seances and visits to fortune tellers, he played credulous innocence off against malevolent cunning.

One of Bates's most important mentors was Max Beckmann, with whom he studied at the Brooklyn Museum Art School in 1949/50. Like Bates, Beckmann was primarily a figure painter whose social comments were often expressed in allegorical terms. Bates emulated his coarse, expressionist-derived technique, frequently employing the same sorts of garish, discordant colors and heavy black-brush drawing. His paintings were generally more simply organized and easily comprehensible than Beckmann's, however, and his love of grids and ornamental patterns also related to cubism and Matisse. Bates's cultural importance to western Canada still appears to be poorly understood in the East, in part because so many of his paintings were so bad or derivative. He often shows to better advantage in his landscapes and watercolors than in the figure paintings for which he is best known.

Bates was close to John Snow, who pulled his prints and shared his taste for social commentary and modern German graphic art. Although there was something indefinite about the expressionism of Snow's early prints, and he eventually turned into a purely decorative lithographer (as well as a highly entertaining sculptor), his early woodcuts provide fascinating insights into the perception of modernism on the prairies during the forties and fifties. Like so many other artists, he turned to German expressionism for his models and themes. It was as if they saw only the winter bleakness, not the effervescent summertime beauty of their surroundings.

This is certainly true of W.L. Stevenson as well, Bates's old friend who returned to Calgary from Vancouver in 1953. Even his early Cézannesque still-lifes were filled with northern intensity and darkness. The paintings that he made after his return were as violent as Goodridge Roberts's late landscapes, with which they have often been compared.

Of the next generation of Calgarian artists to make names for themselves, most did so after leaving the city. Among them were Douglas Morton, Roy Kiyooka, Arthur McKay and Ted Godwin, who all moved to Regina. Morton recalls that while there was "a lot of group thinking and interaction" in Calgary, "there was a general feeling that we needed some tough professional input from outside."[15] The city was too small, too isolated, and with the end of the immediate postwar expansion, teaching jobs became harder to come by.

Judging from the paintings of Kiyooka and Ronald Spickett, many of this next generation were interested in the socially-conscious Mexican muralists and Rico Lebrun, the widely influential Los Angeles figure painter. Both artists studied with the American cubist James Pinto in San Miguel, Mexico, in 1956/57. Before leaving Calgary, Kiyooka made a series of planar, stylized cityscapes and farm scenes, most of which were uncertain and inexpressive. But the Mexican portraits and village scenes that followed were pictorially dynamic, intense and romantic. Kiyooka moved to Regina shortly after returning to Canada, and Spickett returned to Calgary to teach at the Tech. For several years he practised calligraphic "drip" painting based on "the subtle interplay of forms, spaces and textures found in Prairie grass."[16] These met with considerable favor, for critics recognized the affinities with Jackson Pollock, but the dark ecclesiastical figure paintings that followed met with much less favor. Spickett painted these huge religious subjects in Lebrun's grand manner, successfully adopting his wiry contour drawing, patina and virtuoso techniques. "Old fashioned" as they might have been, they were also impressive, and deserve to be better known.

If Calgary had difficulty in consolidating and building upon its postwar gains, Edmonton faced even deeper problems. It was an isolated civil-service community with little to substantiate its claims of cultural superiority over "Cowtown" to the south. It had few artists before 1960, and most of these were amateurs.

H.G. Glyde brought an element of professionalism to the city when he moved to the University of Alberta in 1946. But he had little sympathy for modernist art or the local painters, and his postwar paintings often fell within the well-worn traditions of "Canadian scene" painting, as practised by his friend A.Y. Jackson. J.B. Taylor, who came to the University in 1947, worked in a similar, yet slicker, vein.

Like Thomas Hart Benton, whom he obviously admired, Glyde also painted classical allegories set in the prairie present. And when he put aside the stylistic cliches of Benton and Jackson, and looked directly at his own surroundings, he painted with real originality and force. Similarly, Taylor sometimes transcended the graphic commercial look of most of his paintings with his abstracted landscapes of the early sixties.

Douglas Haynes, who received his training at the Tech, was among the more determined of the second generation of postwar Edmonton artists. As Clement Greenberg noted on his first trip to the city in 1962, Haynes's etchings were "unabashedly" influenced by Adolph Gottlieb's abstract expressionist "burst" paintings.[17] Perhaps because of his interest in this medium, Haynes was also attracted by the high relief and heavy textures of Antoni Tapies's work. His paintings of the late sixties were as much built as they were painted, and often exploited symmetrical cellular images [Fig. 6].

FIGURE 6

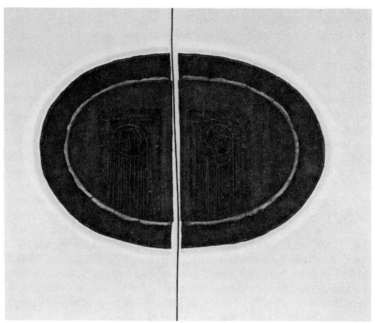

"1-Feb./69" by Douglas Haynes
Courtesy of The Edmonton Art Gallery

Whereas Winnipeg relied too heavily on outside guidance, and ended up with teachers and artists who were unsympathetic to what had gone on before, or who would not stay, Calgary and Edmonton were unable to attract much outside talent. Nor did they seem very open to it. Faced with the task of reinventing the wheel on their own, they struggled, and got off to a slow start after the war. But the seeds that were scattered during these years germinated, and a few took root, and from them has grown the active artistic community that we know today.

Summary

From the first three sections of this six part survey, we can draw several tentative conclusions. First, art galleries and art schools played a vital part in establishing western Canada's art scenes. Private patronage and collectors seem to have been virtually nonexistent during the period in question. Second, there was much travel within the region, but little to or from the East. The "North-South" axis on the contrary actually existed, for many artists felt stronger ties with the American Mid-West and West than with other parts of Canada. Third, Vancouver did indeed exercise some hegemony, but its regional influence was indirect and weak—understandable in light of the great distances between western Canadian cities, and the psychological barrier presented by the Rocky Mountains. Finally, a key ingredient in the establishment of continuity and traditions—without which the art communities did not seem to grow—was the commitment of artists to stay rather than to move on. This brings us back to the public patronage of teaching institutions. Whatever we may think of artists teaching, without teaching jobs, the artists of this survey would have almost all moved on, and our presently lackluster art communities would not exist at all.

Footnotes

1. Vancouver's population was 244,833 in 1951, making it the largest city in western Canada.

2. Or was it 1948/49? Improbable as it seems, there is some confusion about when Plaskett was in Winnipeg. Doris Shadbolt records that he was there in 1947/48 ("Joe Plaskett—An Ode to a Room," *Canadian Art* 13:4 (Summer 1957), p. 318). But the Architecture and Fine Arts Library of the University of Manitoba records that he was there in 1948/49 (Peter Anthony to Christopher Varley, 2 June 1983).

3. *President's Report,* Vancouver Art Gallery, 1944/45.

4. Andrus, Donald F.P., *Bruno Bobak: Selected Works, 1943-1980.* Sir George Williams Art Galleries (Montreal: Concordia University, 1983), p.55.

5. Winnipeg's population was 235,710 in 1951 and 265,429 in 1961, making it the second largest city in western Canada, but the slowest growing.

6. Douglas Morton in conversation with Christopher Varley, 28 July 1981.

7. Ivan Eyre in conversation with Christopher Varley, 28 February 1983.

8. "Clement Greenberg's View of Art on the Prairies: Painting and Sculpture in Prairie Canada." *Canadian Art* 20:2 (March/April 1963), p. 98.

9. Ivan Eyre in conversation with Christopher Varley, 28 February 1983.

10. Bates, Maxwell. "Some Problems of Environment." *Highlights* 2:8 (December 1948), p. 2.

11. Calgary's population was 129,060 in 1951, and Edmonton's was 159,631.

12. Douglas Morton in conversation with Christopher Varley, 28 July 1981.

13. Kiyooka, Roy. "Preface," *Maxwell Bates.* Norman Mackenzie Art Gallery, November 30, 1969-January 2, 1961 (catalogue).

14. Douglas Morton in conversation with Christopher Varley, 28 July 1981.

15. *Ibid.*

16. Ronald Spickett to Christopher Varley, 19 April 1983.

17. "Clement Greenberg's View of Art on the Prairies: Painting and Sculpture in Prairie Canada." *Canadian Art* 20:2 (March/April 1963), p. 95.